Thomas Carlyle, Henry Walcott Boynton

Passages from the French and Italian Note-Books of Nathaniel Hawthorne

Vol. 1

Thomas Carlyle, Henry Walcott Boynton

Passages from the French and Italian Note-Books of Nathaniel Hawthorne
Vol. 1

ISBN/EAN: 9783337058609

Printed in Europe, USA, Canada, Australia, Japan

Cover: Foto ©ninafisch / pixelio.de

More available books at **www.hansebooks.com**

PASSAGES FROM THE FRENCH AND ITALIAN
NOTE-BOOKS OF NATHANIEL HAWTHORNE

VOL. I.

PASSAGES FROM THE

FRENCH AND ITALIAN NOTE-BOOKS
OF NATHANIEL HAWTHORNE

VOL. I.

STRAHAN & CO., PUBLISHERS
56 LUDGATE HILL, LONDON
1871

PASSAGES FROM HAWTHORNE'S NOTE-BOOKS IN FRANCE AND ITALY.

FRANCE.

HOTEL DE LOUVRE, *January 6th*, 1858.—On Tuesday morning, our dozen trunks and half-dozen carpet-bags being all ready packed and labelled, we began to prepare for our journey two or three hours before light. Two cabs were at the door by half-past six, and at seven we set out for the London Bridge station, while it was still dark and bitterly cold. There were already many people in the streets, growing more numerous as we drove city-ward; and, in Newgate Street, there was such a number of market-carts, that we almost came to a dead lock with some of them. At the station we found several persons who were apparently going in the same train with us, sitting round the fire of the waiting-room. Since I came to England there has hardly been a morning when I should have less willingly bestirred myself before daylight; so sharp and inclement was the atmosphere. We started at half-past eight, having taken through tickets to Paris by way of Folkestone and Boulogne. A foot-warmer (a long, flat tin utensil, full of hot water) was put into the carriage just before we started; but it did not make us more than half-comfortable, and the frost soon began to cloud the windows, and shut out the prospect, so that we could only glimpse at the green fields—immortally green, whatever winter can do against them—and, at here and there, a stream or pool, with the ice forming on its borders. It was the first cold weather of a very mild season. The snow began to fall in scattered and almost invisible flakes; and it seemed as if we had stayed our English welcome out, and were to find nothing genial and hospitable there any more.

At Folkestone, we were deposited at a railway station close upon a shingly beach, on which the sea broke in foam, and which J—— reported as strewn with shells and star-fish: behind was the town, with an old church in the midst; and, close at hand, the pier, where lay the steamer in which we were to embark. But the air was so wintry, that I had no heart to explore the town, or pick up shells with

J—— on the beach; so we kept within doors during the two hours of our stay, now and then looking out of the windows at a fishing-boat or two, as they pitched and rolled with an ugly and irregular motion, such as the British Channel generally communicates to the craft that navigate it.

At about one o'clock we went on board, and were soon under steam, at a rate that quickly showed a long line of the white cliffs of Albion behind us. It is a very dusky white, by-the-bye, and the cliffs themselves do not seem, at a distance, to be of imposing height, and have too even an outline to be picturesque.

As we increased our distance from England, the French coast came more and more distinctly in sight, with a low, wavy outline, not very well worth looking at, except because it was the coast of France. Indeed, I looked at it but little; for the wind was bleak and boisterous, and I went down into the cabin, where I found the fire very comfortable, and several people were stretched on sofas in a state of placid wretchedness. . . . . I have never suffered from sea-sickness, but had been somewhat apprehensive of this rough strait between England and France, which seems to have more potency over people's stomachs than ten times the extent of sea in other quarters.

Our passage was of two hours, at the end of which we landed on French soil, and found ourselves immediately in the clutches of the Custom-house officers, who, however, merely made a momentary examination of my passport, and allowed us to pass without opening so much as one of our carpet-bags. The great bulk of our luggage had been registered through to Paris, for examination after our arrival there.

We left Boulogne in about an hour after our arrival, when it was already a darkening twilight. The weather had grown colder than ever, since our arrival in sunny France, and the night was now setting in, wickedly black and dreary. The frost hardened upon the carriage windows in such thickness that I could scarcely scratch a peep-hole through it; but, from such glimpses as I could catch, the aspect of the country seemed pretty much to resemble the December aspect of my dear native land,—broad, bare, brown fields, with streaks of snow at the foot of ridges, and along fences, or in the furrows of ploughed soil. There was ice wherever there happened to be water to form it.

We had feet-warmers in the carriage, but the cold crept in nevertheless; and I do not remember hardly in my life a more disagreeable short journey than this, my first advance into French territory. My impression of France will always be that it is an Arctic region. At any season of the year, the tract over which we passed yesterday must be an uninteresting one as regards its natural features; and the only adornment, as far as I could observe, which art has given it, consists in straight rows of very stiff-looking and slender-stemmed trees. In the dusk they resembled poplar trees.

Weary and frost-bitten—morally, if not physically—we reached Amiens in three or four hours, and here I underwent much annoyance from the French railway officials and attendants, who, I believe, did not mean to incommode me, but rather to forward my purposes as far as they well could. If they would speak slowly and distinctly I might understand them well enough, being perfectly familiar with the written language, and knowing the principles of its pronunciation; but, in their customary rapid utterance, it sounds like a string of mere gabble. When left to myself, therefore, I got into great difficulties. . . . It gives a taciturn personage like myself a new conception as to the value of speech, even to him, when he finds himself unable either to speak or understand.

Finally, being advised on all hands to go to the Hôtel de Rhin, we were carried thither in an omnibus, rattling over a rough pavement, through an invisible and frozen town; and, on our arrival, were ushered into a handsome *salon*, as chill as a tomb. They made a little bit of a wood fire for us in a low and deep chimney-hole, which let a hundred times more heat escape up the flue than it sent into the room.

In the morning we sallied forth to see the Cathedral.

The aspect of the old French town was very different from anything English; whiter, infinitely cleaner; higher and narrower houses—the entrance to most of which seeming to be through a great gateway, affording admission into a central courtyard; a public square, with a statue in the middle, and another statue in a neighbouring street. We met priests in three-cornered hats, long frock-coats, and knee-breeches; also soldiers and gendarmes, and peasants and children, clattering over the pavements in wooden shoes.

It makes a great impression of outlandishness to see the signs over the shop-doors in a foreign tongue. If the cold had not been such as to dull my sense of novelty, and make all my perceptions torpid, I should have taken in a set of new impressions, and enjoyed them very much. As it was, I cared little for what I saw, but yet had life enough left to enjoy the Cathedral of Amiens, which has many features unlike those of English cathedrals.

It stands in the midst of the cold, white town, and has a high-shouldered look to a spectator accustomed to the minsters of England, which cover a great space of ground in proportion to their height. The impression the latter give is of magnitude and mass : this French cathedral strikes one as lofty. The exterior is venerable, though but little time-worn by the action of the atmosphere ; and statues still keep their places in numerous niches, almost as perfect as when first placed there in the thirteenth century. The principal doors are deep, elaborately wrought, pointed arches ; and the interior seemed to us, at the moment, as grand as any that we had seen, and to afford as vast an idea of included space ; it being of such an airy height, and with no screen between the chancel and nave, as in all the English cathedrals. We saw the differences, too, betwixt a church in which the same form of worship for which it was originally built is still kept up, and those of England, where it has been superseded for centuries ; for here, in the recess of every arch of the side aisles, beneath each lofty window, there was a chapel dedicated to some saint, and adorned with great marble sculptures of the crucifixion, and with pictures, execrably bad, in all cases—and various kinds of gilding and ornamentation. Immensely tall wax candles stand upon the altars of these chapels, and before one sat a woman, with a great supply of tapers, one of which was burning. I suppose these were to be lighted as offerings to the saints, by the true believers. Artificial flowers were hung at some of the shrines, or placed under glass. In every chapel, moreover, there was a confessional—a little oaken structure, about as big as a sentry-box, with a closed part for the priest to sit in, and an open one for the penitent to kneel at, and speak, through the open work of the priest's closet. Monuments, mural and others, to long-departed worthies, and images of the Saviour, the Virgin, and saints, were numerous everywhere about the church; and in the chancel there was a great deal of quaint and curious sculpture, fencing in the Holy of Holies, where the High Altar stands. There is not much painted glass; one or two very rich and beautiful rose-windows, however, that looked antique; and the great eastern window, which, I think, is modern. The pavement has, probably, never been renewed, as one piece of work, since the structure was erected, and is footworn by the successive generations, though still in excellent repair. I saw one of the small, square stones in it, bearing the date of 1597, and no doubt there are a thousand older ones. It was gratifying to find the cathedral in such good condition, without any traces of recent repair; and it is perhaps a mark of difference between French and English character, that the Revolution in the former country, though all religious worship disappeared before it, does not seem to have caused such violence to ecclesiastical monuments, as the Reformation and the reign of Puritanism in the latter. I did not see a mutilated shrine, or' even a broken-nosed image in the whole cathedral. But, probably, the very rage of the English fanatics against idolatrous tokens, and their smashing blows at them, were symptoms of sincerer religious faith than the French were capable of. These last did not care enough about their Saviour to beat down his crucified image; and they preserved the works of sacred art, for the sake only of what beauty there was in them.

While we were in the cathedral, we saw several persons kneeling at their devotions on the steps of the chancel and elsewhere. One dipped his fingers in the holy water at the entrance :—by-the-bye, I looked into the stone basin that held it, and saw it full of ice. Could not all that sanctity at least keep it thawed? Priests—jolly, fat, mean-looking fellows, in white robes—went hither and thither, but did not interrupt or accost us.

There were other peculiarities, which I suppose I shall see more of in my visits to other churches, but now we were all glad to make our stay as brief as possible, the atmosphere of the cathedral being so bleak, and its stone pavement so icy cold beneath our feet. We returned to the hotel, and the chambermaid brought me a book, in which she asked me to inscribe my name, age, profession, country, destination, and the authorisation under which I travelled. After the freedom of an English hotel, so much greater than even that of an American one, where they make you disclose your name, this is not so pleasant.

We left Amiens at half-past one; and I can tell as little of the country between that place and Paris, as between Boulogne and Amiens. The windows of our railway carriage were already frosted with French breath when we got into it, and the ice grew thicker and thicker continually. I tried, at various times, to rub a peep-hole through, as before; but the ice immediately shot its crystallised tracery over it again; and, indeed, there was little or nothing to make it worth while to look out,—so bleak was the scene. Now and then a château, too far off for its characteristics to be discerned; now and then a church, with a tall grey tower, and a little peak a-top; here and there a village or a town, which we could not well see. At sunset there was just that clear, cold, wintry sky which I remember so well in America, but have never seen in England.

At five we reached Paris, and were suffered to take a carriage to the Hôtel de Louvre, without any examination of the little luggage we had with us. Arriving, we took a suite of apartments, and the waiter immediately lighted a wax candle in each separate room.

We might have dined at the *table-d'hôte*, but preferred the restaurant connected with and within the hotel. All the dishes were very delicate, and a vast change from the simple English system, with its joints, shoulders, beef steaks, and chops; but I doubt whether English cookery, for the very reason that it is so gross, is not better for men's moral and spiritual nature than French. In the former case, you know that you are gratifying your coarse animal needs and propensities, and are duly ashamed of it; but, in dealing with these French delicacies, you delude yourself into the idea that you are cultivating your taste while satisfying your appetite. This last, however, it requires a good deal of perseverance to accomplish.

In the cathedral at Amiens there were printed lists

of acts of devotion posted on the columns, such as prayers at the shrines of certain saints, whereby plenary indulgences might be gained. It is to be observed, however, that all these external forms were necessarily accompanied with true penitence and religious devotion.

HOTEL DE LOUVRE, *January 8th.*—It was so fearfully cold this morning that I really felt little or no curiosity to see the city. . . . Until after one o'clock, therefore, I knew nothing of Paris except the lights which I had seen beneath our window the evening before, far, far downward, in the narrow Rue St. Honoré, and the rumble of the wheels, which continued later than I was awake to hear it, and began again before dawn. I could see, too, tall houses, that seemed to be occupied in every story, and that had windows on the steep roofs. One of these houses is six stories high. This Rue St. Honoré is one of the old streets in Paris, and is that in which Henry IV. was assassinated; but it has not, in this part of it, the aspect of antiquity.

After one o'clock we all went out and walked along the Rue de Rivoli. . . . We are here, right in the midst of Paris, and close to whatever is best known to those who hear or read about it—the

Louvre being across the street, the Palais Royal but a little way off, the Tuileries joining to the Louvre, the Place de la Concorde just beyond, verging on which is the Champs Elysées. We looked about us for a suitable place to dine, and soon found the Restaurant des Echelles, where we entered at a venture, and were courteously received. It has a handsomely furnished saloon, much set off with gilding and mirrors; and appears to be frequented by English and Americans; its *carte*, a bound volume, being printed in English as well as French. . . .

It was now nearly four o'clock, and too late to visit the galleries of the Louvre, or to do anything else but walk a little way along the street. The splendour of Paris, so far as I have seen, takes me altogether by surprise: such stately edifices, prolonging themselves in unwearying magnificence and beauty, and, ever and anon, a long vista of a street, with a column rising at the end of it, or a triumphal arch, wrought in memory of some grand event. The light stone or stucco, wholly untarnished by smoke and soot, puts London to the blush, if a blush could be seen on its dingy face; but, indeed, London is not to be mentioned with, nor compared even with Paris. I never knew what a palace was till I had a glimpse of the Louvre and the Tuileries—never had my idea of a city been gratified till I trod those stately streets. The life of the scene, too, is infinitely more picturesque than that of London, with its monstrous throng of grim faces and black coats: whereas, here, you see soldiers and priests, policemen in cocked hats, Zouaves with turbans, long mantles, and bronzed, half Moorish faces; and a great many people whom you perceive to be outside of your experience, and know them ugly to look at, and fancy them villainous. Truly, I have no sympathies towards the French people; their eyes do not win me, nor do their glances melt and mingle with mine. But they do grand and beautiful things in the architectural way; and I am grateful for it. The Place de la Concorde is a most splendid square, large enough for a nation to erect trophies in of all its triumphs; and on one side of it is the Tuileries, on the opposite side the Champs Elysées, and, on a third, the Seine, adown which we saw large cakes of ice floating, beneath the arches of a bridge. The Champs Elysées, so far as I saw it, had not a grassy soil beneath its trees; but the bare earth, white and dusty. The very dust, if I saw nothing else, would assure me that I was out of England.

We had time only to take this little walk, when it began to grow dusk; and, being so pitilessly cold, we hurried back to our hotel. Thus far, I think, what I have seen of Paris is wholly unlike what I expected; but very like an imaginary picture which I had conceived of St. Petersburg—new, bright, magnificent, and desperately cold.

A great part of this architectural splendour is due to the present Emperor, who has wrought a great change in the aspect of the city within a very few years. A traveller, if he looks at the thing selfishly, ought to wish him a long reign and arbitrary power, since he makes it his policy to illustrate his capital with palatial edifices, which are, however, better for a stranger to look at, than for his own people to pay for.

We have spent to-day chiefly in seeing—or glimpsing at—some of the galleries of the Louvre. I must confess that the vast and beautiful edifice struck me far more than the pictures, sculpture, and curiosities which it contains—the shell more than the kernel inside: such noble suites of rooms and halls were those through which we first passed, containing Egyptian, and, farther onward, Greek and Roman antiquities; the walls cased in variegated marbles; the ceilings glowing with beautiful frescoes; the whole extended into infinite vistas by mirrors that seemed like vacancy, and multiplied everything for ever. The picture-rooms are not so splendid, and the pictures themselves did not greatly win upon me in this one day. Many artists were employed in copying them, especially in the rooms hung with the productions of French painters. Not a few of these copyists were females; most of them were young men, picturesquely moustached and bearded; but some were elderly, who, it was pitiful to think, had passed through life without so much success as now to paint pictures of their own.

From the pictures we went into a suite of rooms where are preserved many relics of the ancient and later kings of France; more relics of the elder ones, indeed, than I supposed had remained extant through the Revolution. The French seem to like to keep memorials of whatever they do, and of whatever their forefathers have done, even if it be ever so little to their credit; and perhaps they do not take matters sufficiently to heart to detest anything that has ever happened. What surprised me most were the golden sceptre and the magnificent sword and other gorgeous relics of Charlemagne—a person whom I had always associated with a sheepskin cloak. There were suits of armour and weapons that had been worn and handled by a great many of the French kings; and a religious book that had belonged to St. Louis; a dressing-glass, most richly set with precious stones, which formerly stood on the toilette-table of Catherine de Medici, and in which I saw my own face where hers had been. And there were a thousand other treasures, just as well worth mentioning as these. If each monarch could have been summoned from Hades to claim his own relics, we should have had the halls full of the old Childerics, Charleses, Bourbons and Capets, Henrys and Louises, snatching with ghostly hands at sceptres, swords, armour, and mantles; and Napoleon would have seen, apparently, almost everything that personally belonged to him—his coat, his cocked hats, his camp-desk, his field bed, his knives, forks, and plates, and even a lock of his hair. I must let it all go. These things cannot be reproduced by pen and ink.

HOTEL DE LOUVRE, *January 9th*.— . . . . Last evening Mr. Fezandie called. He spoke very freely respecting the Emperor and the hatred entertained against him in France; but said that he is more powerful—that is, more firmly fixed as a ruler, than ever the first Napoleon was. We, who look back upon the first Napoleon as one of the eternal facts of the past—a great boulder in history, cannot well estimate how momentary and unsubstantial the great

Captain may have appeared to those who beheld his rise out of obscurity. They never, perhaps, took the reality of his career fairly into their minds, before it was over. The present Emperor, I believe, has already been as long in possession of the supreme power as his uncle was. I should like to see him, and may, perhaps, do so, as he is our neighbour, across the way.

This morning Miss ——, the celebrated astronomical lady, called. She had brought a letter of introduction to me, while consul; and her purpose now was to see if we could take her as one of our party to Rome, whither she likewise is bound. We readily consented, for she seems to be a simple, strong, healthy-humoured woman, who will not fling herself as a burthen on our shoulders; and my only wonder is that a person evidently so able to take care of herself should wish to have an escort.

We issued forth at about eleven, and went down the Rue St. Honoré, which is narrow, and has houses of five or six stories on either side, between which runs the streets like a gully in a rock. One face of our hotel borders and looks on this street. After going a good way, we came to an insersection with another street, the name of which I forget; but, at this point, Ravaillac sprang at the carriage of Henry IV. and

plunged his dagger into him. As we went down the
Rue St. Honoré, it grew more and more thronged,
and with a meaner class of people. The houses still
were high, and without the shabbiness of exterior
that distinguishes the old part of London, being of
light coloured stone; but I never saw anything that
so much came up to my idea of a swarming city as
this narrow, crowded, and rambling street.

Thence we turned into the Rue St. Denis, which is
one of the oldest streets in Paris, and is said to have
been first marked out by the track of the saint's foot-
steps, where, after his martyrdom, he walked along
it, with his head under his arm, in quest of a burial-
place. This legend may account for any crookedness
of the street, for it could not reasonably be asked of a
headless man that he should walk straight.

Through some other indirections we at last found
the Rue Bergère, down which I went with J—— in
quest of Hottinguer & Co., the bankers, while the
rest of us went along the Boulevards, towards the
Church of the Madeleine. . . . This business accom-
plished, J—— and I threaded our way back, and
overtook the rest of the party, still a good distance
from the Madeleine. I know not why the Boulevards
are called so. They are a succession of broad walks
through broad streets, and were much thronged with

people, most of whom appeared to be bent more on pleasure than business. The sun, long before this, had come out brightly, and gave us the first genial and comfortable sensations which we have had in Paris.

Approaching the Madeleine, we found it a most beautiful church, that might have been adapted from Heathenism to Catholicism; for on each side there is a range of magnificent pillars, unequalled, except by those of the Parthenon. A mourning coach, arrayed in black and silver, was drawn up at the steps, and the front of the church was hung with black cloth, which covered the whole entrance. However, seeing other people going in, we entered along with them. Glorious and gorgeous is the Madeleine. The entrance to the nave is beneath a most stately arch; and three arches of equal height open from the nave to the side aisles; and at the end of the nave is another great arch, rising, with a vaulted half-dome, over the high altar. The pillars supporting these arches are Corinthian, with richly sculptured capitals; and wherever gilding might adorn the church, it is lavished like sunshine; and within the sweeps of the arches there are fresco paintings of sacred subjects, and a beautiful picture covers the hollow of the vault over the altar: all this, besides much sculpture ; and especially a group above and around the high altar, representing the Magdalen, smiling down upon angels and archangels, some of whom are kneeling, and shadowing themselves with their heavy marble wings. There is no such thing as making my page glow with the most distant idea of the magnificence of this church, in its details and in its whole. It was founded a hundred or two hundred years ago; then Bonaparte contemplated transforming it into a Temple of Victory, or building it anew as one. The restored Bourbon remade it into a church; but it still has a heathenish look, and will never lose it.

When we entered we saw a crowd of people, all pressing forward towards the high altar, before which burned a hundred wax lights, some of which were six or seven feet high; and, altogether, they shone like a galaxy of stars. In the middle of the nave, moreover, there was another galaxy of wax candles burning around an immense pall of black velvet, embroidered with silver, which seemed to cover, not only a coffin, but a sarcophagus, or something still more huge. The organ was rumbling forth a deep, lugubrious bass, accompanied with heavy chanting of priests, out of which sometimes rose the clear, young voices of choristers, like light flashing out of the gloom. The church, between the arches, along the nave, and round the altar, was hung with broad expanses of black cloth; and all the priests had their sacred vestments covered with black. They looked exceedingly well: I never saw anything half so well got up on the stage. Some of these ecclesiastical figures were very stately and noble, and knelt and bowed, and bore aloft the cross, and swung the censers in a way that I liked to see. The ceremonies of the Catholic Church were a superb work of art, or perhaps a true growth of man's religious nature; and so long as men felt their original meaning, they must have been full of awe and glory. Being of another parish, I looked on coldly, but not irreverently, and was glad to see the funeral service so well performed, and very glad when it was over. What struck me as singular—the person who performed the part usually performed by a verger, keeping order among the audience, wore a gold-embroidered scarf, a cocked hat, and, I believe, a sword, and had the air of a military man.

Before the close of the service a contribution-box—or, rather, a black velvet bag—was handed about by this military verger; and I gave J—— a franc to put in, though I did not in the least know for what.

Issuing from the church, we inquired of two or

three persons who was the distinguished defunct at whose obsequies we had been assisting, for we had some hope that it might be Rachel, who died last week, and is still above ground. But it proved to be only a Madame Mentel, or some such name, whom nobody had ever before heard of. I forgot to say that her coffin was taken from beneath the illuminated pall, and carried out of the church before us.

When we left the Madeleine we took our way to the Place de la Concorde, and thence through the Elysian Fields (which, I suppose, are the French idea of Heaven), to Bonaparte's Triumphal Arch. The Champs Elysées may look pretty in summer; though I suspect they must be somewhat dry and artificial at whatever season—the trees being slender and scraggy, and requiring to be renewed every few years. The soil is not genial to them. The strangest peculiarity of this place, however, to eyes fresh from moist and verdant England, is, that there is not one blade of grass in all the Elysian Fields, nothing but hard clay, now covered with white dust. It gives the whole scene the air of being a contrivance of man, in which Nature has either not been invited to take any part, or has declined to do so. There were merry-go-rounds, wooden horses, and other provision for children's amusements among the trees; and booths, and tables of cakes, and candy women; and restaurants on the borders of the wood; but very few people there; and doubtless we can form no idea of what the scene might become when alive with French gaiety and vivacity.

As we walked onward, the Triumphal Arch began to loom up in the distance, looking huge and massive, though still a long way off. It was not, however, till we stood almost beneath it that we really felt the grandeur of this great arch, including so large a space of the blue sky in its airy sweep. At a distance it impresses the spectator with its solidity; nearer, with the lofty vacancy beneath it. There is a spiral staircase within one of its immense limbs; and, climbing steadily upward, lighted by a lantern which the doorkeeper's wife gave us, we had a bird's-eye view of Paris, much obscured by smoke or mist. Several interminable avenues shoot with painful directness right towards it.

On our way homeward we visited the Place Vendôme, in the centre of which is a tall column, sculptured from top to bottom, all over the pedestal, and all over the shaft, and with Napoleon himself on the summit. The shaft is wreathed round-and-roundabout with representations of what, as far as I could distinguish, seemed to be the Emperor's victories. It has a very rich effect. At the foot of the column we saw wreaths of artificial flowers, suspended there, no doubt, by some admirer of Napoleon, still ardent enough to expend a franc or two in this way.

HOTEL DE LOUVRE; *January* 10*th*.—We had purposed going to the Cathedral of Notre Dame to-day, but the weather and walking were too unfavourable for a distant expedition; so we merely went across the street to the Louvre. . . .

Our principal object this morning was to see the pencil drawings by eminent artists. Of these the Louvre has a very rich collection, occupying many apartments, and comprising sketches by Annibale Caracci, Claude, Raphael, Leonardo da Vinci, Michel Angelo, Rubens, Rembrandt, and almost all the other great masters, whether French, Italian, Dutch, or whatever else; the earliest drawings of their great pictures, when they had the glory of their pristine idea directly before their minds' eye—that idea which inevitably became overlaid with their own handling of it in the finished painting. No doubt the painters themselves had often a happiness in these rude, off-hand sketches, which they never felt again in the same work, and which resulted in disappointment, after they had done their best. To an artist, the collection must be most deeply interesting : to myself, it was merely curious, and soon grew wearisome.

In the same suite of apartments, there is a collection of miniatures, some of them very exquisite, and absolutely life-like, on their small scale. I observed two of Franklin, both good and picturesque, one of them especially so, with its cloud-like, white hair. I do not think we have produced a man so interesting to contemplate, in many points of view, as he. Most of our great men are of a character that I find it impossible to warm into life by thought, or by lavishing any amount of sympathy upon them. Not so Franklin, who had a great deal of common and uncommon human nature in him.

Much of the time, while my wife was looking at the drawings, I sat observing the crowd of Sunday visitors. They were generally of a lower class than those of week-days; private soldiers in a variety of uniforms, and, for the most part, ugly little men, but decorous and well-behaved. I saw medals on many of their breasts, denoting Crimean service; some wore the English medal, with Queen Victoria's head upon it. A blue coat, with red, baggy trousers, was the most usual uniform. Some had short-breasted

coats, made in the same style as those of the first
Napoleon, which we had seen in the preceding rooms.
The policemen, distributed pretty abundantly about
the rooms, themselves looked military, wearing
cocked hats and swords. There were many women
of the middling classes; some, evidently, of the
lowest, but clean and decent, in coloured gowns and
caps; and labouring men, citizens, Sunday gentlemen, young artists, too, no doubt, looking with edu-
cated eyes, at these art-treasures, and I think as a
general thing, each man was mated with a woman.
The soldiers, however, came in pairs or little squads,
accompanied by women. I did not much like any of
the French faces, and yet I am not sure that there
is not more resemblance between them and the
American physiognomy, than between the latter and
the English. The women are not pretty, but in all
ranks above the lowest they have a trained expression that supplies the place of beauty.

I was wearied to death with the drawings, and
began to have that dreary and desperate feeling
which has often come upon me when the sights last
longer than my capacity for receiving them. As our
time in Paris, however, is brief and precious, we
next inquired our way to the galleries of sculpture,
and these alone are of astounding extent, reaching, I

should think, all round one quadrangle of the Louvre, on the basement floor. Hall after hall opened interminably before us, and on either side of us, paved and encrusted with variegated and beautifully polished marble, relieved against which stand the antique statues and groups, interspersed with great urns and vases, sarcophagi, altars, tablets, busts of historic personages, and all manner of shapes of marble, which consummate art has transmuted into precious stones. Not that I really did feel much impressed by any of this sculpture then, nor saw more than two or three things which I thought very beautiful; but whether it be good or no, I suppose the world has nothing better, unless it be a few world-renowned statues in Italy. I was even more struck by the skill and ingenuity of the French in arranging these sculptural remains, than by the value of the sculptures themselves. The galleries, I should judge, have been recently prepared, and on a magnificent system,— the adornments being yet by no means completed,— for besides the floor and wall-casings of rich, polished marble, the vaulted ceilings of some of the apartments are painted in fresco, causing them to glow as if the sky were opened. It must be owned, however, that the statuary, often time-worn and darkened from its original brilliancy by weather stains, does not suit well as furniture for such splendid rooms. When we see a perfection of modern finish around them, we recognise that most of these statues had been thrown down from their pedestals, hundreds of years ago, and have been battered and externally degraded; and though whatever spiritual beauty they ever had may still remain, yet this is not made more apparent by the contrast betwixt the new gloss of modern upholstery, and their tarnished, even if immortal grace. I rather think the English have given really the more hospitable reception to the maimed Theseus, and his broken-nosed, broken-legged, headless companions, because flouting them with no gorgeous fittings up.

By this time poor J—— (who, with his taste for art yet undeveloped, is the companion of all our visits to sculpture and picture-galleries) was woefully hungry, and for bread we had given him a stone,—not one stone, but a thousand. We returned to the hotel, and it being too damp and raw to go to our Restaurant des Echelles, we dined at the hotel. In my opinion it would require less time to cultivate our gastronomic taste than taste of any other kind; and, on the whole, I am not sure that a man would not be wise to afford himself a little discipline in this line. It is certainly throwing away the bounties of providence, to treat them as the English do, producing from better materials than the French have to work upon, nothing but sirloins, joints, joints — steaks, steaks, steaks—chops, chops, chops, chops! We had a soup to-day, in which twenty kinds of vegetables were represented, and manifested each its own aroma; a fillet of stewed beef, and a fowl, in some sort of delicate fricassee. We had a bottle of Chablis, and renewed ourselves, at the close of the banquet, with a plate of Chateaubriand ice. It was all very good, and we respected ourselves far more than if we had eaten a quantity of red roast beef; but I am not quite sure that we were right. . . . .

Among the relics of kings and princes, I do not know that there was anything more interesting than a little brass cannon, two or three inches long, which had been a toy of the unfortunate Dauphin, son of Louis XVI. There was a map—a hemisphere of the world,—which his father had drawn for this poor boy; very neatly done, too. The sword of Louis XVI., a magnificent rapier, with a beautifully damasked blade; and a jewelled scabbard, but without a hilt, is likewise preserved, as is the hilt of Henry IV.'s sword. But it is useless to begin a catalogue of these things. What a collection it is, including Charlemagne's sword and sceptre, and the last

Dauphin's little toy-cannon, and so much between the two!

HOTEL DE LOUVRE, *January* 11*th*.—This was another chill, raw day, characterised by a spitefulness of atmosphere which I do not remember ever to have experienced in my own dear country. We meant to have visited the Hôtel des Invalides, but J—— and I walked to the Rivoli, the Place de la Concorde, the Champs Elysées, and to the Place de Beaujon, and to the residence of the American minister, where I wished to arrange about my passport. After speaking with the Secretary of Legation, we were ushered into the minister's private room, where he received me with great kindness. Mr. —— is an old gentleman with a white head, and a large, florid face, which has an expression of amiability, not unmingled with a certain dignity. He did not rise from his armchair to greet me—a lack of ceremony which I imputed to the gout, feeling it impossible that he should have willingly failed in courtesy to one of his twenty-five million sovereigns. In response to some remark of mine about the shabby way in which our government treats its officials pecuniarily, he gave a detailed account of his own troubles on that score; then expressed a hope that I had made a good thing out of my consulate, and inquired whether I had received a hint to resign, to which I replied that, for various reasons, I had resigned of my own accord, and before Mr. Buchanan's inauguration. We agreed, however, in disapproving the system of periodical change in our foreign officials; and I remarked that a consul or an ambassador ought to be a citizen both of his native country, and of the one in which he resided; and that his possibility of beneficent influence depended largely on his being so. Apropos to which Mr. —— said that he had once asked a diplomatic friend of long experience, what was the first duty of a minister. "To love his own country, and to watch over its interests," answered the diplomatist. "And his second duty?" asked Mr. ——. "To love and to promote the interests of the country to which he is accredited," said his friend. This is a very Christian and sensible view of the matter; but it can scarcely have happened once in our whole diplomatic history, that a minister can have had time to overcome his first rude and ignorant prejudice against the country of his mission; and if there were any suspicion of his having done so, it would be held abundantly sufficient ground for his recall. I like Mr. ——, a good-hearted, sensible old man.

J—— and I returned along the Champs Elysées,

and, crossing the Seine, kept on our way by the river's brink, looking at the titles of books on the long lines of stalls that extend between the bridges. Novels, fairy-tales, dream books, treatises of behaviour and etiquette, collections of *bon mots* and of songs, were interspersed with volumes in the old style of calf and gilt binding, the works of the classics of French literature. A good many persons, of the poor classes, and of those apparently well to do, stopped transitorily to look at these books. On the other side of the street was a range of tall edifices with shops beneath, and the quick stir of French life hurrying, and babbling, and swarming along the sidewalk. We passed two or three bridges, occurring at short intervals, and at last we re-crossed the Seine by a bridge which oversteps the river, from a point near the National Institute, and reaches the other side, not far from the Louvre. . . . .

Though the day was so disagreeable, we thought it best not to lose the remainder of it, and therefore set out to visit the Cathedral of Notre-Dame. We took a fiacre in the Place de Carrousel, and drove to the door. On entering, we found the interior miserably shut off from view by the stagings erected for the purpose of repairs. Penetrating from the nave towards the chancel, an official personage signified to us, that we must first purchase a ticket for each grown person, at the price of half a franc each. This expenditure admitted us into the sacristy, where we were taken in charge by a guide, who came down upon us with an avalanche or cataract of French, descriptive of a great many treasures reposited in this chapel. I understood hardly more than one word in ten, but gathered doubtfully that a bullet which was shown us was the one that killed the late Archbishop of Paris, on the floor of the cathedral. [But this was a mistake. It was the archbishop who was killed in the insurrection of 1848. Two joints of his backbone were also shown.] Also, that some gorgeously-embroidered vestments, which he drew forth, had been used at the coronation of Napoleon I. There were two large, full-length portraits hanging aloft in the sacristy, and a gold or silver gilt, or, at all events, gilt image of the Virgin, as large as life, standing on a pedestal. The guide had much to say about these, but, understanding him so imperfectly, I have nothing to record.

The guide's supervision of us seemed not to extend beyond this sacristy, on quitting which he gave us permission to go where we pleased, only intimating a hope that we would not forget him; so I gave him half a franc, though thereby violating an inhibition on the printed ticket of entrance.

We had been much disappointed at first by the apparently narrow limits of the interior of this famous church; but now, as we made our way round the choir, gazing into chapel after chapel, each with its painted window, its crucifix, its pictures, its confessional, and afterwards came back into the nave, where arch rises above arch to the lofty roof, we came to the conclusion that it was very sumptuous. It is the greatest of pities that its grandeur and solemnity should just now be so infinitely marred by the workmen's boards, timber, and ladders occupying the whole centre of the edifice, and screening all its best effects. It seems to have been already most richly ornamented, its roof being painted, and the capitals of the pillars gilded, and their shafts illuminated in fresco; and no doubt it will shine out gorgeously when all the repairs and adornments shall be completed. Even now it gave to my actual sight what I have often tried to imagine in my visits to the English cathedrals—the pristine glory of those edifices, when they stood glowing with gold and picture, fresh from the architects' and adorners' hands.

The interior loftiness of Notre-Dame, moreover, gives it a sublimity which would swallow up anything that might look gewgawy in its ornamentation, were we to consider it window by window, or pillar by pillar. It is an advantage of these vast edifices, rising over us and spreading about us in such a firmamental way, that we cannot spoil them by any pettiness of our own, but that they receive (or absorb) our pettiness into their own immensity. Every little fantasy finds its place and propriety in them, like a flower on the earth's broad bosom.

When we emerged from the cathedral, we found it beginning to rain or snow, or both; and, as we had dismissed our fiacre at the door, and could find no other, we were at a loss what to do. We stood a few moments on the steps of the Hôtel Dieu, looking up at the front of Notre-Dame, with its twin towers, and its three deep-pointed arches, piercing through a great thickness of stone, and throwing a cavern-like gloom around these entrances. The front is very rich. Though so huge, and all of grey stone, it is carved and fretted with statues and innumerable devices, as cunningly as any ivory casket in which relics are kept; but its size did not so much impress me. . . .

HOTEL DE LOUVRE, *January 12th.*—This has been a bright day as regards weather; but I have done little or nothing worth recording. After breakfast, I set out in quest of the consul, and found him up a court, at 51, Rue Cammartin, in an office rather smaller, I think, than mine at Liverpool; but, to say the truth, a little better furnished. I was received in the outer apartment by an elderly, brisk-looking man, in whose air, respectful and subservient, and yet with a kind of authority in it, I recognised the vice-consul. He introduced me to Mr. ——, who sat writing in an inner room; a very gentlemanly, courteous, cool man of the world, whom I should take to be an excellent person for consul at Paris. He tells me that he has resided here some years, although his occupancy of the consulate dates only from November last. Consulting him respecting my passport, he gave me what appear good reasons why I should get all the necessary *visés* here; for example, that the *visé* of a minister carries more weight than that of a consul; and especially that an Austrian consul will never *visé* a passport unless he sees his minister's name upon it. Mr. —— has travelled much in Italy, and ought to be able to give me sound advice. His opinion was, that at this season of the year I had better go by steamer to Cività Vecchia, instead of landing at Leghorn, and thence journeying to Rome. On this point I shall decide when the time comes. As I left the office the vice-consul informed me that there was a charge of five francs and some sous for the consul's *visé*, a tax which surprised me—the whole business of passports having been taken from consuls before I quitted office, and the consular fee having been annulled even earlier. However, no doubt Mr. —— had a fair claim to my five francs; but, really, it is not half so pleasant to pay a consular fee as it used to be to receive it.

Afterwards I walked to Notre-Dame, the rich front of which I viewed with more attention than yesterday. There are whole histories, carved in stone figures, within the vaulted arches of the three entrances in this west front, and twelve apostles in a row above, and as much other sculpture as would take a month to see. We then walked quite round it, but I had no sense of immensity from it, not even that of great height, as from many of the cathedrals of England. It stands very near the Seine; indeed, if I mistake not, it is on an island formed by two branches of the river. Behind it, in what seems to be a small public ground (or garden, if a space entirely denuded of grass or other green thing, except a few trees can be called so), with benches, and a monument in the midst. This quarter of the city looks old, and appears to be inhabited by poor people, and to be busied about small and petty affairs; the most picturesque business that I saw being that of the old woman who sells crucifixes of pearl and of wood at the cathedral door. We bought two of these yesterday.

I must again speak of the horrible muddiness, not only of this part of the city, but of all Paris, so far as I have traversed it to-day. My ways, since I came to Europe, have often lain through nastiness, but I never before saw a pavement so universally overspread with mud-padding as that of Paris. It is difficult to imagine where so much filth can come from.

After dinner I walked through the gardens of the Tuileries; but as dusk was coming on, and as I was afraid of being shut up within the iron railing, I did not have time to examine them particularly. There are wide, intersecting walks, fountains, broad basins, and many statues; but almost the whole surface of the gardens is barren earth, instead of the verdure that would beautify an English pleasure-ground of this sort. In the summer it has doubtless an agreeable shade; but at this season the naked branches look meagre, and sprout from slender trunks. Like the trees in the Champs Elysées, those, I presume, in the gardens of the Tuileries need renewing every few years. The same is true of the human race—families becoming extinct after a generation or two of residence in Paris. Nothing really thrives here; man and vegetables have but an artificial life, like flowers stuck in a little mould, but never taking root. I am quite tired of Paris, and long for a home more than ever.

MARSEILLES.

HOTEL D'ANGLETERRE, *January* 15*th*.—On Tuesday morning (12th) we took our departure from the Hôtel de Louvre. It is a most excellent and perfectly ordered hotel, and I have not seen a more magnificent hall, in any palace, than the dining-saloon, with its profuse gilding, and its ceiling, painted in compartments; so that when the chandeliers are all a-light, it looks a fit place for princes to banquet in, and not very fit for the few Americans whom I saw scattered at its long tables. . . . .

By-the-bye, as we drove to the railway, we passed through the public square, where the Bastille formerly stood; and in the centre of it now stands a column, surmounted by a golden figure of Mercury (I think), which seems to be just on the point of casting itself from a gilt ball into the air. This statue is so buoyant, that the spectator feels quite willing to trust it to the viewless element, being as sure that it would be borne up as that a bird would fly.

Our first day's journey was wholly without interest, through a country entirely flat, and looking wretchedly brown and barren. There were rows of trees, very slender, very prim and formal; there was ice wherever there happened to be any water to form it; there were occasional villages, compact little streets, or masses of stone or plastered cottages, very dirty, with gable ends and earthen roofs, and a succession of this same landscape was all that we saw, whenever we rubbed away the congelation of our breath from the carriage windows. Thus we rode on, all day long, from eleven o'clock, with hardly a five minutes' stop, till long after dark, when we came to Dijon, where there was a halt of twenty-five minutes for dinner. Then we set forth again, and rumbled forward, through cold and darkness without, until we reached Lyons at about ten o'clock. We left our luggage at the railway station, and took an omnibus for the Hôtel de Provence, which we chose at a venture, among a score of other hotels.

As this hotel was a little off the direct route of the omnibus, the driver set us down at the corner of a street, and pointed to some lights, which he said designated the Hôtel de Provence; and thither we proceeded, all seven of us, taking along a few carpet-bags and shawls, our equipage for the night. The porter of the hotel met us near its doorway, and ushered us, through an arch, into the inner quadrangle, and then up some old and worn steps,— very broad, — and appearing to be the principal staircase. At the first landing-place, an old woman and a waiter or two received us; and we went up two or three more flights of the same broad and worn stone staircases. What we could see of the house looked very old, and had the musty odour with which I first became acquainted at Chester.

After ascending to the proper level, we were conducted along a corridor, paved with octagonal earthen tiles; on one side, were windows, looking into the courtyard, on the other doors opening into the sleeping chambers. The corridor was of immense length, and seemed still to lengthen itself before us, as the glimmer of our conductor's candle went farther and farther into the obscurity. Our own chamber was at a vast distance along this passage; those of the rest of the party were on the hither side, but all this immense suite of rooms appeared to communicate by doors from one to another, like the chambers through which the reader wanders at midnight, in Mrs. Radcliffe's romances. And they were really splendid rooms, though of an old fashion, lofty, spacious, with floors of oak or other wood, inlaid in squares and crosses, and waxed till they were slippery, but without carpets. Our own sleeping-room had a deep fireplace, in which we ordered a fire, and asked if there were not some saloon already warmed, where we could get a cup of tea.

Hereupon the waiter led us back along the endless corridor, and down the old stone staircases, and out into the quadrangle, and journeyed with us along an exterior arcade, and finally threw open the door of the *salle à manger*, which proved to be a room of lofty height, with a vaulted roof, a stone floor and interior spaciousness sufficient for a baronial hall, the whole bearing the same aspect of times gone by, that characterised the rest of the house. There were two or three tables covered with white cloth, and we sat down at one of them and had our tea. Finally we wended back to our sleeping rooms, a considerable journey, so endless seemed the ancient hotel. I should like to know its history.

The fire made our great chamber look comfortable, and the fireplace threw out the heat better than the little square hole, over which we cowered in our saloon at the Hôtel de Louvre. . . . .

In the morning we began our preparations for starting at ten. Issuing into the corridor, I found a soldier of the line, pacing to and fro there as sentinel. Another was posted in another corridor, into which I wandered by mistake; another stood in the inner courtyard, and another at the *porte-cochère*. They were not there the night before, and I know not whence nor why they came, unless that some officer of rank may have taken up his quarters at the hotel. Miss M—— says she heard at Paris, that a considerable number of troops had recently been drawn together at Lyons, in consequence of symptoms of disaffection that have recently shown themselves here.

Before breakfast I went out to catch a momentary glimpse of the city. The street in which our hotel stands is near a large public square; in the centre is a bronze equestrian statue of Louis XIV.; and the square itself is called the Place de Louis le Grand. I wonder where this statue hid itself while the Revolution was raging in Lyons, and when the guillotine, perhaps, stood on that very spot.

The square was surrounded by stately buildings, but had what seemed to be barracks for soldiers— at any rate—mean little huts, deforming its ample space; and a soldier was on guard before the statue of Louis le Grand. It was a cold, misty morning, and a fog lay throughout the area, so that I could scarcely see from one side of it to the other.

Returning towards our hotel, I saw that it had an immense front, along which ran in gigantic letters, its title—

HOTEL DE PROVENCE ET DES AMBASSADEURS.

The excellence of the hotel lay rather in the faded pomp of its sleeping-rooms, and the vastness of its *salle à manger*, than in anything very good to eat or drink.

We left it, after a poor breakfast, and went to the railway station. Looking at the mountainous heap of our luggage the night before, we had missed a great carpet bag; and we now found that Miss M——'s trunk had been substituted for it, and, there being the proper number of packages as registered, it was impossible to convince the officials that anything was wrong. We, of course, began to generalise forthwith, and pronounce the incident to be characteristic of French morality. They love a certain system and external correctness, but do not trouble themselves to be deeply in the right; and Miss M—— suggested that there used to be parallel cases in the French Revolution, when, so long as the assigned number were sent out of prison to be guillotined, the jailer did not much care whether they were the persons designated by the tribunal or not. At all events, we could get no satisfaction about the carpet-bag, and shall very probably be compelled to leave Marseilles without it.

This day's ride was through a far more picturesque country than that we saw yesterday. Heights began to rise imminent above our way, with sometimes a ruined castle wall upon them; on our left, the rail track kept close to the hills; on the other side there was the level bottom of a valley, with heights descending upon it a mile or a few miles away. Farther off we could see blue hills, shouldering high above the intermediate ones, and themselves worthy to be called mountains. These hills arranged themselves in beautiful groups, affording openings between them, and vistas of what lay beyond, and gorges which I suppose held a great deal of romantic scenery. By-and-by a river made its appearance, flowing swiftly in the same direction that we were travelling—a beautiful and cleanly river, with white pebbly shores, and itself of a peculiar blue. It rushed along very fast, sometimes whitening over shallow descents, and even in its calmer intervals its surface was all covered with whirls and eddies, indicating that it dashed onward in haste. I do not now know the name of this river, but have set it down as the "Arrowy Rhone." It kept us company a long while, and I think we did not part with it as long as daylight remained. I have seldom seen hill-scenery that struck me more than some that we saw to-day, and the old feudal towers and old villages at their feet; and the old churches, with spires shaped just like extinguishers, gave it an interest accumulating from many centuries past.

Still going southward, the vineyards began to border our track, together with what I at first took to be orchards, but soon found were plantations of olive trees, which grow to a much larger size than I supposed, and look almost exactly like very crabbed and eccentric apple trees. Neither they nor the vineyards add anything to the picturesqueness of the landscape.

On the whole, I should have been delighted with all this scenery if it had not looked so bleak, barren, brown, and bare; so like the wintry New England before the snow has fallen. It was very cold, too; ice along the borders of streams, even among the vineyards and olives. The houses are of rather a different shape here than farther northward, their roofs being not nearly so sloping. They are almost invariably covered with white plaster; the farm-houses have their outbuildings in connection with the dwelling—the whole surrounding three sides of a quadrangle.

We travelled far into the night, swallowed a cold and hasty dinner at Avignon, and reached Marseilles sorely wearied, at about eleven o'clock. We took a cab to the Hôtel d'Angleterre (two cabs, to be quite accurate), and find it a very poor place.

To go back a little, as the sun went down, we looked out of the window of our railway-carriage, and saw a sky that reminded us of what we used to see day after day in America, and what we have not seen since; and, after sunset, the horizon burned and glowed with rich crimson and orange lustre, looking at once warm and cold. After it grew dark, the stars brightened, and Miss M—— from her window pointed out some of the planets to the children, she being as familiar with them as a gardener with his flowers. They were as bright as diamonds.

We had a wretched breakfast, and J—— and I then went to the railway station to see about our luggage. On our walk back we went astray, passing by a triumphal arch, erected by the Marseillais, in honour of Louis Napoleon; but we inquired our way of old women and soldiers, who were very kind and courteous — especially the latter — and were directed aright. We came to a large, oblong, public place, set with trees, but devoid of grass, like all public places in France. In the middle of it was a bronze statue of an ecclesiastical personage, stretching forth his hands in the attitude of addressing the people, or of throwing a benediction over them. It was some archbishop, who had distinguished himself by his humanity and devotedness, during the plague of 1720. At the moment of our arrival, the piazza was quite thronged with people, who seemed to be talking amongst themselves with considerable earnestness, although without any actual excitement. They were smoking cigars; and we judged that they were only loitering here for the sake of the sunshine, having no fires at home, and nothing to do. Some looked like gentlemen, others like peasants; most of them I should have taken for the lazzaroni of this southern city—men with cloth caps, like the classic liberty-cap, or with wide-awake hats. There were one or two women of the lower classes, without bonnets, the elder ones with white caps, the younger bareheaded. I have hardly seen a lady in Marseilles; and I suspect, it being a commercial city, and dirty to the last degree, ill-built, narrow-streeted, and sometimes pestilential, there are few or no families of gentility resident here.

Returning to the hotel, we found the rest of the party ready to go out; so, we all issued forth in a body, and inquired our way to the telegraph-office, in order to send my message about the carpet-bag. In a street through which we had to pass (and which seemed to be the Exchange, or its precincts), there was a crowd even denser—yes, much denser—than that which we saw in the square of the Archbishop's statue; and each man was talking to his neighbour in a vivid, animated way, as if business were very brisk to-day.

At the telegraph-office, we discovered the cause that had brought out these many people. There had been attempts on the Emperor's life—unsuccessful, as they seem fated to be, though some mischief was done to those near him. I rather think the good people of Marseilles were glad of the attempt, as an item of news and gossip, and did not very greatly care whether it were successful or no. It seemed to have roused their vivacity rather than their interest. The only account I have seen of it was in the brief public dispatch from the Syndic (or whatever he be) of Paris to the chief authority of Marseilles, which was printed and posted in various conspicuous places. The only chance of knowing the truth with any fulness of detail would be to come across an English paper. We have had a banner hoisted half-mast in front of our hotel to-day as a token, the head-waiter tells me, of sympathy and sorrow for the General and other persons who were slain by this treasonable attempt.

J—— and I now wandered by ourselves along a circular line of quays, having, on one side of us, a thick forest of masts, while, on the other, was a sweep of shops, book-stalls, sailors' restaurants and drinking houses, fruit-sellers, candy - women, and all manner of open-air dealers and pedlars; little children playing, and jumping the rope, and such a babble and bustle as I never saw or heard before; the sun lying along the whole sweep, very hot, and evidently very grateful to those who basked in it. Whenever I passed into the shade, immediately from too warm, I became too cold. The sunshine was like hot air; the shade, like the touch of cold steel—sharp, hard, yet exhilarating. From the broad street of the quays, narrow, threadlike lanes pierced up between the edifices, calling themselves streets, yet so narrow, that a person in the middle could almost touch the houses on either hand. They ascended steeply, bordered on each side by long, contiguous walls of high houses, and, from the time of their first being built, could never have had a gleam of sunshine in them,— always in shadow, always unutterably nasty, and often pestiferous. The nastiness which I saw in Marseilles exceeds my heretofore experience. There is dirt in the hotel, and everywhere else; and it evidently troubles nobody, — no more than if all the people were pigs in a pigsty. . . . .

Passing by all this sweep of quays, J—— and I ascended to an elevated walk, overlooking the harbour, and far beyond it; for here we had our first view of the Mediterranean, blue as heaven, and bright with sunshine. It was a bay, widening forth into the open deep, and bordered with heights, and bold, picturesque headlands, some of which had either fortresses or convents on them. Several boats and one brig were under sail, making their way towards the port. I have never seen a finer sea-view. Behind the town, there seemed to be a mountainous landscape, imperfectly visible, in consequence of the intervening edifices.

THE MEDITERRANEAN SEA.

STEAMER "CALABRESE," *January* 17*th.*—If I had remained at Marseilles, I might have found many peculiarities and characteristics of that southern city to notice; but I fear that these will not be recorded if I leave them till I touch the soil of Italy. Indeed, I doubt whether there be anything really worth recording in the little distinctions between one nation and another; at any rate, after the first novelty is over, new things seem equally commonplace with the old. There is but one little interval when the mind is in such a state that it can catch the fleeting aroma of a new scene. And it is always so much pleasanter to enjoy this delicious newness than to attempt arresting it, that it requires great force of will to insist with one's self upon sitting down to write. I can do nothing with Marseilles, especially here, on the Mediterranean, long after nightfall, and when the steamer is pitching in a pretty lively way.

(Later.)—I walked out with J—— yesterday morning, and reached the outskirts of the city, whence we could see the bold and picturesque heights that surround Marseilles as with a semicircular wall. They rise into peaks, and the town being on their lower slope, descends from them towards the sea with a gradual sweep. Adown the streets that descend these declivities come little rivulets, running along over the pavement, close to the side-walks, as over a pebbly bed; and though they look vastly like kennels, I saw women washing linen in these streams, and others dipping up the water for household purposes. The women appear very much in public at Marseilles. In the squares and places you see half-a-dozen of them together, sitting in a social circle on the bottoms of upturned baskets, knitting, talking, and enjoying the public sunshine, as if it were their own household fire. Not one in a thousand of them, probably, ever has a household fire for the purpose of keeping themselves warm, but only to do their little cookery; and when there is sunshine they take advantage of it, and in the short season of rain and frost they shrug their shoulders, put on what warm garments they have, and get through the winter somewhat as grasshoppers and butterflies do—being summer insects like them. There certainly is a very keen and cutting air—sharp as a razor—and I saw ice along the borders of the little rivulets almost at noonday. To be sure, it is mid winter, and yet in the sunshine I found myself uncomfortably warm, but in the shade the air was like the touch of death itself. I do not like the climate.

There are a great number of public places in Marseilles, several of which are adorned with statues or fountains, or triumphal arches or columns, and set out with trees, and otherwise furnished as a kind of drawing-rooms, where the populace may meet together and gossip. I never before heard from human lips anything like this bustle and babble, this thousandfold talk which you hear all round about you in the crowd of a public square; so entirely different is it from the dulness of a crowd in England, where, as a rule, everybody is silent, and hardly half-a-dozen monosyllables will come from the lips of a thousand people. In Marseilles, on the contrary, a stream of unbroken talk seems to bubble from the lips of every individual. A great many interesting scenes take place in these squares. From the window of our hotel (which looked into the Place Royal) I saw a juggler displaying his art to a crowd, who stood in a regular square about him, none pretending to press nearer than the prescribed limit. While the juggler wrought his miracles his wife supplied him with his magic materials out of a box; and when the exhibition was over she packed up the white cloth with which his table was covered, together with cups, cards, balls, and whatever else, and they took their departure.

I have been struck with the idle curiosity, and, at the same time, the courtesy and kindliness of the populace of Marseilles, and I meant to exemplify it by recording how Miss S—— and I attracted their notice, and became the centre of a crowd of at least fifty of them, while doing no more remarkable thing than settling with a cab-driver. But really this pitch and swell is getting too bad, and I shall go to bed, as the best chance of keeping myself in an equable state.

ROME.

37, PALAZZO LARAZANI, VIA PORTA PINCIANA, *January 24th.*—We left Marseilles in the Neapolitan steamer *Calabrese*, as noticed above, a week ago this morning. There was no fault to be found with the steamer, which was very clean and comfortable, contrary to what we had understood beforehand, except for the coolness of the air (and I know not that this was greater than that of the Atlantic in July), our voyage would have been very pleasant; but for myself, I enjoyed nothing, having a cold upon me, or a low fever, or something else that took the light and warmth out of everything.

I went to bed immediately after my last record, and was rocked to sleep pleasantly enough by the billows of the Mediterranean; and, coming on deck about sunrise next morning, found the steamer approaching Genoa. We saw the city, lying at the foot of a range of hills, and stretching a little way up their slopes, the hills sweeping round it in the segment of a circle, and looking like an island rising abruptly out of the sea; for no connection with the mainland was visible on either side. There was snow scattered on their summits and streaking their sides a good way down. They looked bold, and barren, and brown, except where the snow whitened them. The city did not impress me with much expectation of size or splendour. Shortly after coming into the port our whole party landed, and we found ourselves at once in the midst of a crowd of cab-drivers, hotel-runners, and commissionnaires, who assaulted us with a volley of French, Italian, and broken English, which beat pitilessly about our ears; for really it seemed as if all the dictionaries in the world had been torn to pieces, and blown around us by a hurricane. Such a pother! We took a commissionnaire, a respectable-looking man, in a cloak, who said his name was Salvator Rosa; and he engaged to show us whatever was interesting in Genoa.

In the first place, he took us through narrow streets to an old church, the name of which I have forgotten and, indeed, its peculiar features; but I know that I found it pre-eminently magnificent; its whole interior being encased in polished marble, of various kinds and colours, its ceiling painted, and its chapels adorned with pictures. However, this church was dazzled out of sight by the Cathedral of San Lorenzo, to which we were afterwards conducted, whose exterior front is covered with alternate slabs of black and white marble, which were brought, either in whole or in part, from Jerusalem. Within, there was a prodigious richness of precious marbles, and a pillar, if I mistake not, from Solomon's temple; and a picture of the Virgin by St. Luke; and others (rather more intrinsically valuable, I imagine), by old masters, set in superb marble frames, within the arches of the chapels. I used to try to imagine how the English cathedrals must have looked in their primeval glory, before the Reformation, and before the whitewash of Cromwell's time had overlaid their marble pillars; but I never imagined anything at all approaching what my eyes now beheld: this sheen of polished and variegated marble covering every inch of its walls; this glow of brilliant frescoes all over the roof, and up within the domes; these beautiful pictures by great masters, painted for the places which they now occupied, and making an actual portion of the edifice; this wealth of silver, gold, and gems, that adorned the shrines of the saints, before which wax candles burned, and were kept burning, I suppose, from year's end to year's end; in short, there is no imagining nor remembering a hundredth part of the rich details. And even the cathedral (though I give it up as indescribable) was nothing at all in comparison with a church to which the commissionnaire afterwards led us; a church that had been built four or five hundred years ago, by a pirate, in expiation of his sins, and out of the profit of his rapine. This last edifice, in its interior, absolutely shone with burnished gold, and glowed with pictures; its walls were a quarry of precious stones, so valuable were the marbles out of which they were wrought; its columns and pillars were of inconceivable costliness; its pavement was a mosaic of wonderful beauty, and there were four twisted pillars made out of stalactites. Perhaps the best way to form some dim conception of it is to fancy a little casket, inlaid inside with precious stones, so that there shall not a hair's-breadth be left un-precious-stoned, and then to conceive this little bit of a casket increased to the magnitude of a great church, without losing anything of the excessive glory that was compressed into its original small compass; but all its pretty lustre made sublime by the consequent immensity. At any rate, nobody who has not seen a church like this can imagine what a gorgeous religion it was that reared it.

In the cathedral, and in all the churches, we saw priests, and many persons, kneeling at their devotions; and our Salvator Rosa, whenever we passed a chapel or shrine, failed not to touch the pavement with one knee, crossing himself the while; and once, when a priest was going through some form of devotion, he stopped a few moments to share in it.

He conducted us, too, to the Balbi Palace, the stateliest and most sumptuous residence, but not more so than another which he afterwards showed us, nor perhaps than many others which exist in Genoa, THE SUPERB. The painted ceilings in these palaces are a glorious adornment; the walls of the saloons, encrusted with various-coloured marbles, give an idea of splendour which I never gained from anything else. The floors, laid in mosaic, seem too precious to tread upon. In the royal palace, many of the floors were of various woods, inlaid by an English artist, and they looked like a magnification of some exquisite piece of Tunbridge ware; but, in all respects, this palace was inferior to others which we saw. I say nothing of the immense pictorial treasures which hung upon the walls of all the rooms through which we passed; for I soon grew so weary of admirable things, that I could neither enjoy nor understand them. My receptive faculty is very limited, and when the utmost of its small capacity is full, I become perfectly miserable, and the more so the better worth seeing are the things I am forced to reject. I do not know a greater misery: to see sights, after such repletion, is to the mind what it would be to the body to have dainties forced down the throat, long after the appetite were satiated.

All this while, whenever we emerged into the vault-like streets, we were wretchedly cold. The commissionnaire took us to a sort of pleasure-garden, occupying the ascent of a hill, and presenting seven different views of the city, from as many stations. One of the objects pointed out to us was a large yellow house, on a hill-side, in the outskirts of Genoa, which was formerly inhabited for six months by Charles Dickens. Looking down from the elevated part of the pleasure-gardens, we saw orange trees beneath us, with the golden fruit hanging upon them, though their trunks were muffled in straw; and, still lower down, there was ice and snow.

Gladly (so far as I myself was concerned) we dismissed the commissionnaire, after he had brought us to the hotel of the Cross of Malta, where we dined; needlessly, as it proved, for another dinner awaited us, after our return on board the boat.

We set sail for Leghorn before dark, and I retired early, feeling still more ill from my cold than the night before. The next morning we were in the crowded port of Leghorn. We all went ashore, with some idea of taking the rail for Pisa, which is within an hour's distance, and might have been seen in time for our departure with the steamer. But a necessary visit to a banker's, and afterwards some unnecessary formalities about our passports, kept us wandering through the streets nearly all day; and we saw nothing in the slightest degree interesting, except the tomb of Smollett, in the burial-place attached to the English Chapel. It is surrounded by an iron railing, and marked by a slender obelisk of white marble, the pattern of which is many times repeated over surrounding graves.

We went into a Jewish Synagogue,—the interior cased in marbles, and surrounded with galleries, resting upon arches above arches. There were lights burning at the altar, and it looked very like a Christian church; but it was dirty, and had an odour not of sanctity.

In Leghorn, as everywhere else, we were chilled

to the heart, except when the sunshine fell directly upon us; and we returned to the steamer with a feeling as if we were getting back to our home; for this life of wandering makes a three days' residence in one place seem like home.

We found several new passengers on board, and among others a monk, in a long brown frock of woollen cloth, with an immense cape, and a little black covering over his tonsure. He was a tall figure, with a grey beard, and might have walked, just as he stood, out of a picture by one of the old masters. This holy person addressed me very affably in Italian; but we found it impossible to hold much conversation.

The evening was beautiful, with a bright young moonlight, not yet sufficiently powerful to overwhelm the stars, and as we walked the deck, Miss M—— showed the children the constellations, and told their names. J—— made a slight mistake as to one of them, pointing it out to me as " O'Brien's belt!"

Elba was presently in view, and we might have seen many other interesting points, had it not been for our steamer's practice of resting by day, and only pursuing its voyage by night. The next morning we found ourselves in the harbour of Cività Vecchia, and, going ashore with our luggage, went through a blind turmoil with custom-house officers, inspectors of passports, soldiers, and vetturino people. My wife and I strayed a little through Città Vecchia, and found its streets narrow, like clefts in a rock,(which seems to be the fashion of Italian towns), and smelling nastily. I had made a bargain with a vetturino to send us to Rome in a carriage, with four horses, in eight hours; and as soon as the custom-house and passport people would let us, we started, lumbering slowly along with our mountain of luggage. We had heard rumours of robberies lately committed on this route; especially of a Nova Scotia bishop, who was detained on the road an hour and a half, and utterly pillaged; and certainly there was not a single mile of the dreary and desolate country over which we passed, where we might not have been robbed and murdered with impunity. Now and then, at long distances, we came to a structure that was either a prison, a tavern, or a barn, but did not look very much like either, being strongly built of stone, with iron-grated windows, and of ancient and rusty aspect. We kept along by the sea-shore a great part of the way, and stopped to feed our horses at a village, the wretched street of which stands close along the shore of the Mediterranean, its loose, dark sand being made nasty by the vicinity. The vetturino cheated us, one of the horses giving out, as he must have known it would do, half-way on our journey; and we staggered onward through cold and darkness, and peril, too, if the banditti were not a myth—reaching Rome not much before midnight. I perpetrated unheard-of briberies on the custom-house officers at the gates, and was permitted to pass through and establish myself at Spillman's Hotel, the only one where we could gain admittance, and where we have been half-frozen, and have continued so ever since.

And this is sunny Italy, and genial Rome!

PALAZZO LARAZANI, VIA PORTA PINCIANA, *February 3rd.*—We have been in Rome a fortnight to-day, or rather at eleven o'clock to-night; and I have seldom or never spent so wretched a time anywhere. Our impressions were very unfortunate, arriving at midnight, half frozen in the wintry rain, and being received into a cold and cheerless hotel, where we shivered during two or three days; meanwhile seeking lodgings among the sunless, dreary alleys which are called streets in Rome. One cold, bright day after another, has pierced me to the heart, and cut me in twain as with a sword, keen and sharp and poisoned at point and edge. I did not think that cold weather could have made me so very miserable. Having caught a feverish influenza, I was really glad of being muffled up comfortably in the fever heat. The atmosphere certainly has a peculiar quality of malignancy. After a day or two we settled ourselves in a suite of ten rooms, comprehending one flat, or what is called the second *piano* of this house. The rooms, thus far, have been very uncomfortable, it being impossible to warm them by means of the deep, old-fashioned inartificial fire-places, unless we had the great logs of a New England forest to burn in them; so I have sat in my corner by the fireside with more clothes on than I ever wore before, and my thickest great-coat over all. In the middle of the day I generally venture out for an hour or two, but have only once been warm enough even in the sunshine, and out of the sun never at any time. I understand now the force of that story of Diogenes when he asked the Conqueror, as the only favour he could do him, to stand out of his sunshine, there being such a difference in these southern climes of Europe between sun and shade. If my wits had not been too much congealed, and my fingers too numb, I should like to have kept a minute journal of my feelings and impressions during the past fortnight. It would have shown modern Rome in an aspect in which it has never yet been depicted. But I have now grown somewhat acclimated, and the first freshness of my discomfort has worn off, so that I shall never be able to express how I dislike the place, and how wretched I have been in it; and soon, I suppose, warmer weather will come, and perhaps reconcile me to Rome against my will. Cold, narrow lanes, between tall, ugly, mean-looking whitewashed houses, sour bread, pavements most uncomfortable to the feet, enormous prices for poor living; beggars, pickpockets, ancient temples and broken monuments, and clothes hanging to dry about them; French soldiers, monks, and priests of every degree; a shabby population, smoking bad cigars — these would have been some of the points of my description. Of course there are better and truer things to be said. . . . . .

It would be idle for me to attempt any sketches of these famous sites and edifices — St. Peter's, for example — which have been described by a thousand people, though none of them have ever given me an idea of what sort of place Rome is. . . . . .

The Coliseum was very much what I had preconceived it, though I was not prepared to find it turned into a sort of Christian church, with a pulpit on the verge of the open space. . . . . The French soldiers, who keep guard within it, as in other public places in

Rome, have an excellent opportunity to secure the welfare of their souls.

February 7th.—I cannot get fairly into the current of my journal since we arrived, and already I perceive that the nice peculiarities of Roman life are passing from my notice before I have recorded them. It is a very great pity. During the past week I have plodded daily, for an hour or two, through the narrow, stony streets, that look worse than the worst backside lanes of any other city; indescribably ugly and disagreeable they are, . . . without side walks, but provided with a line of larger square stones, set crosswise to each other, along which there is somewhat less uneasy walking. . . . . Ever and anon, even in the meanest streets—though, generally speaking, one can hardly be called meaner than another—we pass a palace, extending far along the narrow way on a line with the other houses, but distinguished by its architectural windows, iron-barred on the basement story, and by its portal arch, through which we have glimpses, sometimes of a dirty courtyard, or perhaps of a clean, ornamented one, with trees, a colonnade, a fountain, and a statue in the vista; though, more likely, it resembles the entrance to a stable, and may, perhaps, really be one. The lower regions of palaces come to strange uses in

Rome. . . . . . In the basement story of the Barberini palace, a regiment of French soldiers (or soldiers of some kind*) seems to be quartered, while no doubt princes have magnificent domiciles above. Be it palace or whatever other dwelling, the inmates climb through rubbish often to the comforts, such as they may be, that await them above. I vainly try to get down upon paper the dreariness, the ugliness, shabbiness, un-home-likeness of a Roman street. It is also to be said that you cannot go far in any direction without coming to a piazza, which is sometimes little more than a widening and enlarging of the dingy street, with the lofty façade of a church or basilica on one side, and a fountain in the centre, where the water squirts out of some fantastic piece of sculpture into a great stone basin. These fountains are often of immense size and most elaborate design. . . . . . .

There are a great many of these fountain-shapes, constructed under the orders of one pope or another, in all parts of the city; and only the very simplest, such as a jet springing from a broad marble or porphyry vase, and falling back into it again, are really ornamental. If an antiquary were to accompany me through the streets, no doubt he would point out ten thousand interesting objects that I now pass over

* We find them to be retainers of the Barberini family, not French.

unnoticed, so general is the surface of plaster and whitewash; but often I can see fragments of antiquity built into the walls, or perhaps a church that was a Roman temple, or a basement of ponderous stones that were laid above twenty centuries ago. It is strange how our ideas of what antiquity is become altered here in Rome; the sixteenth century, in which many of the churches and fountains seem to have been built or re-edified, seems close at hand, even like our own days; a thousand years, or the days of the latter empire, is but a modern date, and scarcely interests us; and nothing is really venerable of a more recent epoch than the reign of Constantine. And the Egyptian obelisks that stand in several of the piazzas, put even the Augustan or Republican antiquities to shame. I remember reading in a New York newspaper an account of one of the public buildings of that city—a relic of "the olden time," the writer called it; for it was erected in 1825! I am glad I saw the castles and gothic churches and cathedrals of England before visiting Rome, or I never could have felt that delightful reverence for their grey and ivy-hung antiquity after seeing these so much older remains. But, indeed, old things are not so beautiful in this dry climate and clear atmosphere as in moist England. . . . .

Whatever beauty there may be in a Roman ruin is the remnant of what was beautiful originally; whereas an English ruin is more beautiful often in its decay than even it was in its primal strength. If we ever build such noble structures as these Roman ones, we can have just as good ruins, after two thousand years, in the United States; but we never can have a Furness Abbey or a Kenilworth. The Corso, and perhaps some other streets, does not deserve all the vituperation which I have bestowed on the generality of Roman *vias*, though the Corso is narrow, not averaging more than nine paces, if so much, from side-walk to side-walk. But palace after palace stands along almost its whole extent—not, however, that they make such architectural show on the street as palaces should. The enclosed courts were perhaps the only parts of these edifices which the founders cared to enrich architecturally. I think Linlithgow palace, of which I saw the ruins during my last tour in Scotland, was built by an architect who had studied these Roman palaces. There was never any idea of domestic comfort, or of what we include in the name of home, at all implicated in such structures; they being generally built by wifeless and childless churchmen, for the display of pictures and statuary, in galleries and long suites of rooms.

I have not yet fairly begun the sight-seeing of Rome. I have been four or five times to St. Peter's, and always with pleasure, because there is such a delightful, summer-like warmth the moment we pass beneath the heavy, padded leather curtains that protect the entrances. It is almost impossible not to believe that this genial temperature is the result of furnace-heat; but, really, it is the warmth of last summer, which will be included within those massive walls and in that vast immensity of space till, six months hence, this winter's chill will just have made its way thither. It would be an excellent plan for a valetudinarian to lodge during the winter in St. Peter's, perhaps establishing his household in one of the papal tombs. I become, I think, more sensible of the size of St. Peter's, but am as yet far from being overwhelmed by it. It is not, as one expects, so big as all out of doors, nor is its dome so immense as that of the firmament. It looked queer, however, the other day, to see a little ragged boy, the very least of human things, going round and kneeling at shrine after shrine, and a group of children standing on tiptoe to reach the vase of holy water. . . . .

On coming out of St. Peter's, at my last visit, I saw a great sheet of ice around the fountain on the right hand, and some little Romans awkwardly sliding on it. I, too, took a slide, just for the sake of doing what I never thought to do in Rome. This inclement weather, I should suppose, must make the whole city very miserable; for the native Romans, I am told, never keep any fire, except for culinary purposes, even in the severest winter. They flee from their cheerless houses into the open air, and bring their firesides along with them, in the shape of small earthen vases or pipkins, with a handle, by which they carry them up and down the streets, and so warm at least their hands with the lighted charcoal. I have had glimpses through open doorways into interiors, and saw them as dismal as tombs. Wherever I pass my summers, let me spend my winters in a cold country.

We went yesterday to the Pantheon. . . . .

When I first came to Rome, I felt embarrassed and unwilling to pass, with my heresy, between a devotee and his saint; for they often shoot their prayers at a shrine almost quite across the church. But there seems to be no violation of etiquette in so doing. A women begged of us in the Pantheon, and accused my wife of impiety for not giving her an alms. . . . People of very decent appearance are often unexpectedly converted into beggars as you approach them; but in general they take a "No" at once.

February 9th.—For three or four days it has been cloudy and rainy, which is the greater pity, as this should be the gayest and merriest part of the Carnival. I go out but little—yesterday only as far as Pakenham and Hooker's bank, in the Piazza di Spagna, where I read *Galignani* and the American papers. At last, after seeing in England more of my fellow-compatriots than ever before, I really am disjoined from my country.

To-day I walked out along the Pincian Hill. . . . . As the clouds still threatened rain, I deemed it my safest course to go to St. Peter's for refuge. Heavy and dull as the day was, the effect of this great world of a church was still brilliant in the interior, as if it had a sunshine of its own, as well as its own temperature; and, by-and-by, the sunshine of the outward world came through the windows, hundreds of feet aloft, and fell upon the beautiful inlaid pavement. . . . . Against a pillar, on one side of the nave, is a mosaic copy of Raphael's Transfiguration, fitly framed within a great arch of gorgeous marble; and, no doubt, the indestructible mosaic has preserved it far more completely than the fading and darkening tints in which the artist painted it. At any rate, it seemed to me the one glorious picture that I have ever seen. The pillar nearest the great entrance, on the left of the nave, supports the monument to the Stuart family, where two winged figures, with inverted torches, stand on either side of a marble door, which is closed for ever. It is an impressive monument, for you feel as if the last of the race had passed through that door.

Emerging from the church, I saw a French sergeant drilling his men in the piazza. These French soldiers are prominent objects everywhere about the city, and make up more of its sight and sound than anything else that lives. They stroll about individually; they pace as sentinels in all the public places; and they march up and down in squads, companies, and battalions, always with a very great din of drum, fife, and trumpet; ten times the proportion of music that the same number of men would require elsewhere; and it reverberates with ten times the noise between the high edifices of these lanes than it would make in broader streets. Nevertheless, I have no quarrel with the French soldiers; they are fresh, healthy, smart, honest-looking young fellows enough, in blue coats and red trousers; . . . . and, at all events, they serve as an efficient police, making Rome as safe as London; whereas, without them, it would very likely be a den of banditti.

On my way home I saw a few tokens of the Carnival, which is now in full progress; though, as it was only about one o'clock, its frolics had not commenced for the day. .... I question whether the Romans themselves take any great interest in the Carnival. The balconies along the Corso were almost entirely taken by English and Americans, or other foreigners.

As I approached the bridge of St. Angelo, I saw several persons engaged, as I thought, in fishing in the Tiber, with very strong lines; but on drawing nearer I found that they were trying to hook up the branches and twigs, and other drift wood, which the recent rains might have swept into the river. There was a little heap of what looked chiefly like willow twigs, the poor result of their labour. The hook was a knot of wood, with the lopped-off branches projecting in three or four prongs. The Tiber has always the hue of a mud-puddle; but now, after a heavy rain, which has washed the clay into it, it looks like pease-soup. It is a broad and rapid stream, eddying along as if it were in haste to disgorge its impurities into the sea. On the left side, where the city mostly is situated, the buildings hang directly over the stream; on the other, where stand the Castle of St. Angelo and the Church of St. Peter, the town does not press so imminent upon the shore. The banks are clayey, and look as if the river had been digging them away for ages; but I believe its bed is higher than of yore.

February 10*th.*—I went out to-day, and, going along the Via Felice and the Via delle Quattro Fontane, came unawares to the Basilica of Santa Maria Maggiore, on the summit of the Esquiline Hill. I entered it, without in the least knowing what church it was, and found myself in a broad and noble nave, both very simple and very grand. There was a long row of Ionic columns of marble, twenty or thereabouts on each side, supporting a flat roof. There were vaulted side-aisles, and, at the farther end, a bronze canopy over the high altar; and all along the length of the side aisles were shrines with pictures, sculpture, and burning lamps; the whole church, too, was lined with marble; the roof was gilded; and yet the general effect of severe and noble simplicity triumphed over all the ornament. I should have taken it for a Roman temple, retaining nearly its pristine aspect; but Murray tells us that it was founded A.D. 342 by Pope Liberius, on the spot precisely marked out by a miraculous fall of snow in the month of August, and it has undergone many alterations since his time. But it is very fine, and gives the beholder the idea of vastness, which seems harder to attain than anything else. On the right hand, approaching the high altar, there is a chapel, separated from the rest of the church by an iron paling; and, being admitted into it with another party, I found it most elaborately magnificent. But one magnificence outshone another, and made itself the brightest conceivable for the moment. However, this chapel was as rich as the most precious marble could make it in pillars and pilasters, and broad, polished slabs, covering the whole walls (except where there were splendid and glowing frescoes, or where some monumental statuary or bas-relief, or mosaic picture filled up an arched niche). Its architecture was a dome, resting on four great arches; and in size it would alone have been a church. In the centre of the mosaic pavement there was a flight of steps, down which we went, and saw a group in marble representing the nativity of Christ, which, judging by the unction with which our guide talked about it, must have been of peculiar sanctity. I hate to leave this chapel and church without being able to say any one thing that may reflect a portion of their beauty, or of the feeling which they excite. Kneeling against many of the pillars there were persons in prayer, and I stepped softly, fearing lest my tread on the marble pavement should disturb them—a needless precaution, however, for nobody seems to expect it, nor to be disturbed by the lack of it.

The situation of the church, I should suppose, is the loftiest in Rome: it has a fountain at one end, and a column at the other; but I did not pay particular attention to either, nor to the exterior of the church itself.

On my return, I turned aside from the Via delle Quattro Fontane into the Via Quirinalis, and was led by it into the Piazza di Monte Cavallo. The street through which I passed was broader, cleaner, and statelier than most streets in Rome, and bordered by palaces; and the piazza had noble edifices around it, and a fountain, an obelisk, and two nude statues in the centre. The obelisk was, as the inscription indicated, a relic of Egypt: the basin of the fountain was an immense bowl of oriental granite, into which poured a copious flood of water, discoloured by the rain; the statues were colossal; two beautiful young men, each holding a fiery steed. On the pedestal of one was the inscription, OPUS PHIDIÆ; on the other, OPUS PRAXITELIS. What a city is this, when one may stumble, by mere chance—at a street corner, as it were—on the works of two such sculptors! I do not know the authority on which these statues (Castor and Pollux, I presume) are attributed to

Phidias and Praxiteles; but they impressed me as noble and godlike, and I feel inclined to take them for what they purport to be. On one side of the piazza is the Pontifical Palace; but, not being aware of this at the time, I did not look particularly at the edifice.

I came home by way of the Corso, which seemed a little enlivened by Carnival time; though, as it was not yet two o'clock, the fun had not begun for the day. The rain throws a dreary damper on the festivities.

February 13*th.* — Day before yesterday we took J—— and R—— in a carriage, and went to see the Carnival, by driving up and down the Corso. It was as ugly a day, as respects weather, as has befallen us since we came to Rome: cloudy, with an indecisive wet, which finally settled into a rain; and people say that such is generally the weather in Carnival time. There is very little to be said about the spectacle. Sunshine would have improved it, no doubt; but a person must have very broad sunshine within himself to be joyous on such shallow provocation. The street, at all events, would have looked rather brilliant under a sunny sky, the balconies being hung with bright-coloured draperies, which were also flung out of some of the windows. . . . . Soon I had my first experience of the Carnival, in a handful of *confetti*, right slap in my face. . . . . Many of the ladies wore loose, white dominoes, and some of the gentlemen had on defensive armour of blouses; and wire masks over the face were a protection for both sexes; not a needless one, for I received a shot in my right eye which cost me many tears. It seems to be a point of courtesy (though often disregarded by Americans and English) not to fling confetti at ladies, or at non-combatants, or quiet by-standers; and the engagements with these missiles were generally between open carriages, manned with youths, who were provided with confett for such encounters, and with bouquets for the ladies. We had one real enemy on the Corso; for our former friend Mrs. T—— was there, and as often as we passed and repassed her, she favoured us with a handful of lime. Two or three times, somebody ran by the carriage and puffed forth a shower of winged seeds through a tube into our faces and over our clothes; and, in the course of the afternoon, we were hit with perhaps half a dozen sugar-plums. Possibly we may not have received our fair share of these last salutes, for J—— had on a black mask, which made him look like an imp of Satan, and drew many volleys of confetti that we might otherwise have escaped. A good many bouquets were flung at our little R——, and at us generally. .... This was what is called masquing day, when it is the rule to wear masques in the Corso, but the great majority of people appeared without them. ..... Two fantastic figures, with enormous heads, set round with frizzly hair, came and grinned into our carriage, and J—— tore out a handful of hair (which proved to be sea-weed) from one of their heads, rather to the discomposure of the owner, who muttered his indignation in Italian. .... On comparing notes with J—— and R——, indeed, with U——, too, I find that they all enjoyed the Carnival much more than I did. Only the young ought to write descriptions of such scenes. My cold criticism chills the life out of it.

February 14*th.*—Friday, 12th, was a sunny day,—the first that we had had for some time,—and my wife and I went forth to see sights as well as to make some calls that had long been due. We went first to the church of Santa Maria Maggiore, which I have already mentioned, and, on our return, we went to the Piazza di Monte Cavallo, and saw those admirable ancient statues of Castor and Pollux, which seem to me sons of the morning, and full of life and strength. The atmosphere, in such a length of time, has covered the marble surface of these statues with a grey rust, that envelops both the men and horses as with a garment; besides which, there are strange discoloration, such as patches of white moss on the elbows, and reddish streaks down the sides; but the glory of form overcomes all these defects of colour. It is pleasant to observe how familiar some little birds are with these colossal statues—hopping about on their heads and over their huge fists, and very likely they have nests in their ears or among their hair.

We called at the Barberini Palace, where William Story has established himself and family for the next seven years, or more, on the third piano, in apartments that afford a very fine outlook over Rome, and have the sun in them through most of the day. Mrs. S—— invited us to her fancy ball, but we declined.

On the staircase ascending to their piano we saw the ancient Greek bas-relief of a lion, whence Canova is supposed to have taken the idea of his lions on the monument in St. Peter's. Afterwards we made two or three calls in the neighbourhood of the Piazza di Spagna, finding only Mr. Hamilton Fish and family, at the Hôtel d'Europe, at home, and next visited the studio of Mr. C. G. Thompson, whom I knew in Boston. He has very greatly improved since those days, and being always a man of delicate mind, and earnestly desiring excellence for its own sake, he has won himself the power of doing beautiful and elevated works. He is now meditating a series of pictures from Shakspere's *Tempest*, the sketches of one or two of which he showed us, likewise a copy of a small Madonna, by Raphael, wrought with a minute faithfulness which it makes one a better man to observe. . . . . Mr. Thompson is a true artist, and whatever his pictures have of beauty comes from very far beneath the surface; and this, I suppose, is one weighty reason why he has but moderate success. I should like his pictures for the mere colour, even if they represented nothing. His studio is in the Via Sistina; and, at a little distance on the other side of the same street, is William Story's, where we likewise went, and found him at work on a sitting statue of "Cleopatra."

William Story looks quite as vivid, in a graver way, as when I saw him last, a very young man. His perplexing variety of talents and accomplishments—he being a poet, a prose writer, a lawyer, a painter, a musician, and a sculptor—seems now to be concentrating itself into this latter vocation, and I cannot see why he should not achieve something very good. He has a beautiful statue, already finished, of Goethe's Margaret, pulling a flower to pieces to discover whether Faust loves her; a very type of virginity and simplicity. The statue of "Cleopatra," now only fourteen days advanced in the clay, is as wide a step from the little maidenly Margaret as any artist could take; it is a grand subject, and he is conceiving it with depth and power, and working it out with adequate skill. He certainly is sensible of something deeper in his art than merely to make beautiful nudities and baptize them by classic names. By-the-bye, he told us several queer stories of American visitors to his studio: one of them, after long inspecting Cleopatra, into which he has put all possible characteristics of her time and nation and of her own individuality, asked, "Have you baptized your statue yet?" as if the sculptor were waiting till his statue were finished before he chose the subject of it—as, indeed, I should think many sculptors do. Another remarked of a statue of "Hero," who is seeking Leander by torch-light, and in momentary expectation of finding his drowned body, "Is not the face a little sad?" Another time a whole party of Americans filed into his studio, and ranged themselves round his father's statue, and, after much silent examination, the spokesman of the party inquired, "Well, sir, what is this intended to represent?" William Story, in telling these little anecdotes, gave the Yankee twang to perfection. . . . .

The statue of his father—his first work—is very noble, as noble and fine a portrait-statue as I ever saw. In the outer room of his studio a stone-cutter, or whatever this kind of artisan is called, was at work, transferring the statue of "Hero" from the plaster-cast into marble ; and already, though still in some respects a block of stone, there was a wonderful degree of expression in the face. It is not quite pleasant to think that the sculptor does not really do the whole labour on his statues, but that they are all but finished to his hand by merely mechanical people. It is generally only the finishing touches that are given by his own chisel.

Yesterday, being another bright day, we went to the basilica of St. John Lateran, which is the basilica next in rank to St. Peter's, and has the precedence of it as regards certain sacred privileges. It stands on a most noble site, on the outskirts of the city, commanding a view of the Sabine and Alban hills, blue in the distance, and some of them hoary with sunny snow. The ruins of the Claudian aqueduct are close at hand. The church is connected with the Lateran palace and museum, so that the whole is one edifice; but the façade of the church distinguishes it, and is very lofty and grand, more so, it seems to me, than that of St. Peter's. Under the portico is an old statue of Constantine, representing him as a very stout and sturdy personage. The inside of the church disappointed me, though, no doubt, I should have been wonder-struck had I seen it a month ago. We went into one of the chapels, which was very rich in coloured marbles; and going down a winding staircase, found ourselves among the tombs and sarcophagi of the Corsini family, and in presence of a marble Pietà, very beautifully sculptured. On the other side of the church we looked into the Torlonia chapel, very rich and rather profusely gilded, but, as it seemed to me, not tawdry, though the white newness of the marble is not perfectly agreeable after being accustomed to the milder tint which time bestows on sculpture. The tombs and statues appeared like shapes and images of new-fallen snow. The most interesting thing which we saw in this church (and, admitting its authenticity, there can scarcely be a more interesting one anywhere) was the table at which the Last Supper was eaten. It is preserved in a corridor, on one side of the tribune or chancel, and is shown by torch-light suspended upon the wall beneath a covering of glass. Only the top of the table is shown, presenting a broad, flat surface of wood, evidently very old, and showing traces of dry rot in one or two places. There are nails in it, and the attendant said that it had formerly been covered with bronze. As well as I can remember, it may be five or six feet square, and I suppose would accommodate twelve persons, though not if they reclined in the Roman fashion, nor if they sat as they do in Leonardo da Vinci's picture. It would be very delightful to believe in this table.

There are several other sacred relics preserved in the church; for instance, the staircase of Pilate's house up which Jesus went, and the porphyry slab on which the soldiers cast lots for his garments. These, however, we did not see. There are very glowing frescoes on portions of the walls; but, there being much whitewash instead of encrusted marble, it has not the pleasant aspect which one's eye learns to demand in Roman churches. There is a good deal of statuary along the columns of the nave, and in the monuments of the side aisles.

In reference to the interior splendour of Roman churches, I must say that I think it a pity that painted windows are exclusively a Gothic ornament; for the elaborate ornamentation of these interiors puts the ordinary daylight out of countenance, so that a window with only the white sunshine coming through it, or even with a glimpse of the blue Italian sky, looks like a portion left unfinished, and therefore a blotch in the rich wall. It is like the one spot in Aladdin's palace which he left for the king, his father-in-law, to finish, after his fairy architects had exhausted their magnificence on the rest, and the sun, like the king, fails in the effort. It has what is called a Porta Santa, which we saw walled up, in the front of the church, one side of the main entrance. I know not what gives it its sanctity, but it appears to be opened by the Pope on a year of jubilee, once every quarter of a century.

After our return .... I took R—— along the Pincian Hill, and finally, after witnessing what of the Carnival could be seen in the Piazza del Popolo from that safe height, we went down into the Corso, and some little distance along it. Except for the sunshine, the scene was much the same as I have already described; perhaps fewer confetti and more bouquets. Some Americans and English are said to have been brought before the police authorities, and fined for throwing lime. It is remarkable that the jollity, such as it is, of the Carnival does not extend an inch beyond the line of the Corso; there it flows along in a narrow stream, while in the nearest street we see nothing but the ordinary Roman gravity.

February 15*th.*—Yesterday was a bright day, but I did not go out till the afternoon, when I took an hour's walk along the Pincian, stopping a good while to look at the old beggar who, for many years past, has occupied one of the platforms of the flight of steps leading from the Piazza di Spagna to the Trinità di Monti. Hillard commemorates him in his book. He is an unlovely object, moving about on his hands and knees, principally by aid of his hands, which are fortified with a sort of wooden shoes, while his poor, wasted lower shanks stick up in the air behind him, loosely vibrating as he progresses. He is grey, old, ragged, a pitiable sight, but seems very active in his own fashion, and bestirs himself, on the approach of his visitors, with the alacrity of a spider when a fly touches the remote circumference of his web. While I looked down at him he received alms from three persons, one of whom was a young woman of the lower orders, the other two were gentlemen, probably either English or American. I could not quite make out the principle on which he let some persons pass without molestation, while he shuffled from one end of the platform to the other to intercept an occasional individual. He is not persistent in his demands; nor, indeed, is this a usual fault among Italian beggars.

A shake of the head will stop him when wriggling towards you from a distance. I fancy he reaps a pretty fair harvest, and no doubt leads as contented and as interesting a life as most people, sitting there all day on those sunny steps, looking at the world, and making his profit out of it. It must be pretty much such an occupation as fishing, in its effect upon the hopes and apprehensions; and probably he suffers no more from the many refusals he meets with than the angler does, when he sees a fish smell at his bait and swim away. One success pays for a hundred disappointments, and the game is all the better for not being entirely in his own favour.

Walking onward, I found the Pincian thronged with promenaders, as also with carriages, which drove round the verge of the gardens in an unbroken ring.

To-day has been very rainy. I went out in the forenoon, and took a sitting for my bust in one of a suite of rooms formerly occupied by Canova. It was large, high, and dreary from the want of a carpet, furniture, or anything but clay and plaster. A sculptor's studio has not the picturesque charm of that of a painter, where there are colour, warmth, and cheerfulness, and where the artist continually turns towards you the glow of some picture, which is resting against the wall. . . . . I was asked not to look at the bust at the close of the sitting, and, of course, I obeyed; though I have a vague idea of a heavy-browed physiognomy, something like what I have seen in the glass, but looking strangely in that guise of clay. . . . .

It is a singular fascination that Rome exercises upon artists. There is clay elsewhere, and marble enough, and heads to model, and ideas may be made sensible objects at home as well as here. I think it is the peculiar mode of life that attracts, and its freedom from the enthralments of society, more than the artistic advantages which Rome offers; and, no doubt, though the artists care little about one another's works, yet they keep each other warm by the presence of so many of them.

The Carnival still continues, though I hardly see how it can have withstood such a damper as this rainy day. There were several people — three, I think — killed in the Corso on Saturday: some accounts say that they were run over by the horses in the race; others, that they were ridden down by the dragoons in clearing the course.

After leaving Canova's studio, I stepped into the church of San Luigi de' Franchesi, in the Via di Ripetta. It was built, I believe, by Catherine di Medici, and is under the protection of the French

Government, and is a most shamefully dirty place of worship, the beautiful marble columns looking dingy, for the want of loving and pious care. There are many tombs and monuments of French people, both of the past and present :—artists, soldiers, priests, and others, who have died in Rome. It was so dusky within the church that I could hardly distinguish the pictures in the chapels and over the altar, nor did I know that there were any worth looking for. Nevertheless, there were frescoes by Domenichino, and oil-paintings by Guido and others. I found it peculiarly touching to read the records, in Latin or French, of persons who had died in this foreign land, though they were not my own country-people, and though I was even less akin to them than they to Italy. Still, there was a sort of relationship in the fact that neither they nor I belonged here.

February 17*th*.—Yesterday morning was perfectly sunny, and we went out betimes to see churches; going first to the Capuchins', close by the Piazza Barberini.

["The Marble Faun" takes up this description of the church, and of the dead monk, which we really saw, just as recounted, even to the sudden stream of blood, which flowed from the nostrils, as we looked at him.—ED.]

We next went to the Trinità di Monti, which stands at the head of the steps, leading, in several flights, from the Piazza di Spagna. It is now connected with a convent of French nuns, and when we rang at a side door, one of the sisterhood answered the summons, and admitted us into the church. This, like that of the Capuchins, had a vaulted roof over the nave, and no side aisles, but rows of chapels instead. Unlike the Capuchins', which was filthy, and really disgraceful to behold, this church was most exquisitely neat, as women alone would have thought it worth while to keep it. It is not a very splendid church—not rich in gorgeous marbles—but pleasant to be in, if it were only for the sake of its godly purity. There was only one person in the nave—a young girl, who sat perfectly still, with her face towards the altar, as long as we stayed. Between the nave and the rest of the church there is a high iron railing, and on the other side of it were two kneeling figures in black—so motionless, that I at first thought them statues; but they proved to be two nuns at their devotions; and others of the sisterhood came by-and-by, and joined them. Nuns—at least these nuns, who are French, and probably ladies of refinement, having the education of young girls in charge—are far pleasanter objects to see and think about than monks; the odour of sanctity, in the latter, not being an agreeable fragrance. But these holy sisters, with their black crape and white muslin, looked really pure and unspotted from the world.

On the iron railing above mentioned was the representation of a golden heart, pierced with arrows; for these are nuns of the Sacred Heart. In the various chapels there are several paintings in fresco, some by Daniele da Volterra; and one of them—the "Descent from the Cross"—has been pronounced the third greatest picture in the world. I never should have had the slighest suspicion that it was a great picture at all—so worn and faded it looks, and so hard; so difficult to be seen, and so undelightful when one does see it.

From the Trinità we went to the Santa Maria del Popolo, a church built on a spot where Nero is said to have been buried, and which was afterwards made horrible by devilish phantoms. It now being past twelve, and all the churches closing from twelve till two, we had not time to pay much attention to the frescoes, oil-pictures, and statues, by Raphael and other famous men, which are to be seen here. I remember dimly the magnificent chapel of the Chigi family, and little else, for we stayed but a short time; and went next to the sculptor's studio, where I had another sitting for my bust. After I had been moulded for about an hour, we turned homeward; but my wife concluded to hire a balcony for this last afternoon and evening of the Carnival, and she took possession of it, while I went home to send to her Miss S—— and the two elder children. For my part, I took R——, and walked, by way of the Pincian, to the Piazza del Popolo, and thence along the Corso, where, by this time, the warfare of bouquets and confetti raged pretty fiercely. The sky being blue and the sun bright, the scene looked much gayer and brisker than I had before found it; and I can conceive of its being rather agreeable than otherwise, up to the age of twenty. We got several volleys of confetti. R—— received a bouquet and a sugarplum, and I a resounding hit from something that looked more like a cabbage than a flower. Little as I have enjoyed the Carnival, I think I could make quite a brilliant sketch of it, without very widely departing from truth.

February 19*th.*—Day before yesterday, pretty early, we went to St. Peter's, expecting to see the Pope cast ashes on the heads of the cardinals, it being Ash Wednesday. On arriving, however, we found no more than the usual number of visitants and devotional people scattered through the broad interior of

St. Peter's; and thence concluded that the ceremonies were to be performed in the Sistine Chapel. Accordingly, we went out of the cathedral, through the door in the left transept, and passed round the exterior, and through the vast courts of the Vatican, seeking for the chapel. We had blundered into the carriage-entrance of the palace: there is an entrance from some point near the front of the church, but this we did not find. The papal guards, in the strangest antique and antic costume that was ever seen,—a parti-coloured dress, striped with blue, red, and yellow, white and black, with a doublet and ruff, and trunk-breeches, and armed with halberds—were on duty at the gateways, but suffered us to pass without question. Finally, we reached a large court, where some cardinals' red equipages and other carriages were drawn up, but were still at a loss as to the whereabouts of the chapel. At last an attendant kindly showed us the proper door, and led us up flights of stairs, along passages and galleries, and through halls, till at last we came to a spacious and lofty apartment adorned with frescoes: this was the Sala Regia, and the ante-chamber to the Sistine Chapel.

The attendant, meanwhile, had informed us that my wife could not be admitted to the chapel in her bonnet, and that I myself could not enter at all, for lack of a dress-coat; so my wife took off her bonnet, and, covering her head with her black lace veil, was readily let in, while I remained in the Sala Regia, with several other gentlemen, who found themselves in the same predicament as I was. There was a wonderful variety of costume to be seen and studied among the persons around me, comprising garbs that have been elsewhere laid aside for at least three centuries—the broad, plaited, double ruff, and black velvet cloak, doublet, trunk-breeches, and sword of Queen Elizabeth's time—the papal guard, in their striped and parti-coloured dress as before described, looking not a little like harlequins; other soldiers in helmets and jackboots; French officers of various uniform; monks and priests; attendants, in old-fashioned and gorgeous livery; gentlemen, some in black dress-coats and pantaloons, others in wide-awake hats and tweed overcoats; and a few ladies in the prescribed costume of black; so that, in any other country, the scene might have been taken for a fancy ball. By-and-by, the cardinals began to arrive, and added their splendid purple robes and red hats to make the picture still more brilliant. They were old men—one or two very aged and infirm—and generally men of bulk and substance, with heavy faces, fleshy about the chin. Their red hats, trimmed with gold lace, are a beautiful piece of finery, and are identical in shape with the black, loosely-cocked beavers worn by the Catholic ecclesiastics generally. Wolsey's hat, which I saw at the Manchester Exhibition, might have been made on the same block, but apparently was never cocked, as the fashion now is. The attendants changed the upper portions of their masters' attire, and put a little cap of scarlet cloth on each of their heads, after which the cardinals, one by one, or two by two, as they happened to arrive, went into the chapel, with a page behind each holding up his purple train. In the meanwhile, within the chapel, we heard singing and chanting; and whenever the voluminous curtains that hung before the entrance were slightly drawn apart, we outsiders glanced through, but could see only a mass of people, and beyond them still another chapel, divided from the hither one by a screen. When almost everybody had gone in, there was a stir among the guards and attendants, and a door opened, apparently communicating with the inner apartments of the Vatican. Through this door came —not the Pope, as I had partly expected, but a bulky old lady in black, with a red face, who bowed towards the spectators with an aspect of dignified complaisance as she passed towards the entrance of the chapel. I took off my hat, unlike certain English gentlemen who stood nearer, and found that I had not done amiss, for it was the Queen of Spain.

There was nothing else to be seen; so I went back through the ante-chambers (which are noble halls, richly frescoed on the walls and ceilings), endeavouring to get out through the same passages that had let me in. I had already tried to descend what I now suppose to be the Scala Santa, but had been turned back by a sentinel. After wandering to and fro a good while, I at last found myself in a long, long gallery, on each side of which were innumerable inscriptions, in Greek and Latin, on slabs of marble, built into the walls; and classic altars and tablets were ranged along, from end to end. At the extremity was a closed iron grating, from which I was retreating; but a French gentleman accosted me, with the information that the custode would admit me, if I chose, and would accompany me through the sculpture department of the Vatican. I acceded, and thus took my first view of those innumerable art-treasures, passing from one object to another, at an easy pace, pausing hardly a moment anywhere, and dismissing even the Apollo, and the Laocoon, and the Torso of

Hercules, in the space of half a dozen breaths. I was well enough content to do so, in order to get a general idea of the contents of the galleries, before settling down upon individual objects.

Most of the world-famous sculptures presented themselves to my eye with a kind of familiarity, through the copies and casts which I had seen; but I found the originals more different than I anticipated. The Apollo, for instance, has a face which I have never seen in any cast or copy. I must confess, however, taking such transient glimpses as I did, I was more impressed with the extent of the Vatican, and the beautiful order in which it is kept, and its great, sunny, open courts, with fountains, grass and shrubs, and the views of Rome and the Campagna from its windows—more impressed with these, and with certain vastly capacious vases, and two great sarcophagi—than with the statuary. Thus I went round the whole, and was dismissed through the grated barrier into the gallery of inscriptions again; and after a little more wandering, I made my way out of the palace. . . . . .

Yesterday, I went out betimes, and strayed through some portion of ancient Rome, to the column of Trajan, to the Forum, thence along the Tarpeian

Way; after which I lost myself among the intricacies of the streets, and finally came out at the bridge of St. Angelo. The first observation which a stranger is led to make, in the neighbourhood of Roman ruins, is that the inhabitants seem to be strangely addicted to the washing of clothes; for all the precincts of Trajan's Forum, and of the Roman Forum, and wherever else an iron railing affords opportunity to hang them, were whitened with sheets, and other linen and cotton, drying in the sun. It must be that washerwomen burrow among the old temples. The second observation is not quite so favourable to the cleanly character of the modern Romans; indeed, it is so very unfavourable, that I hardly know how to express it. But the fact is, that, through the forum, ... and any where out of the commonest foot-track and road-way, you must look well to your steps. . . . . If you.tread beneath the triumphal arch of Titus or Constantine, you had better look downward than upward, whatever be the merit of the sculptures aloft. . . . .

After awhile, the visitant finds himself getting accustomed to this horrible state of things; and the associations of moral sublimity and beauty seem to throw a veil over the physical meannesses to which I allude. Perhaps there is something in the mind of the people of these countries that enables them quite to dissever small ugliness from great sublimity and beauty. They spit upon the glorious pavement of St. Peter's, and wherever else they like; they place paltry-looking, wooden confessionals beneath its sublime arches, and ornament them with cheap little coloured prints of the crucifixion; they hang tin hearts and other tinsel and trumpery at the gorgeous shrines of the saints, in chapels that are encrusted with gems, or marbles almost as precious; they put pasteboard statues of saints beneath the dome of the Pantheon; in short, they let the sublime and the ridiculous come close together, and are not in the least troubled by the proximity. It must be that their sense of the beautiful is stronger than in the Anglo-Saxon mind, and that it observes only what is fit to gratify it.

To-day, which was bright and cool, my wife and I set forth immediately after breakfast, in search of the Baths of Diocletian, and the Church of Santa Maria degl' Angeli. We went too far along the Via di Porta Pia, and after passing by two or three convents, and their high garden walls, and the villa Bonaparte on one side, and the villa

Torlonia on the other, at last issued through the city gate. Before us, far away, were the Alban hills, the loftiest of which was absolutely silvered with snow and sunshine, and set in the bluest and brightest of skies. We now retraced our steps, to the Fountain of the Termini, where is a ponderous heap of stone, representing Moses striking the rock—a colossal figure, not without a certain enormous might and dignity, though rather too evidently looking his awfullest. This statue was the death of its sculptor, whose heart was broken, on account of the ridicule it excited. There are many more absurd aquatic devices in Rome, however, and few better.

We turned into the Piazza di Termini, the entrance of which is at this fountain; and after some inquiry of the French soldiers, a numerous detachment of whom appear to be quartered in the vicinity, we found our way to the portal of Santa Maria degl' Angeli. The exterior of this church has no pretensions to beauty or majesty, or, indeed, to architectural merit of any kind, or to any architecture whatever; for it looks like a confused pile of ruined brickwork, with a façade resembling half the inner curve of a large oven. No one would imagine that there was a church under that enormous heap of ancient rubbish. But the door admits you into a circular vestibule, once an apartment of Diocletian's Baths, but now a portion of the nave of the church, and surrounded with monumental busts; and thence you pass into what was the central hall; now, with little change, except of detail and ornament, transformed into the body of the church. This space is so lofty, broad, and airy, that the soul forthwith swells out and magnifies itself, for the sake of filling it. It was Michel Angelo who contrived this miracle; and I feel even more grateful to him for rescuing such a noble interior from destruction, than if he had originally built it himself. In the ceiling above, you see the metal fixtures, whereon the old Romans hung their lamps; and there are eight gigantic pillars of Egyptian granite, standing as they stood of yore. There is a grand simplicity about the church, more satisfactory than elaborate ornament; but the present Pope has paved and adorned one of the large chapels of the transept in very beautiful style; and the pavement of the central part is likewise laid in rich marbles. In the choir there are several pictures, one of which was veiled, as celebrated pictures frequently are, in churches. A person, who seemed to be at his devotions, withdrew the veil for us, and we saw a martyrdom of St. Sebastian, by Domenichino, originally, I believe, painted in fresco in St. Peter's, but since transferred to canvas, and removed hither. Its place at St. Peter's is supplied by a mosaic copy. I was a good deal impressed by this picture—the dying saint, amid the sorrow of those who loved him, and the fury of his enemies, looking upward, where a company of angels, and Jesus with them, are waiting to welcome him and crown him;—and I felt what an influence pictures might have upon the devotional part of our nature. The nail-marks in the hands and feet of Jesus, ineffaceable, even after he had passed into bliss and glory, touched my heart with a sense of his love for us. I think this really a great picture. We walked round the church, looking at other paintings and frescoes, but saw no others that greatly interested us. In the vestibule there are monuments to Carlo Maratti and Salvator Rosa, and there is a statue of St. Bruno, by Houdon, which is pronounced to be very fine. I thought it good, but scarcely worthy of vast admiration. Houdon was the sculptor of the first statue of Washington, and of the bust whence, I suppose, all subsequent statues have been, and will be, mainly modelled.

After emerging from the church, I looked back with wonder at the stack of shapeless old brick work that hid the splendid interior. I must go there again, and breathe freely in that noble space.

February 20*th*.—This morning, after breakfast, I walked across the city, making a pretty straight course to the Pantheon, and thence to the bridge of St. Angelo, and to St. Peter's. It had been my purpose to go to the Fontana Paolina; but finding that the distance was too great, and being weighed down with a Roman lassitude, I concluded to go into St. Peter's. Here I looked at Michael Angelo's Pietà, a representation of the dead Christ in his mother's lap. Then I strolled round the great church, and find that it continues to grow upon me both in magnitude and beauty, by comparison with the many interiors of sacred edifices which I have lately seen. At times, a single, casual, momentary glimpse of its magnificence gleams upon my soul, as it were, when I happen to glance at arch opening beyond arch, and I am surprised into admiration. I have experienced that a landscape and the sky unfold the deepest beauty in a similar way; not when they are gazed at of set purpose, but when the spectator looks suddenly through a vista, among a crowd of other thoughts. Passing near the confessional for foreigners to day, I saw a Spaniard, who had just come out of the one devoted to his native tongue, taking leave of his confessor, with an affectionate reverence which—as well as the benign dignity of the good father—it was good to behold. . . . .

I returned home early, in order to go with my wife to the Barberini Palace at two o'clock. We entered through the gateway, through the Via delle Quattro Fontane, passing one or two sentinels; for there is apparently a regiment of dragoons quartered on the ground floor of the palace; and I stumbled upon a room containing their saddles, the other day, when seeking for Mr. Story's staircase. The entrance to the picture gallery is by a door on the right hand, affording us a sight of a beautiful spiral staircase, which goes circling upward from the very basement to the very summit of the palace, with a perfectly easy ascent, yet confining its sweep within a moderate compass. We looked up through the interior of the spiral, as through a tube, from the bottom to the top. The pictures are contained in three contiguous rooms of the lower piano, and are few in number, comprising barely half a dozen which I should care to see again, though doubtless all have value in their way. One that attracted our attention was a picture of "Christ disputing with the Doctors," by Albert Dürer, in which was represented the ugliest, most evil-minded, stubborn, pragmatical, and contentious old Jew that ever lived under the law of Moses; and he and the child Jesus were arguing, not only with their tongues, but making hieroglyphics, as it were, by the motion of their hands and fingers. It is a very queer, as well as a very remarkable picture. But we passed hastily by this, and almost all others, being eager to see the two which chiefly make the collection famous—Raphael's Fornarina, and Guido's portrait of Beatrice Cenci. These were found in the last of the three rooms, and as regards Beatrice Cenci, I might as well not try to say anything; for its spell is indefinable, and the painter has wrought it in a way more like magic than anything else. . . . .

It is the most profoundly wrought picture in the world; no artist did it, nor could do it again. Guido may have held the brush, but he painted better than he knew. I wish, however, it were possible for some spectator, of deep sensibility, to see the picture without knowing anything of its subject or history; for, no doubt, we bring all our knowledge of the Cenci tragedy to the interpretation of it.

Close beside Beatrice Cenci hangs the Fornarina. . . . .

While we were looking at these works Miss M——
unexpectedly joined us, and we went, all three together, to the Rospigliosi Palace, in the Piazza di
Monte Cavallo. A porter, in cocked hat, and with a
staff of office, admitted us into a spacious court before the palace, and directed us to a garden on one
side, raised as much as twenty feet above the level on
which we stood. The gardener opened the gate for
us, and we ascended a beautiful stone staircase, with
a carved balustrade, bearing many marks of time
and weather. Reaching the garden-level, we found
it laid out in walks, bordered with box and ornamental shrubbery, amid which were lemon trees, and
one large old exotic from some distant clime. In the
centre of the garden, surrounded by a stone balustrade, like that of the staircase, was a fish-pond, into
which several jets of water were continually spouting; and on pedestals, that made part of the
balusters, stood eight marble statues of Apollo,
Cupid, nymphs, and other such sunny and beautiful
people of classic mythology. There had been many
more of these statues, but the rest had disappeared, and
those which remained had suffered grievous damage
—here to a nose, there to a hand or foot, and often a
fracture of the body, very imperfectly mended. There
was a pleasant sunshine in the garden, and a spring-

like, or rather a genial, autumnal atmosphere, though elsewhere it was a day of poisonous Roman chill.

At the end of the garden, which was of no great extent, was an edifice, bordering on the piazza, called the Casino, which, I presume, means a garden-house. The front is richly ornamented with bas-reliefs and statues in niches, as if it were a place for pleasure and enjoyment, and therefore ought to be beautiful. As we approached it, the door swung open, and we went into a large room on the ground floor, and looking up to the ceiling, beheld Guido's Aurora. The picture is as fresh and brilliant as if he had painted it with the morning sunshine which it represents. It could not be more lustrous in its hues, if he had given it the last touch an hour ago. Three or four artists were copying it at that instant, and positively their colours did not look brighter, though a great deal newer than his. The alacrity and movement, briskness and morning stir and glow of the picture are wonderful. It seems impossible to catch its glory in a copy. Several artists, as I said, were making the attempt, and we saw two other attempted copies leaning against the wall; but it was easy to detect failure in just the essential points. My memory, I believe, will be somewhat enlivened by this picture hereafter: not that I remember it very distinctly even now; but bright things leave a sheen and glimmer in the mind, like Christian's tremulous glimpse of the celestial city.

In two other rooms of the Casino, we saw pictures by Domenichino, Rubens, and other famous painters, which I do not mean to speak of, because I cared really little or nothing about them. Returning into the garden, the sunny warmth of which was most grateful after the chill air and cold pavement of the Casino, we walked round the laguna, examining the statues, and looking down at some little fishes that swarmed at the stone margin of the pool. There were two infants of the Rospigliosi family: one, a young child playing with a maid and head-servant; another, the very chubbiest and rosiest boy in the world, sleeping on its nurse's bosom. The nurse was a comely woman enough, dressed in bright colours, which fitly set off the deep hues of her Italian face. An old painter very likely would have beautified and refined the pair into a Madonna, with the child Jesus; for an artist need not go far in Italy to find a picture ready composed and tinted, needing little more than to be literally copied.

Miss M—— had gone away before us; but my wife and I, after leaving the Palazzo Rospigliosi, and on our way home, went into the church of St. Andrea,

which belongs to a convent of Jesuits. I have long
ago exhausted all my capacity of admiration for splendid interiors of churches, but methinks this little, little
temple (it is not more than fifty or sixty feet across) has
a more perfect and gem-like beauty than any other.
Its shape is oval, with an oval dome, and, above that,
another little dome, both of which are magnificently
frescoed. Around the base of the larger dome is
wreathed a flight of angels, and the smaller and
upper one is encircled by a garland of cherubs—
cherub and angel all of pure white marble. The
oval centre of the church is walled round with precious and lustrous marble of a red-veined variety,
interspersed with columns and pilasters of white;
and there are arches opening through this rich wall,
forming chapels, which the architect seems to have
striven hard to make even more gorgeous than the
main body of the church. They contain beautiful
pictures, not dark and faded, but glowing, as if just
from the painter's hands; and the shrines are adorned
with whatever is most rare, and in one of them was
the great carbuncle—at any rate, a bright, fiery gem
as big as a turkey's egg. The pavement of the
church was one star of various-coloured marble, and
in the centre was a mosaic, covering, I believe, the
tomb of the founder. I have not seen, nor expect

VOL. I. I

to see, anything else so entirely and satisfactorily finished as this small oval church; and I only wish I could pack it in a large box, and send it home.

I must not forget, that on our way from the Barberini Palace we stopped an instant to look at the house, at the corner of the street of the four fountains, where Milton was a guest while in Rome. He seems quite a man of our own day, seen so nearly at the hither extremity of the vista through which we look back, from the epoch of railways to that of the oldest Egyptian obelisk. The house (it was then occupied by the Cardinal Barbarini) looks as if it might have been built within the present century; for mediæval houses in Rome do not assume the aspect of antiquity; perhaps because the Italian style of architecture, or something similar, is the one more generally in vogue in most cities.

February 21*st.*—This morning I took my way through the Porta del Popolo, intending to spend the forenoon in the Campagna; but getting weary of the straight, uninteresting street that runs out of the gate, I turned aside from it, and soon found myself on the shores of the Tiber. It looked, as usual, like a saturated solution of yellow mud, and eddied hastily along between deep banks of clay, and over a clay bed, in which doubtless are hidden many a richer treasure than we now possess. The French once proposed to draw off the river, for the purpose of recovering all the sunken statues and relics; but the Romans made strenuous objection, on account of the increased virulence of malaria which would probably result. I saw a man on the immediate shore of the river, fifty feet or so beneath the bank on which I stood, sitting patiently, with an angling rod; and I waited to see what he might catch. Two other persons likewise sat down to watch him; but he caught nothing so long as I stayed, and at last seemed to give it up. The banks and vicinity of the river are very bare and uninviting, as I then saw them; no shade, no verdure—a rough, neglected aspect, and a peculiar shabbiness about the few houses that were visible. Farther down the stream, the dome of St. Peter's showed itself on the other side, seeming to stand on the outskirts of the city. I walked along the banks, with some expectation of finding a ferry, by which I might cross the river; but my course was soon interrupted by the wall, and I turned up a lane that led me straight back again to the Porta del Popolo. I stopped a moment, however, to see some young men pitching quoits, which they appeared to do with a good deal of skill.

I went along the Via di Ripetta, and through other

streets, stepping into two or three churches, one of which was the Pantheon. . . . . .

There are, I think, seven deep, pillared recesses around the circumference of it, each of which becomes a sufficiently capacious chapel; and alternately with these chapels there is a marble structure, like the architecture of a doorway, beneath which is the shrine of a saint; so that the whole circle of the Pantheon is filled up with the seven chapels and seven shrines. A number of persons were sitting or kneeling around; others came in while I was there, dipping their fingers in the holy water, and bending the knee, as they passed the shrines and chapels, until they reached the one which, apparently, they had selected as the particular altar for their devotions. Everybody seemed so devout, and in a frame of mind so suited to the day and place, that it really made me feel a little awkward not to be able to kneel down along with them. Unlike the worshippers in our own churches, each individual here seems to do his own individual acts of devotion, and I cannot but think it better so than to make an effort for united prayer as we do. It is my opinion that a great deal of devout and reverential feeling is kept alive in people's hearts by the Catholic mode of worship.

Soon leaving the Pantheon, a few minutes' walk

towards the Corso brought me to the church of St. Ignazio, which belongs to the College of the Jesuits. It is spacious and of beautiful architecture, but not strikingly distinguished, in the latter particular, from many others; a wide and lofty nave, supported upon marble columns, between which arches open into the side aisles, and, at the junction of the nave and transept, a dome, resting on four great arches. The church seemed to be purposely somewhat darkened, so that I could not well see the details of the ornamentation, except the frescoes on the ceiling of the nave, which were very brilliant, and done in so effectual a style, that I really could not satisfy myself that some of the figures did not actually protrude from the ceiling;—in short, that they were not coloured bas-reliefs, instead of frescoes. No words can express the beautiful effect, in an upholstery point of view, of this kind of decoration. Here, as at the Pantheon, there were many persons sitting silent, kneeling, or passing from shrine to shrine.

I reached home at about twelve, and, at one, set out again, with my wife, towards St. Peter's, where we meant to stay till after vespers. We walked across the city, and through the Piazza de Navona, where we stopped to look at one of Bernini's absurd fountains, of which the water makes but the smallest part—a little squirt or two amid a prodigious fuss of gods and monsters. Thence we passed by the poor, battered down torso of Pasquin, and came, by devious ways, to the bridge of St. Angelo; the streets bearing pretty much their week-day aspect, many of the shops open, the market-stalls doing their usual business, and the people brisk and gay, though not indecorously so. I suppose there was hardly a man or woman who had not heard mass, confessed, and said their prayers; a thing which—the prayers, I mean—it would be absurd to predicate of London, New York, or any Protestant city. In however adulterated a guise, the Catholics do get a draught of devotion to slake the thirst of their souls, and methinks it must needs do them good, even if not quite so pure as if it came from better cisterns, or from the original fountain-head.

Arriving at St. Peter's shortly after two, we walked round the whole church, looking at all the pictures and most of the monuments, ... and paused longest before Guido's "Archangel Michael overcoming Lucifer." This is surely one of the most beautiful things in the world, one of the human conceptions that are imbued most deeply with the celestial. . . . . .

We then sat down in one of the aisles and awaited the beginning of vespers, which we supposed would take place at half-past three. Four o'clock came, however, and no vespers; and as our dinner hour is five, ... we at last came away without hearing the vesper hymn.

February 23*rd*.—Yesterday, at noon, we set out for the Capitol, and after going up the acclivity (not from the Forum, but from the opposite direction), stopped to look at the statues of Castor and Pollux, which, with other sculptures, look down the ascent. Castor and his brother seem to me to have heads disproportionately large, and are not so striking, in any respect, as such great images ought to be. But we heartily admired the equestrian statue of Marcus Aurelius Antoninus, ... and looked at a fountain, principally composed, I think, of figures representing the Nile and the Tiber, who loll upon their elbows and preside over the gushing water; and between them, against the façade of the Senator's Palace, there is a statue of Minerva, with a petticoat of red porphyry. Having taken note of these objects, we went to the Museum, in an edifice on our left, entering the Piazza, and here, in the vestibule, we found various old statues and relics. Ascending the stairs, we passed through a long gallery, and, turning to our left, examined somewhat more carefully a suite of rooms running parallel with it. The first of these contained busts of the Cæsars and their kindred, from the epoch of the mightiest Julius downward, eighty-three, I believe, in all. I had seen a bust of Julius Cæsar in the British Museum, and was surprised at its thin and withered aspect: but this head is of a very ugly old man indeed — wrinkled, puckered, shrunken, lacking breadth and substance; careworn, grim, as if he had fought hard with life, and had suffered in the conflict; a man of schemes, and of eager effort to bring his schemes to pass. His profile is by no means good, advancing from the top of his forehead to the tip of his nose, and retreating, at about the same angle, from the latter point to the bottom of his chin, which seems to be thrust forcibly down into his meagre neck—not that he pokes his head forward, however, for it is particularly erect.

The head of Augustus is very beautiful, and appears to be that of a meditative, philosophic man, saddened with the sense that it is not very much worth while to be at the summit of human greatness after all. It is a sorrowful thing to trace the decay of civilisation through this series of busts, and to observe how the artistic skill, so requisite at first, went on declining through the dreary dynasty of the Cæsars, till at length the master of the world could not get his head carved in better style than the figure-head of a ship.

In the next room there were better statues than we had yet seen; but in the last room of the range we found the "Dying Gladiator," of which I had already caught a glimpse in passing by the open door. It had made all the other treasures of the gallery tedious in my eagerness to come to that. I do not believe that so much pathos is wrought into any other block of stone. Like all works of the highest excellence, however, it makes great demands upon the spectator. He must make a generous gift of his sympathies to the sculptor, and help out his skill with all his heart, or else he will see little more than a skilfully wrought surface. It suggests far more than it shows. I looked long at this statue, and little at anything else, though, among other famous works, a statue of Antinous was in the same room.

I was glad when we left the Museum, which, by-the-bye, was piercingly chill, as if the multitude of statues radiated cold out of their marble substance. We might have gone to see the pictures in the Palace of the Conservatori, and S——, whose receptivity is unlimited and for ever fresh, would willingly have done so; but I objected, and we went towards the Forum. I had noticed, two or three times, an inscription over a mean-looking door in this neighbourhood, stating that here was the entrance to the prison of the holy Apostles, Peter and Paul; and we soon found the spot, not far from the Forum, with two wretched frescoes of the Apostles above the inscription. We knocked at the door without effect; but a lame beggar, who sat at another door of the same house (which looked exceedingly like a liquor shop), desired us to follow him, and began to ascend to the Capitol, by the causeway leading from the Forum. A little way upward we met a woman, to whom the beggar delivered us over, and she led us into a church or chapel door, and pointed to a long flight of steps, which descended through twilight into utter darkness. She called to somebody in the lower regions, and then went away, leaving us to get down this mysterious staircase by ourselves. Down we went, farther and farther from the daylight, and found ourselves, anon, in a dark chamber or cell, the shape or boundaries of which we could not make out, though it seemed to be of stone, and black and dungeon-like. Indistinctly, and from a still farther depth in the earth, we heard voices,—one voice, at least,— apparently not addressing ourselves, but some other persons; and soon, directly beneath our feet, we saw a glimmering of light through a round, iron-grated hole in the bottom of the dungeon. In a few moments the glimmer and the voice came up through this hole, and the light disappeared, and it and the voice came glimmering and babbling up a flight of stone stairs, of which we had not hitherto been aware. It was the custode, with a party of visitors, to whom he had been showing St. Peter's dungeon. Each visitor was provided with a wax taper, and the custode gave one to each of us, bidding us wait a moment while he conducted the other party to the upper air. During his absence we examined the cell, as well as our dim lights would permit, and soon found an indentation in the wall, with an iron grate put over it for protection, and an inscription above, informing us that the Apostle Peter had here left the imprint of his visage; and, in truth, there is a profile there—forehead, nose, mouth, and chin—plainly to be seen, an intaglio in the solid rock. We touched it with the tips of our fingers, as well as saw it with our eyes.

The custode soon returned, and led us down the darksome steps, chattering in Italian all the time. It is not a very long descent to the lower cell, the roof of which is so low, that I believe I could have reached it with my hand. We were now in the deepest and ugliest part of the old Mamertine Prison, one of the few remains of the kingly period of Rome, and which served the Romans as a state-prison for hundreds of years before the Christian era. A multitude of criminals or innocent persons, no doubt, have languished here in misery, and perished in darkness. Here Jugurtha starved; here Catiline's adherents were strangled; and, methinks, there cannot be in the world another such an evil den, so haunted with black memories and indistinct surmises of guilt and suffering. In old Rome, I suppose, the citizens never spoke of this dungeon above their breath. It looks just as bad as it is:—round, only seven paces across, yet so obscure that our tapers could not illuminate it from side to side—the stones of which it is constructed being as black as midnight. The custode showed us a stone post, at the side of the cell, with the hole in the top of it, into which, he said, St. Peter's chain had been fastened; and he uncovered a spring of water, in the middle of the stone floor, which he told us had miraculously gushed up to enable the saint to baptize his jailer. The miracle was perhaps the more easily wrought, inasmuch as Jugurtha had found the floor of the dungeon oozy with wet. However, it is best to be as simple and childlike as we can in these matters; and whether St. Peter stamped his visage into the stone, and wrought this other miracle or no, and whether or no he ever was in the prison at all, still the belief of a thousand years and more gives a sort of reality and substance to such traditions. The custode dipped an iron ladle into the miraculous water, and we each of us drank a sip; and what is very remarkable, to me it seemed hard water, and almost brackish, while many persons think it the sweetest in Rome. I suspect that St. Peter still dabbles in this water, and tempers its qualities according to the faith of those who drink it.

The staircase descending into the lower dungeon is comparatively modern, there having been no entrance of old, except through the small circular opening in the roof. In the upper cell the custode showed us an ancient flight of stairs, now built into the wall, which used to lead from the Capitol. The whole precincts are now consecrated, and I believe the upper portion —perhaps both upper and lower—are a shrine or a chapel.

I now left S—— in the Forum, and went to call on Mr. J. P. K—— at the Hôtel d'Europe. I found him just returned from a drive—a gentleman of about sixty, or more, with grey hair, a pleasant, intellectual face, and penetrating, but not unkindly, eyes. He moved infirmly, being on the recovery from an illness. We went up to his saloon together, and had a talk, or rather, he had it nearly all to himself—and particularly sensible talk, too, and full of the results of learning and experience. In the first place, he settled the whole Kansas difficulty; then he made havoc of St. Peter, who came very shabbily out of his hands, as regarded his early character in the Church, and his claims to the position he now holds in it. Mr. K—— also gave a curious illustration, from something that happened to himself, of the little dependence that can be placed on tradition purporting to be ancient, and I capped his story by telling him how the site of my town pump, so plainly indicated in the sketch itself, has already been mistaken in the City council and in the public prints.

February 24th.—Yesterday I crossed the Ponte Sisto, and took a short ramble on the other side of the river; and it rather surprised me to discover, pretty nearly opposite the Capitoline Hill, a quay, at which several schooners and barques, of two or three hundred tons burden, were moored. There was also a steamer, armed with a large gun, and two brass swivels on her forecastle, and I know not what artillery besides. Probably she may have been a revenue cutter.

Returning, I crossed the river by way of the island of St. Bartholomew, over two bridges. The island is densely covered with buildings, and is a separate small fragment of the city. It was a tradition of the ancient Romans that it was formed by the aggregation of soil and rubbish brought down by the river, and accumulating round the nucleus of some sunken baskets.

On reaching the hither side of the river, I soon struck upon the ruins of the theatre of Marcellus, which are very picturesque, and the more so from being closely linked in—indeed, identified with the shops, habitations, and swarming life of modern Rome. The most striking portion was a circular edifice, which seemed to have been composed of a row of Ionic columns, standing upon a lower row of Doric, many of the antique pillars being yet perfect; but the intervening arches built up with brickwork, and the whole once magnificent structure now tenanted by poor and squalid people, as thick as mites within the round of an old cheese. From this point I cannot very clearly trace out my course; but I passed, I think, between the Circus Maximus and the Palace of the Cæsars, and near the Baths of Caracalla, and went into the cloisters of the church of San Gregorio. All along I saw massive ruins, not particularly picturesque or beautiful, but huge, mountainous piles, chiefly of brickwork, somewhat weed-grown here and there, but oftener bare and dreary. . . . . All the successive ages since Rome began to decay have done their best to ruin the very ruins by taking away the marble and the hewn stone for their own structures, and leaving only the inner filling up of brickwork, which the ancient architects never designed to be seen. The consequence of all this is that, except for the lofty and poetical associations connected with it,—and except, too, for the immense difference in magnitude, —a Roman ruin may be in itself not more picturesque than I have seen an old cellar, with a shattered brick chimney half crumbling down into it, in New England.

By this time I knew not whither I was going, and turned aside from a broad, paved road (it was the Appian Way) into the Via Latina, which I supposed would lead to one of the city gates. It was a lonely path : on my right hand extensive piles of ruin, in strange shapes or shapelessness, built of the broad and thin old Roman bricks, such as may be traced everywhere when the stucco has fallen away from a modern Roman house; for I imagine there has not been a new brick made here for a thousand years. On my left, I think, was a high wall, and before me, grazing in the road, . . [the buffalo calf of the Marble Faun.—ED.] The road went boldly on, with a well-worn track up to the very walls of the city; but there it abruptly terminated at an ancient, closed-up gateway. From a notice posted against a door, which appeared to be the entrance to the ruins on my left, I found that these were the remains of columbaria, where the dead used to be put away in pigeon-holes. Reaching the paved road again, I kept on my course, passing the tomb of the Scipios, and soon came to the gate of San Sebastiano, through which I entered the Campagna. Indeed, the scene around was so rural, that I had fancied myself already beyond the walls. As the afternoon was getting advanced, I did not proceed any farther towards the blue hills which I saw in the distance, but turned to my left, following a road that runs round the exterior of the city wall. It was very dreary and solitary—not a house on the whole track, with the broad and shaggy Campagna on one side, and the high, bare wall, looking down over my head, on the other. It is not, any more than the other objects of the scene, a very picturesque wall, but is little more than a brick garden-fence seen through a magnifying glass, with now and then a tower, however, and frequent buttresses, to keep its height of fifty feet from toppling over. The top

VOL. I.   K

was ragged, and fringed with a few weeds; there had been embrasures for guns and eyelet-holes for musketry, but these were plastered up with brick or stone. I passed one or two walled-up gateways (by-the-bye, the Porta Latina was the gate through which Belisarius first entered Rome), and one of these had two high, round towers, and looked more Gothic and venerable with antique strength than any other portion of the wall. Immediately after this I came to the gate of San Giovanni, just within which is the Basilica of St. John Lateran, and there I was glad to rest myself upon a bench before proceeding homeward.

There was a French sentinel at this gateway, as at all the others; for the Gauls have always been a pest to Rome, and now gall her worse than ever. I observed, too, that an official, in citizen's dress, stood there also, and appeared to exercise a supervision over some carts with country produce that were entering just then.

February 25th.—We went this forenoon to the Palazzo Borghese, which is situated on a street that runs at right angles with the Corso, and very near the latter. Most of the palaces in Rome, and the Borghese among them, were built somewhere about the sixteenth century; this in 1590, I believe. It is an immense edifice, standing round the four sides of a quadrangle; and though the suite of rooms, comprising the picture-gallery, forms an almost interminable vista, they occupy only a part of the ground-floor of one side. We enter from the street into a large court, surrounded with a corridor, the arches of which support a second series of arches above. The picture-rooms open from one into another, and have many points of magnificence, being large and lofty, with vaulted ceilings and beautiful frescoes, generally of mythological subjects, in the flat central part of the vault. The cornices are gilded; the deep embrasures of the windows are panelled with woodwork; the door-ways are of polished and variegated marble, or covered with a composition as hard, and seemingly as durable. The whole has a kind of splendid shabbiness thrown over it, like a slight coating of rust; the furniture, at least the damask chairs, being a good deal worn, though there are marble and mosaic tables which may serve to adorn another palace when this one crumbles away with age. One beautiful hall, with a ceiling more richly gilded than the rest, is panelled all round with large looking-glasses, on which are painted pictures, both landscapes and human figures, in oil; so that the effect is somewhat as if you saw these objects represented in the mirrors. These glasses must be of old date, perhaps coeval with the first building of the palace; for they are so much dimmed, that one's own figure appears indistinct in them, and more difficult to be traced than the pictures which cover them half over. It was very comfortless—indeed, I suppose nobody ever thought of being comfortable there, since the house was built—but especially uncomfortable on a chill, damp day like this. My fingers were quite numb before I got half way through the suite of apartments, in spite of a brazier of charcoal which was smouldering into ashes in two or three of the rooms. There was not, so far as I remember, a single fire-place in the suite. A considerable number of visitors were there, and a good many artists; and three or four ladies among them were making copies of the more celebrated pictures, and in all or in most cases missing the especial points that made their celebrity and value. The Prince Borghese certainly demeans himself like a kind and liberal gentleman, in throwing open this invaluable collection to the public to see, and for artists to carry away with them, and diffuse all over the world, so far as their own power and skill will permit. It is open every day of the week, except Saturday and Sunday, without any irksome restriction or supervision; and the fee, which custom requires the visitor to pay to the custode, has the good effect of making us feel that we are not intruders, nor received in an exactly eleemosynary way. The thing could not be better managed.

The collection is one of the most celebrated in the world, and contains between eight and nine hundred pictures, many of which are esteemed masterpieces. I think I was not in a frame for admiration to-day, nor could achieve that free and generous surrender of myself which I have already said is essential to the proper estimate of anything excellent. Besides, how is it possible to give one's soul, or any considerable part of it, to a single picture, seen for the first time, among a thousand others, all of which set forth their own claims in an equally good light? Furthermore, there is an external weariness, and sense of a thousandfold sameness to be overcome, before we can begin to enjoy a gallery of the old Italian masters. . . . . I remember but one painter, Francia, who seems really to have approached this awful class of subjects [Christs and Madonnas] in a fitting spirit; his pictures are very singular and awkward, if you look at them with merely an external eye, but they are full of the beauty of holiness and evidently wrought out as acts of devotion with the deepest sincerity, and are veritable prayers upon canvas. . . .

I was glad, in the very last of the twelve rooms, to come upon some Dutch and Flemish pictures, very few, but very welcome; Rubens, Rembrandt, Vandyke, Paul Potter, Teniers, and others—men of flesh and blood, and warm fists and human hearts. As compared with them, these mighty Italian masters seem men of polished steel; not human, nor addressing themselves so much to human sympathies as to a formed, intellectual taste.

March 1st.—To-day began very unfavourably; but we ventured out at about eleven o'clock, intending to visit the gallery of the Colonna Palace. Finding it closed, however, on account of the illness of the custode, we determined to go to the picture-gallery of the Capitol, and on our way thither we stepped into Il Gesù, the grand and rich church of the Jesuits, where we found a priest in white preaching a sermon with vast earnestness of action and variety of tone, insomuch that I fancied sometimes that two priests were in the agony of sermonising at once. He had a pretty large and seemingly attentive audience clustered round him from the entrance of the church half way down the nave, while in the chapels of the transepts, and in the remoter distances, were persons occupied with their own individual devotion. We sat down near the chapel of St. Ignazio, which is adorned with a picture over the altar, and with marble sculptures of the Trinity aloft, and of angels fluttering at the sides. What I particularly noted (for the angels were not very real personages, being neither earthly nor celestial) was the great ball of lapis-lazuli, the biggest in the world, at the feet of the First Person in the Trinity. The church is a splendid one, lined with a great variety of precious marbles, . . . but partly, perhaps, owing to the dusky light, as well as to the want of cleanliness, there was a dingy effect upon the whole. We made but a very short stay, our New England breeding causing us to feel shy of moving about the church in sermon time.

It rained when we reached the Capitol, and, as the Museum was not yet open, we went into the Palace of the Conservators, on the opposite side of the piazza. Around the inner court of the ground floor, partly under two opposite arcades, and partly under the sky, are several statues and other ancient sculptures: among them a statue of Julius Cæsar, said to be the only authentic one, and certainly giving an impression of him more in accordance with his character than the withered old face in the Museum; also, a statue of Augustus in middle age, still retaining a resemblance to the bust of him in youth;

some gigantic heads and hands and feet, in marble and bronze; a stone lion and horse, which lay long at the bottom of a river, broken and corroded, and were repaired by Michael Angelo; and other things which it were wearisome to set down. We inquired of two or three French soldiers the way into the picture gallery; but it is our experience that French soldiers in Rome never know anything of what is around them, not even the name of the palace or public place over which they stand guard; and though invariably civil, you might as well put a question to a statue of an old Roman as to one of them. While we stood under the Loggia, however, looking at the rain plashing into the court, a soldier of the Papal Guard kindly directed us up the staircase, and even took pains to go with us to the very entrance of the picture-rooms. Thank heaven, there are but two of them, and not many pictures which one cares to look at very long.

Italian galleries are at a disadvantage as compared with English ones, inasmuch as the pictures are not nearly such splendid articles of upholstery; though, very likely, having undergone less cleaning and varnishing, they may retain more perfectly the finer touches of the masters. Nevertheless, I miss the mellow glow, the rich and mild external lustre, and even the brilliant frames of the pictures I have seen in England. You feel that they have had loving care taken of them: even if spoiled, it is because they have been valued so much. But these pictures in Italian galleries look rusty and lustreless, as far as the exterior is concerned; and really the splendour of the painting, as a production of intellect and feeling, has a good deal of difficulty in shining through such clouds.

There is a picture at the Capitol—"the Rape of Europa," by Paul Veronese—that would glow with wonderful brilliancy if it were set in a magnificent frame, and covered with a sunshine of varnish; and it is a kind of picture that would not be desecrated, as some deeper and holier ones might be, by any splendour of external adornment that could be bestowed on it. It is deplorable and disheartening to see it in faded and shabby plight—this joyous, exuberant, warm, voluptuous work. There is the head of a cow thrust into the picture, and staring with wild, ludicrous wonder at the godlike bull, so as to introduce quite a new sentiment.

Here, and at the Borghese Palace, there were some pictures by Garofalo, an artist of whom I never heard before, but who seemed to have been a man of power. A picture by Marie Subleyras—a miniature copy from one by her husband, of the woman anointing the feet of Christ—is most delicately and beautifully finished, and would be an ornament to a drawing-room; a thing that could not truly be said of one in a hundred of these grim masterpieces. When they were painted life was not what it is now, and the artists had not the same ends in view. . . . . It depresses the spirits to go from picture to picture, leaving a portion of your vital sympathy at every one, so that you come with a kind of half-torpid desperation to the end. On our way down the staircase we saw several noteworthy bas-reliefs, and among them a very ancient one of Curtius plunging on horseback into the chasm in the Forum. It seems to me, however, that old sculpture affects the spirits even more dolefully than old painting; it strikes colder to the heart, and lies heavier upon it, being marble, than if it were merely canvas.

My wife went to revisit the Museum, which we had already seen, on the other side of the piazza; but, being cold, I left her there, and went out to ramble in the sun, for it was now brightly, though fitfully, shining again. I walked through the Forum (where a thorn thrust itself out and tore the sleeve of my talma), and under the arch of Titus, towards the Coliseum. About a score of French drummers were beating a long, loud roll-call, at the base of the Coliseum, and under its arches; and a score of trumpeters responded to these from the rising ground opposite the arch of Constantine; and the echoes of the old Roman ruins, especially those of the palace of the Cæsars, responded to this martial uproar of the barbarians. There seemed to be no cause for it, but the drummers beat and the trumpeters blew as long as I was within hearing.

I walked along the Appian Way as far as the baths of Caracalla. The palace of the Cæsars, which I have never yet explored, appears to be crowned by the walls of a convent, built, no doubt, out of some of the fragments that would suffice to build a city; and I think there is another convent among the baths. The Catholics have taken a peculiar pleasure in planting themselves in the very citadels of paganism, whether temples or palaces. There has been a good deal of enjoyment in the destruction of old Rome. I often think so when I see the elaborate pains that have been taken to smash and demolish some beautiful column, for no purpose whatever except the mere delight of annihilating a noble piece of work. There is something in the impulse with which one sympathises, though I am afraid the destroyers were not sufficiently aware of the mischief they did to enjoy it fully. Probably, too, the early Christians were impelled by religious zeal to destroy the pagan temples, before the happy thought occurred of converting them into churches.

March 3rd.—This morning was U——'s birthday, and we celebrated it by taking a barouche, and driving (the whole family) out on the Appian Way as far as the tomb of Cecilia Metella. For the first time since we came to Rome, the weather was really warm—a kind of heat producing languor and disinclination to active movement, though still a little breeze which was stirring threw an occasional coolness over us, and made us distrust the almost sultry atmosphere. I cannot think the Roman climate healthy in any of its moods that I have experienced.

Close on the other side of the road are the ruins of a Gothic chapel, little more than a few bare walls and painted windows, and some other fragmentary structures which we did not particularly examine. U—— and I clambered through a gap in the wall, extending from the basement of the tomb, and thus getting into the field beyond, went quite round the mausoleum and the remains of the castle connected with it. The latter, though still high and stalwart, showed few or no architectural features of interest, being built, I think, principally of large bricks, and not to be compared to English ruins as a beautiful or venerable object.

A little way beyond Cecilia Metella's tomb, the road still shows a specimen of the ancient Roman pavement, composed of broad, flat flagstones, a good deal cracked and worn, but sound enough, probably, to outlast the little cubes which make the other portions of the road so uncomfortable. We turned back from this point, and soon re-entered the gate of St. Sebastian, which is flanked by two small towers, and just within which is the old triumphal arch of Drusus —a sturdy construction, much dilapidated as regards its architectural beauty, but rendered far more picturesque than it could have been in its best days by a crown of verdure on its head. Probably so much of the dust of the highway has risen in clouds and settled there, that sufficient soil for shrubbery to root itself has thus been collected, by small annual contributions, in the course of two thousand years. A little farther towards the city we turned aside from the Appian Way, and came to the site of some ancient columbaria, close by what seemed to partake of the character of a villa and a farm-house. A man came out of the house and unlocked a door in a low building, apparently quite modern; but on entering we found ourselves looking into a large, square chamber, sunk entirely beneath the surface of the ground. A very narrow and steep staircase of stone, and evidently ancient, descended into this chamber; and going down, we found the walls hollowed on all sides into little semi-circular niches, of which, I believe, there were nine rows, one above another, and nine niches in each row. Thus they looked somewhat like the little entrances to a pigeon-house, and hence the name of Columbarium. Each semi-circular niche was about a foot in its semi-diameter. In the centre of this subterranean chamber was a solid square column, or pier, rising to the roof, and containing other niches of the same pattern, besides one that was high and deep, rising to the height of a man from the floor on each of the four sides. In every one of the semicircular niches were two round holes covered with an earthen plate, and in each hole were ashes and little fragments of bones— the ashes and bones of the dead, whose names were inscribed in Roman capitals on marble slabs inlaid into the wall over each individual niche. Very likely the great ones in the central pier had contained statues, or busts or large urns; indeed, I remember that some such things were there, as well as bas-reliefs in the walls; but hardly more than the general aspect of this strange place remains in my mind.

It was the columbarium of the connections or dependents of the Cæsars; and the impression left on me was, that this mode of disposing of the dead was infinitely preferable to any which has been adopted since that day. The handful or two of dry dust and bits of dry bones in each of the small round holes had nothing disgusting in them, and they are no drier now than they were when first deposited there. I would rather have my ashes scattered over the soil, to help the growth of the grass and daisies; but still I should not murmur much at having them decently pigeon-holed in a Roman tomb.

After ascending out of this chamber of the dead, we looked down into another similar one containing the ashes of Pompey's household, which was discovered only a very few years ago. Its arrangement was the same as that first described, except that it had no central pier with a passage round it as the former had.

While we were down in the first chamber the proprietor of the spot—a half-gentlemanly and very affable kind of person—came to us, and explained the arrangements of the columbarium, though, indeed, we understood them better by their own aspect than by his explanation. The whole soil around his dwelling is elevated much above the level of the road, and it is probable that, if he chose to excavate, he might bring to light many more sepulchral chambers, and find his profits in them too, by disposing of the urns and busts. What struck me as much as anything was the neatness of these subterranean apartments, which were quite as fit to sleep in as most of those occupied by living Romans; and having undergone no wear and tear, they were in as good condition as on the day they were built.

In this columbarium, measuring about twenty feet square, I roughly estimate that there have been deposited together the remains of at least seven or eight hundred persons, reckoning two little heaps of bones and ashes in each pigeon-hole, nine pigeon-holes in each row, and nine rows on each side, besides those on the middle pier. All difficulty in finding space for the dead would be obviated by returning to the ancient fashion of reducing them to ashes—the only objection, though a very serious one, being the quantity of fuel that it would require. But perhaps future chemists may discover some better means of consuming or dissolving this troublesome mortality of ours.

We got into the carriage again, and driving farther towards the city, came to the tomb of the Scipios, of the exterior of which I retain no very definite idea. It was close upon the Appian Way, however, though separated from it by a high fence, and accessible through a gateway, leading into a court. I think the tomb is wholly subterranean, and that the ground above it is covered with the buildings of a farm-house; but of this I cannot be certain, as we were led immediately into a dark, underground passage, by an elderly peasant, of a cheerful and affable demeanour. As soon as he had brought us into the twilight of the tomb, he lighted a long wax taper for each of us, and led us groping into blacker and blacker darkness. Even little R—— followed courageously in the procession, which looked very picturesque, as we glanced backward or forward, and beheld a twinkling line of seven lights, glimmering faintly on our faces, and showing nothing beyond. The passages and niches of the tomb seem to have been hewn and hollowed out of the rock, not built by any art of masonry; but the walls were very dark, almost black, and our tapers so dim that I could not gain a sufficient breadth of view to ascertain what kind of place it was. It was very dark, indeed; the Mammoth Cave of Kentucky could not be darker. The rough-hewn roof was within touch, and sometimes we had to stoop to avoid hitting our heads; it was covered with damps, which collected and fell upon us in occasional drops. The passages, besides being narrow, were so irregular and crooked, that, after going a little way, it would have been impossible to return upon our steps without the help of the guide; and we appeared to be taking quite an extensive ramble underground, though, in reality, I suppose the tomb includes no great space. At several turns of our dismal way, the guide pointed to inscriptions in Roman capitals, commemorating various members of the Scipio family who were buried here; among them, a son of Scipio Africanus, who himself had his death and burial in a foreign land. All these inscriptions, however, are copies—the originals, which were really found here, having been removed to the Vatican. Whether any bones and ashes have been left, or whether any were found, I do not know. It is not, at all events, a particularly interesting spot, being such shapeless blackness, and a mere dark hole, requiring a stronger illumination than that of our tapers to distinguish it from any other cellar. I did, at one place, see a sort of frieze, rather roughly sculptured; and, as we returned towards the twilight of the entrance-passage, I discerned a large spider, who fled hastily away from our tapers—the solitary living inhabitant of the tomb of the Scipios.

One visit that we made—and I think it was before entering the city gates—I forgot to mention. It was to an old edifice, formerly called the Temple of Bacchus, but now supposed to have been the Temple of Virtue and Honour. The interior consists of a vaulted hall, which was converted from its pagan consecration into a church or chapel, by the early Christians; and the ancient marble pillars of the temple may still be seen, built in with the brick and stucco of the later occupants. There is an altar, and other tokens of a Catholic church, and high towards the ceiling there are some frescoes of saints or angels, very curious specimens of mediæval, and earlier than mediæval art. Nevertheless, the place impressed me as still rather pagan than Christian. What is most remarkable about this spot or this vicinity, lies in the fact that the fountain of Egeria was formerly supposed to be close at hand: indeed, the custode of the chapel still claims the spot as the identical one consecrated by the legend. There is a dark grove of trees not far from the door of the temple, but Murray—a highly essential nuisance on such excursions as this—throws such overwhelming doubt, or rather incredulity, upon the site, that I seized upon it as a pretext for not going thither. In fact, my small capacity for sight-seeing was already more than satisfied.

On account of —— I am sorry that we did not see the grotto, for her enthusiasm is as fresh as the waters of Egeria's well can be, and she has poetical faith enough to light her cheerfully through all these mists of incredulity.

Our visits to sepulchral places ended with Scipio's tomb, whence we returned to our dwelling, and Miss M—— came to dine with us.

March 10th.—On Saturday last, a very rainy day, we went to the Sciarra Palace, and took U—— with us. It is on the Corso, nearly opposite to the Piazza Colonna. It has (Heaven be praised!) but four rooms of pictures, among which, however, are several very celebrated ones. Only a few of these remain in my memory,—Raphael's "Violin Player," which I am willing to accept as a good picture; and Leonardo da Vinci's "Vanity and Modesty," which also I can bring up before my mind's eye, and find it very beautiful, although one of the faces has an affected smile, which I have since seen on another picture by the same artist—Joanna of Arragon. The most striking picture in the collection, I think, is Titian's "Bella Donna"— the only one of Titian's works that I have yet seen which makes an impression on me corresponding with his fame. It is a very splendid and very scornful lady, as beautiful and as scornful as Gainsborough's

"Lady Lyndoch," though of an entirely different type. There were two Madonnas by Guido, of which I liked the least celebrated one best; and several pictures by Garofalo, who always produces something noteworthy. All the pictures lacked the charm (no doubt I am a barbarian to think it one) of being in brilliant frames, and looked as if it were a long, long while since they were cleaned or varnished. The light was so scanty, too, on that heavily clouded day, and in those gloomy old rooms of the palace, that scarcely anything could be fairly made out.

[I cannot refrain from observing here that Mr. Hawthorne's inexorable demand for perfection in all things leads him to complain of grimy pictures and tarnished frames and faded frescoes, distressing beyond measure to eyes that never failed to see everything before him with the keenest apprehension. The usual careless observation of people both of the good and the imperfect is much more comfortable in this imperfect world. But the insight which Mr. Hawthorne possessed was only equalled by his outsight, and he suffered in a way not to be readily conceived, from any failure in beauty—physical, moral, or intellectual. It is not, therefore, mere love of upholstery that impels him to ask for perfect settings to priceless gems of art; but a native idiosyncrasy, which always made me feel that "the New Jerusalem," "even like a jasper stone, clear as crystal," "where shall in no wise enter anything that defileth, neither what worketh abomination nor maketh a lie," would alone satisfy him, or rather alone not give him actual pain. It may give an idea of this exquisite nicety of feeling to mention, that one day he took in his fingers a half-bloomed rose, without blemish, and smiling with an infinite joy, remarked—"This is perfect: on earth a flower only can be perfect."— ED.]

The palace is about two hundred and fifty years old, and looks as if it had never been a very cheerful place; most shabbily and scantily furnished, moreover, and as chill as any cellar. There is a small balcony, looking down on the Corso, which probably has often been filled with a merry little family party, in the Carnivals of days long past. It has faded frescoes, and tarnished gilding, and green blinds, and a few damask chairs still remain in it.

On Monday we all went to the sculpture gallery of the Vatican, and saw as much of the sculpture as we could in the three hours during which the public are admissible. There were a few things which I really enjoyed, and a few moments during which I really seemed to see them; but it is in vain to attempt giving the impression produced by masterpieces of art, and most in vain when we see them best. They are a language in themselves, and if they could be expressed as well any way except by themselves, there would have been no need of expressing those particular ideas and sentiments by sculpture. I saw the Apollo Belvidere as something ethereal and godlike; only for a flitting moment, however, and as if he had alighted from heaven, or shone suddenly out of the sunlight, and then had withdrawn himself again. I felt the Laocoön very powerfully, though very quietly; an immortal agony, with a strange calmness diffused through it, so that it resembles the vast rage of the sea, calm on account of its immensity; or the tumult of Niagara, which does not seem to be tumult, because it keeps pouring on for ever and ever. I have not had so good a day as this (among works of art) since we came to Rome; and I impute it partly to the magnificence of the arrangements of the Vatican,—its long vistas and beautiful courts, and the aspect of immortality which marble statues acquire by being kept free from dust. A very hungry boy, seeing in one of the cabinets a vast porphyry vase, forty-four feet in circumference, wished that he had it full of soup.

Yesterday, we went to the Pamfili Doria palace, which, I believe, is the most splendid in Rome. The entrance is from the Corso into a court, surrounded by a colonnade, and having a space of luxuriant verdure and ornamental shrubbery in the centre. The apartments containing pictures and sculptures are fifteen in number, and run quite round the court; in the first piano, all the rooms, halls, and galleries of beautiful proportion, with vaulted roofs, some of which glow with frescoes; and all are colder and more comfortless than can possibly be imagined without having been in them. The pictures, most of them, interested me very little. I am of opinion that good pictures are quite as rare as good poets; and I do not see why we should pique ourselves on admiring any but the very best. One in a thousand, perhaps, ought to live in the applause of men, from generation to generation, till its colours fade or blacken out of sight, and its canvas rots away; the rest should be put in garrets, or painted over by newer artists, just as tolerable poets are shelved when their little day is over. Nevertheless, there was one long gallery containing many pictures that I should be glad to see again under more favourable circumstances—that is, separately, and where I might contemplate them quite undisturbed, reclining in an easy-chair. At one end of the long vista of this gallery is a bust of the present Prince Doria—a smooth, sharp-nosed, rather handsome young man—and at the other end his princess, an English lady of the Talbot family, apparently a blonde, with a simple and sweet expression. There is a noble and striking portrait of the old Venetian admiral, Andrea Doria, by Sebastian del Piombo, and some other portraits and busts of the family.

In the whole immense range of rooms I saw but a single fire-place, and that so deep in the wall that no amount of blaze would raise the atmosphere of the room ten degrees. If the builder of the palace, or any of his successors, have committed crimes worthy of Tophet, it would be a still worse punishment for him to wander perpetually through this suite of rooms on the cold floors of polished brick tiles or marble, or mosaic, growing a little chiller and chiller through every moment of eternity—or, at least, till the palace crumbles down upon him.

Neither would it assuage his torment in the least to be compelled to gaze up at the dark old pictures—the ugly ghosts of what may once have been beautiful. I am not going to try any more to receive pleasure from a faded, tarnished, lustreless picture, especially if it be a landscape. There were two or three landscapes of Claude in this palace, which I doubt not would have been exquisite if they were in the condition of those in the British National Gallery;

but here they looked most forlorn, and even their sunshine was sunless. The merits of historical painting may be quite independent of the attributes that give pleasure, and a superficial ugliness may even heighten the effect; but not so of landscapes.

VIA PORTA, PALAZZO LARAZANI, *March* 11*th*.— To-day we called at Mr. Thompson's studio, and . . . He had on the easel a little picture of St. Peter released from prison by the angel, which I saw once before. It is very beautiful indeed, and deeply and spiritually conceived, and I wish I could afford to have it finished for myself. I looked again, too, at his Georgian Slave, and admired it as much as at first view; so very warm and rich it is, so sensuously beautiful, and with an expression of higher life and feeling within. I do not think there is a better painter than Mr. Thompson living—among Americans, at least; not one so earnest, faithful, and religious in his worship of art. I had rather look at his pictures than at any except the very finest of the old masters, and—taking into consideration only the comparative pleasure to be derived—I would not except more than one or two of those. In painting, as in literature, I suspect there is something in the productions of the day that takes the fancy more than the works of any past age;—not greater merit, nor nearly so great, but better suited to this very present time. . . . .

After leaving him, we went to the Piazza di Termini, near the Baths of Diocletian, and found our way with some difficulty to Crawford's studio. It occupies several great rooms, connected with the offices of the Villa Negroni; and all these rooms were full of plaster casts, and a few works in marble—principally portions of his huge Washington monument, which he left unfinished at his death. Close by the door at which we entered stood a gigantic figure of Mason, in bag-wig, and the coat, waistcoat, breeches, and knee and shoe buckles of the last century—the enlargement of these unheroic matters to far more than heroic size having a very odd effect. There was a figure of Jefferson, on the same scale; another of Patrick Henry, besides a horse's head, and other portions of the equestrian group, which is to cover the summit of the monument. In one of the rooms was a model of the monument itself, on a scale, I should think, of about an inch to a foot. It did not impress me as having grown out of any great and genuine idea in the artist's mind, but as being merely an ingenious contrivance enough. There were also casts of statues that seemed to be intended for some other monument, referring to revolutionary times and personages; and with these were intermixed some ideal statues or groups—a naked boy playing marbles, very beautiful; a girl with flowers; the cast of his Orpheus, of which I long ago saw the marble statue; Adam and Eve; Flora,—all with a good deal of merit, no doubt, but not a single one that justifies Crawford's reputation, or that satisfies me of his genius. They are but commonplaces in marble and plaster, such as we should not tolerate on a printed page. He seems to have been a respectable man, highly respectable, but no more, although those who knew him seem to have rated him much higher. It is said that he exclaimed, not very long before his death, that he had fifteen years of good work still in him; and he appears to have considered all his life and labour, heretofore, as only preparatory to the great things that he was to achieve hereafter. I should say, on the contrary, that he was a man who had done his best, and had done it early; for his Orpheus is quite as good as anything else we saw in his studio.

People were at work chiselling several statues in marble from the plaster models—a very interesting process, and what I should think a doubtful and hazardous one; but the artists say that there is no risk of mischief, and that the model is sure to be accurately repeated in the marble. These persons, who do what is considered the mechanical part of the business, are often themselves sculptors, and of higher reputation than those who employ them.

It is rather sad to think that Crawford died before he could see his ideas in the marble, where they gleam with so pure and celestial a light as compared with the plaster. There is almost as much difference as between flesh and spirit.

The floor of one of the rooms was burthened with immense packages, containing parts of the Washington monument, ready to be forwarded to its destination. When finished, and set up, it will probably make a very splendid appearance, by its height, its mass, its skilful execution ; and will produce a moral effect through its images of illustrious men, and the associations that connect it with our Revolutionary History; but I do not think it will owe much to artistic force of thought or depth of feeling. It is certainly, in one sense, a very foolish and illogical piece of work—Washington, mounted on an uneasy steed, on a very narrow space, aloft in the air, whence a single step of the horse backward, forward, or on either side, must precipitate him ; and several of his contemporaries standing beneath him, not looking up to wonder at his predicament, but each intent on manifesting his own personality to the world around. They have nothing to do with one another, nor with Washington, nor with any great purpose which all are to work out together.

March 14*th.*—On Friday evening I dined at Mr. T. B. Reade's, the poet and artist, with a party composed of painters and sculptors—the only exceptions being the American banker and an American tourist who has given Mr. Reade a commission. Next to me at table sat Mr. Gibson, the English sculptor, who, I suppose, stands foremost in his profession at this day. He must be quite an old man now, for it was whispered about the table that he is known to have been in Rome forty-two years ago, and he himself spoke to me of spending thirty-seven years here, before he once returned home. I should hardly take him to be sixty, however, his hair being more dark than grey, his forehead unwrinkled, his features unwithered, his eye undimmed, though his beard is somewhat venerable. . . . . .

He has a quiet, self-contained aspect, and being a bachelor, has doubtless spent a calm life among his clay and marble, meddling little with the world, and entangling himself with no cares beyond his studio. He did not talk a great deal; but enough to show that he is still an Englishman in many sturdy traits, though his accent has something foreign about it. His conversation was chiefly about India, and other topics of the day, together with a few reminiscences of people in Liverpool, where he once resided. There was a kind of simplicity both in his manner and matter, and nothing very remarkable in the latter. . . . . . .

The gist of what he said (upon art) was condemnatory of the Pre-Raphaelite modern school of painters, of whom he seemed to spare none, and of their works nothing ; though he allowed that the old Pre-Raphaelites had some exquisite merits, which the moderns entirely omit in their imitations. In his own art, he said the aim should be to find out the principles on which the Greek sculptors wrought, and to do the work of this day on those principles and in their spirit : a fair doctrine enough, I should think, but which Mr. Gibson can scarcely be said to practise. . . . The difference between the Pre-Raphaelites and himself is deep and genuine, they being literalists and realists, in a certain sense, and he a pagan idealist. Methinks they have hold of the best end of the matter.

March 18*th*.—To-day, it being very bright and mild, we set out, at noon, for an expedition to the Temple of Vesta, though I did not feel much inclined for walking, having been ill and feverish for two or three days past with a cold, which keeps renewing itself faster than I can get rid of it. We kept along on this side of the Corso, and crossed the Forum, skirting along the Capitoline Hill, and thence towards the Circus Maximus. On our way, looking down a cross street, we saw a heavy arch, and, on examination, made it out to be the Arch of Janus Quadrifrons, standing in the Forum Boarium. Its base is now considerably below the level of the surrounding soil, and there is a church or basilica close by, and some mean edifices looking down upon it. There is something satisfactory in this arch, from the immense solidity of its structure. It gives the idea, in the first place, of a solid mass constructed of huge blocks of marble, which time can never wear away, nor earthquakes shake down; and then this solid mass is penetrated by two arched passages, meeting in the centre. There are empty niches, three in a row, and, I think, two rows, on each face; but there seems to have been very little effort to make it a beautiful object. On the top is some brickwork, the remains of a mediæval fortress built by the Frangipanis, looking very frail and temporary being brought thus in contact with the antique strength of the arch.

A few yards off, across the street, and close beside the basilica, is what appears to be an ancient portal, with carved bas-reliefs, and an inscription which I could not make out. Some Romans were lying dormant in the sun, on the steps of the basilica; indeed, now that the sun is getting warmer, they seem to take advantage of every quiet nook to bask in, and perhaps to go to sleep.

We had gone but a little way from the arch, and across the Circus Maximus, when we saw the Temple of Vesta before us, on the bank of the Tiber, which, however, we could not see behind it. It is a most perfectly preserved Roman ruin, and very beautiful, though so small that, in a suitable locality, one would take it rather for a garden-house than an ancient temple. A circle of white marble pillars, much time-worn and a little battered, though but one of them broken, surround the solid structure of the temple, leaving a circular walk between it and the pillars, the whole covered by a modern roof which looks like wood, and disgraces and deforms the elegant little building. This roof resembles, as much as anything else, the round wicker cover of a basket, and gives a very squat aspect to the temple. The pillars are of the Corinthian order, and when they were new and the marble snow-white, and sharply carved and cut, there could not have been a prettier object in all Rome; but so small an edifice does not appear well as a ruin.

Within view of it, and, indeed, a very little way off, is the Temple of Fortuna Virilis, which likewise retains its antique form in better preservation than we generally find a Roman ruin, although the Ionic pillars are now built up with blocks of stone and patches of brickwork, the whole constituting a church which is fixed against the side of a tall edifice, the nature of which I do not know.

I forgot to say that we gained admittance into the Temple of Vesta, and found the interior a plain cylinder of marble, about ten paces across, and fitted up as a chapel, where the Virgin takes the place of Vesta.

In very close vicinity we came upon the Ponte Rotto, the old Pons Emilius, which was broken down long ago, and has recently been pieced out by connecting a suspension bridge with the old piers. We crossed by this bridge, paying a toll of a baioccho each, and stopped in the midst of the river to look at the Temple of Vesta, which shows well, right on the brink of the Tiber. We fancied, too, that we could discern, a little farther down the river, the ruined and almost submerged piers of the Sublician bridge, which Horatius Cocles defended. The Tiber here whirls rapidly along, and Horatius must have had a perilous swim for his life, and the enemy a fair mark at his head with their arrows. I think this is the most picturesque part of the Tiber in its passage through Rome.

After crossing the bridge, we kept along the right bank of the river, through the dirty and hard-hearted streets of Trastevere (which have, in no respect, the advantage over those of hither Rome), till we reached St. Peter's. We saw a family sitting before their door on the pavement in the narrow and sunny street, engaged in their domestic avocations—the old woman spinning with a wheel. I suppose the people now begin to live out of doors. We entered beneath the colonnade of St. Peter's, and immediately became sensible of an evil odour—the bad odour of our fallen nature, which there is no escaping in any nook of Rome. . . . .

Between the pillars of the colonnade, however, we had the pleasant spectacle of the two fountains, sending up their lily-shaped gush, with rainbows shining in their falling spray. Parties of French soldiers, as usual, were undergoing their drill in the piazza. When we entered the church, the long, dusty sunbeams were falling aslantwise through the dome, and through the chancel behind it. . . . .

March 23rd. — On the 21st we all went to the Coliseum, and enjoyed ourselves there in the bright, warm sun—so bright and warm that we were glad to get into the shadow of the walls and under the arches, though, after all, there was the freshness of March in the breeze that stirred now and then. J—— and baby found some beautiful flowers growing round about the Coliseum; and far up towards the top of the walls we saw tufts of yellow wallflowers and a great deal of green grass growing along the ridges between the arches. The general aspect of the place, however, is somewhat bare, and does not compare favourably with an English ruin, both on account of the lack of ivy, and because the material is chiefly brick, the stone and marble having been stolen away by popes and cardinals to build their palaces. While we sat within the circle, many people of both sexes passed through, kissing the iron cross which stands in the centre, thereby gaining an indulgence of seven years, I believe. In front of several churches I have seen an inscription in Latin, "INDULGENTIA PLENARIA ET PERPETUA PRO CUNCTIS MORTUIS ET VIVIS;" than which, it seems to me, nothing more could be asked or desired. The terms of this great boon are not mentioned.

Leaving the Coliseum, we went and sat down in the vicinity of the Arch of Constantine, and J——

and R—— went in quest of lizards. J—— soon caught a large one with two tails; one a sort of after thought, or appendix, or corollary to the original tail, and growing out from it instead of from the body of the lizard. These reptiles are very abundant, and J—— has already brought home several, which make their escape, and appear occasionally, darting to and fro on the carpet. Since we have been here, J—— has taken up various pursuits in turn. First he devoted himself to gathering snail-shells, of which there are many sorts; afterwards he had a fever for marbles, pieces of which he found on the banks of the Tiber, just on the edge of its muddy waters, and in the Palace of the Cæsars, the Baths of Caracalla, and indeed wherever else his fancy led him — verde antique, rosso antico, porphyry, giallo antico, serpentine, sometimes fragments of bas-reliefs and mouldings, bits of mosaic, still firmly stuck together, on which the foot of a Cæsar had perhaps once trodden; pieces of Roman glass, with the iridescence glowing on them; and all such things, of which the soil of Rome is full. It would not be difficult, from the spoil of his boyish rambles, to furnish what would be looked upon as a curious and valuable museum in America.

Yesterday we went to the sculpture galleries of

the Vatican. I think I enjoy these noble galleries and their contents and beautiful arrangement better than anything else in the way of art, and often I seem to have a deep feeling of something wonderful in what I look at. The Laocoon on this visit impressed me not less than before; it is such a type of human beings, struggling with an inextricable trouble, and entangled in a complication which they cannot free themselves from by their own efforts, and out of which Heaven alone can help them. It was a most powerful mind, and one capable of reducing a complex idea to unity, that imagined this group. I looked at Canova's Perseus, and thought it exceedingly beautiful, but found myself less and less contented after a moment or two, though I could not tell why. Afterwards, looking at the Apollo, the recollection of the Perseus disgusted me, and yet really I cannot explain how one is better than the other.

I was interested in looking at the busts of the Triumvirs, Antony, Augustus, and Lepidus. The first two are men of intellect, evidently, though they do not recommend themselves to one's affections by their physiognomy; but Lepidus has the strangest, most commonplace countenance that can be imagined — small-featured, weak, such a face as you meet anywhere in a man of no mark, but are amazed to find in one of the three foremost men of the world. I suppose that it is these weak and shallow men, when chance raises them above their proper sphere, who commit enormous crimes without any such restraint as stronger men would feel, and without any retribution in the depth of their conscience. These old Roman busts, of which there are so many in the Vatican, have often a most life-like aspect, a striking individuality. One recognises them as faithful portraits, just as certainly as if the living originals were standing beside them. The arrangement of the hair and beard too, in many cases, is just what we see now, the fashions of two thousand years ago having come round again.

March 25th.—On Tuesday we went to breakfast at William Story's in the Palazzo Barberini. We had a very pleasant time. He is one of the most agreeable men I know in society. He showed us a note from Thackeray, an invitation to dinner, written in hieroglyphics, with great fun and pictorial merit. He spoke of an expansion of the story of Blue Beard, which he himself had either written or thought of writing, in which the contents of the several chambers which Fatima opened, before arriving at the fatal one, were to be described. This idea has haunted my mind ever since, and if it had but been my own I am pretty sure that it would develop itself into something very rich. I mean to press William Story to work it out. The chamber of Blue Beard, too (and this was a part of his suggestion), might be so handled as to become powerfully interesting. Were I to take up the story I would create an interest by suggesting a secret in the first chamber, which would develop itself more and more in every successive hall of the great palace, and lead the wife irresistibly to the chamber of horrors.

After breakfast, we went to the Barberini Library, passing through the vast hall, which occupies the central part of the palace. It is the most splendid domestic hall I have seen, eighty feet in length at least, and of proportionate breadth and height; and the vaulted ceiling is entirely covered, to its utmost edge and remotest corners, with a brilliant painting in fresco, looking like a whole heaven of angelic people descending towards the floor. The effect is indescribably gorgeous. On one side stands a Baldacchino, or canopy of state, draped with scarlet cloth, and fringed with gold embroidery; the scarlet indicating that the palace is inhabited by a cardinal. Green would be appropriate to a prince. In point of fact, the Palazzo Barberini is inhabited by a cardinal, a prince, and a duke, all belonging to the Barberini family, and each having his separate portion of the palace, while their servants have a common territory and meeting-ground in this noble hall.

After admiring it for a few minutes, we made our exit by a door on the opposite side, and went up the spiral staircase of marble to the library, where we were received by an ecclesiastic, who belongs to the Barberini household, and I believe was born in it. He is a gentle, refined, quiet-looking man, as well he may be, having spent all his life among these books, where few people intrude, and few cares can come. He showed us a very old Bible in parchment, a specimen of the earliest printing, beautifully ornamented with pictures, and some monkish illuminations of indescribable delicacy and elaboration. No artist could afford to produce such work, if the life that he thus lavished on one sheet of parchment had any value to him, either for what could be done or enjoyed in it. There are about eight thousand volumes in this library, and judging by their outward aspect, the collection must be curious and valuable; but having another engagement, we could spend only a little time here. We had a hasty glance, however, of some poems of Tasso, in his own autograph.

We then went to the Palazzo Galitzin, where dwell

the Misses Weston, with whom we lunched, and where we met a French abbé, an agreeable man, and an antiquarian, under whose auspices two of the ladies and ourselves took carriage for the Castle of St. Angelo. Being admitted within the external gateway, we found ourselves in the court of guard, as I presume it is called, where the French soldiers were playing with very dirty cards, or lounging about in military idleness. They were well-behaved and courteous, and when we had intimated our wish to see the interior of the castle, a soldier soon appeared, with a large unlighted torch in his hand, ready to guide us. There is an outer wall surrounding the solid structure of Hadrian's tomb, to which there is access by one or two drawbridges; the entrance to the tomb, or castle, not being at the base, but near its central height. The ancient entrance, by which Hadrian's ashes and those of other imperial personages were probably brought into this tomb, has been walled up—perhaps ever since the last emperor was buried here. We were now in a vaulted passage, both lofty and broad, which circles round the whole interior of the tomb, from the base to the summit. During many hundred years the passage was filled with earth and rubbish, and forgotten, and it is but partly excavated even now, although we found it a long, long, and gloomy descent by torch-light to the base of the vast mausoleum. The passage was once lined and vaulted with precious marbles (which are now entirely gone), and paved with fine mosaics, portions of which still remain ; and our guide lowered his flaming torch to show them to us, here and there, amid the earthy dampness over which we trod. It is strange to think what splendour and costly adornment were here wasted on the dead.

After we had descended to the bottom of this passage, and again retraced our steps to the highest part, the guide took a large cannon-ball, and sent it, with his whole force, rolling down the hollow, arched way, rumbling and reverberating and bellowing forth long thunderous echoes, and winding up with a loud, distant crash, that seemed to come from the very bowels of the earth.

We saw the place, near the centre of the mausoleum, and lighted from above, through an immense thickness of stone and brick, where the ashes of the emperor and his fellow-slumberers were found. It is as much as twelve centuries, very likely, since they were scattered to the winds, for the tomb has been nearly or quite that space of time, a fortress. The tomb itself is merely the base and foundation of the castle, and being so massively built, it serves just as well for the purpose as if it were a solid granite rock. The mediæval fortress, with its antiquity of more than a thousand years, and having dark and deep dungeons of its own, is but a modern excrescence on the top of Hadrian's tomb.

We now ascended towards the upper region, and were led into the vaults which used to serve as a prison, but which, if I mistake not, are situated above the ancient structure, although they seem as damp and subterranean as if they were fifty feet under the earth. We crept down to them through narrow and ugly passages, which the torch-light would not illuminate, and stooping under a low, square entrance, we followed the guide into a small, vaulted room—not a room, but an artificial cavern, remote from light or air, where Beatrice Cenci was confined before her execution. According to the abbé, she spent a whole year in this dreadful pit, her trial having dragged on through that length of time. How ghost-like she must have looked when she came forth! Guido never painted that beautiful picture from her blanched face, as it appeared after this confinement. And how rejoiced she must have been to die at last, having already been in a sepulchre so long!

Adjacent to Beatrice's prison, but not communicating with it, was that of her stepmother; and next to the latter was one that interested me almost as much as Beatrice's—that of Benvenuto Cellini, who was confined here, I believe, for an assassination. All these prison vaults are more horrible than can be imagined without seeing them; but there are worse places here, for the guide lifted a trap-door in one of the passages, and held his torch down into an inscrutable pit beneath our feet. It was an *oubliette*, a dungeon where the prisoner might be buried alive, and never come forth again, alive or dead. Groping about among these sad precincts, we saw various other things that looked very dismal; but at last emerged into the sunshine, and ascended from one platform and battlement to another, till we found ourselves right at the feet of the Archangel Michael. He has stood there in bronze for I know not how many hundred years, in the act of sheathing a (now) rusty sword, such being the attitude in which he appeared to one of the popes in a vision, in token that a pestilence which was then desolating Rome was to be stayed.

There is a fine view from the lofty station, over Rome and the whole adjacent country, and the abbé pointed out the site of Ardea, of Corioli, of Veii, and other places renowned in story. We were ushered, too, into the French commandant's quarters in the castle. There is a large hall, ornamented with frescoes, and accessible from this a drawing-room, comfortably fitted up, and where we saw modern furniture and a chess-board, and a fire burning clear, and other symptoms that the place had perhaps just been vacated by civilised and kindly people. But in one corner of the ceiling the abbé pointed out a ring, by which, in the times of mediæval anarchy, when popes, cardinals, and barons were all by the ears together, a cardinal was hanged. It was not an assassination, but a legal punishment, and he was executed in the best apartment of the castle as an act of grace.

The fortress is a straight-lined structure on the summit of the immense round tower of Hadrian's tomb; and to make out the idea of it we must throw in drawbridges, esplanades, piles of ancient marble balls for cannon; battlements and embrasures, lying high in the breeze and sunshine, and opening views round the whole horizon; accommodation for the soldiers; and many small beds in a large room.

How much mistaken was the emperor in his expectation of a stately, solemn repose for his ashes through all the coming centuries, as long as the world should endure! Perhaps his ghost glides up and down, disconsolate, in that spiral passage which goes from top to bottom of the tomb, while the barbarous Gauls plant themselves in his very mausoleum to keep the imperial city in awe.

Leaving the Castle of St. Angelo, we drove, still on the same side of the Tiber, to the Villa Pamfila, which lies a short distance beyond the walls. As we passed through one of the gates (I think it was that of San Pancrazio), the abbé pointed out the spot where the Constable de Bourbon was killed while attempting to scale the walls. If we are to believe Benvenuto Cellini, it was he who shot the Constable. The road to the villa is not very interesting, lying (as the roads in the vicinity of Rome often do) between very high walls, admitting not a glimpse of the surrounding country; the road itself white and dusty, with no verdant margin of grass or border of shrubbery. At the portal of the villa we found many carriages in waiting, for the Prince Doria throws open the grounds to all comers, and on a pleasant day like this they are probably sure to be thronged. We left our carriage just within the entrance, and rambled among these beautiful groves, admiring the live oak trees, and the stone pines, which latter are truly a majestic tree, with tall columnar stems, supporting a cloud-like density of boughs far aloft, and not a straggling branch between them and the ground. They stand in straight rows, but are now so ancient and venerable as to have lost the formal look of a plantation, and seem like a wood that might have arranged itself almost of its own will. Beneath them is a flower-strewn turf, quite free of underbrush. We found open fields and lawns, moreover, all a-bloom with anemones, white and rose-coloured, and purple and golden, and far larger than could be found out of Italy, except in hothouses. Violets, too, were abundant and exceedingly fragrant. When we consider that all this floral exuberance occurs in the midst of March, there does not appear much ground for complaining of the Roman climate; and so long ago as the first week of February I found daisies among the grass, on the sunny side of the basilica of St. John Lateran. At this very moment I suppose the country within twenty miles of Boston may be two feet deep with snow, and the streams solid with ice.

We wandered about the grounds, and found them very beautiful indeed, nature having done much for them by an undulating variety of surface, and art having added a good many charms, which have all the better effect now that decay and neglect have thrown a natural grace over them likewise. There is an artificial ruin, so picturesque that it betrays itself;

weather-beaten statues, and pieces of sculpture, scattered here and there; an artificial lake, with up-gushing fountains; cascades, and broad-bosomed coves, and long, canal-like reaches, with swans taking their delight upon them. I never saw such a glorious and resplendent lustre of white as shone between the wings of two of these swans. It was really a sight to see, and not to be imagined beforehand. Angels, no doubt, have just such lustrous wings as those. English swans partake of the dinginess of the atmosphere, and their plumage has nothing at all to be compared to this; in fact, there is nothing like it in the world, unless it be the illuminated portion of a fleecy, summer-cloud.

While we were sauntering along beside this piece of water, we were surprised to see U—— on the other side. She had come hither with E—— S—— and her two little brothers, and with our R——, the whole under the charge of Mrs. Story's nursery-maids. U—— and E—— crossed, not over, but beneath the water, through a grotto, and exchanged greetings with us. Then, as it was getting towards sunset and cool, we took our departure, the abbé, as we left the grounds, taking me aside to give me a glimpse of a Columbarium, which descends into the earth to about the depth to which an ordinary house might rise above it. These grounds, it is said, formed the country residence of the Emperor Galba, and he was buried here after his assassination. It is a sad thought that so much natural beauty and long refinement of picturesque culture is thrown away, the villa being uninhabitable during all the most delightful season of the year on account of malaria. There is truly a curse on Rome and all its neighbourhood.

On our way home we passed by the great Paolina fountain, and were assailed by many beggars during the short time we stopped to look at it. It is a very copious fountain, but not so beautiful as the Trevi, taking into view merely the water-gush of the latter.

March 26th.—Yesterday, between twelve and one, our whole family went to the Villa Ludovisi, the entrance to which is at the termination of a street which passes out of the Piazza Barberini, and it is no very great distance from our own street, Via Porta Pinciana. The grounds, though very extensive, are wholly within the walls of the city, which skirt them, and comprise a part of what were formerly the gardens of Sallust. The villa is now the property of Prince Piombini, a ticket from whom procured us admission. A little within the gateway, to the right, is a casino, containing two large rooms filled with sculpture, much of which is very valuable. A colossal head of Juno, I believe, is considered the greatest treasure of the collection, but I did not myself feel it to be so, nor indeed did I receive any strong impression of its excellence. I admired nothing so much, I think, as the face of Penelope (if it be her face), in the group supposed also to represent Electra and Orestes. The sitting statue of Mars is very fine; so is the Aria and Pætus; so are many other busts and figures.

By-and-by we left the casino and wandered among the grounds, threading interminable alleys of cypress, through the long vistas of which we could see here and there a statue, an urn, a pillar, a temple, or garden-house, or a bas-relief against the wall. It seems as if there must have been a time—and not so very long ago—when it was worth while to spend money and thought upon the ornamentation of grounds in the neighbourhood of Rome. That time is past, however, and the result is very melancholy; for great beauty has been produced, but it can be enjoyed in its perfection only at the peril of one's life. . . . . For my part, and judging from my own experience, I suspect that the Roman atmosphere, never wholesome, is always more or less poisonous.

We came to another and larger casino remote from the gateway, in which the Prince resides during two months of the year. It was now under repair, but we gained admission, as did several other visitors, and saw in the entrance-hall the Aurora of Guercino, painted in fresco on the ceiling. There is beauty in the design; but the painter certainly was most unhappy in his black shadows, and in the work before us they give the impression of a cloudy and lowering morning, which is likely enough to turn to rain by-and-by. After viewing the fresco we mounted by a spiral staircase to a lofty terrace, and found Rome at our feet, and, far off, the Sabine and Alban mountains, some of them still capped with snow. In another direction there was a vast plain, on the horizon of which, could our eyes have reached to its verge, we might perhaps have seen the Mediterranean Sea. After enjoying the view and the warm sunshine, we descended, and went in quest of the gardens of Sallust, but found no satisfactory remains of them.

One of the most striking objects in the first casino was a group by Bernini—Pluto—an outrageously masculine and strenuous figure, heavily bearded, ravishing away a little, tender Proserpine, whom he holds aloft, while his forcible gripe impresses itself into her soft, virgin flesh. It is very disagreeable, but it makes one feel that Bernini was a man of great ability. There are some works in literature that bear an analogy to his works in sculpture—when great power is lavished a little outside of nature, and therefore proves to be only a fashion, and not permanently adapted to the tastes of mankind.

March 27th.—Yesterday forenoon my wife and I went to St. Peter's, to see the Pope pray at the chapel of the Holy Sacrament. We found a good many people in the church, but not an inconvenient number; indeed, not so many as to make any remarkable show in the great nave, nor even in front of the chapel. A detachment of the Swiss Guard, in their strange, picturesque, harlequin-like costume, were on duty before the chapel, in which the wax-tapers were all lighted, and a *prie-dieu* was arranged near the shrine, and covered with scarlet velvet. On each side, along the breadth of the side aisle, were placed seats, covered with rich tapestry or carpeting; and some gentlemen and ladies—English, probably, or American—had comfortably deposited themselves here, but were compelled to move by the guards before the Pope's entrance. His holiness should have appeared precisely at twelve, but we waited nearly half an hour beyond that time; and it seemed to me particularly ill-mannered in the Pope, who owes the courtesy of being punctual to the people, if not to St. Peter. By-and-by, however, there was a stir; the guard motioned to us to stand away from the benches, against the backs of which we had been leaning; the spectators in the nave looked towards the door, as if they beheld something approaching; and first, there appeared some cardinals, in scarlet skull-caps and purple robes, intermixed with some of the Noble Guard and other attendants. It was not a very formal and stately procession, but rather straggled onward, with ragged edges, the spectators standing aside to let it pass, and merely bowing, or perhaps slightly bending the knee, as good Catholics are accustomed to do when passing before the shrines of saints. Then, in the midst of the purple cardinals, all of whom were grey-haired men, appeared a stout old man, with a white skull-cap, a scarlet gold-embroidered cape falling over his shoulders, and a white silk robe, the train of which was borne up by an attendant. He walked slowly, with a sort of dignified movement, stepping out broadly, and planting his feet (on which were red shoes) flat upon the pavement, as if he were not much accustomed to locomotion, and perhaps had known a twinge of the gout. His face was kindly and venerable, but not particularly impressive. Arriving at the scarlet-covered prie-dieu, he kneeled down and took off his white skull-cap; the cardinals also kneeled behind and on either side of him, taking off their scarlet skull-caps;

while the Noble Guard remained standing, six on one side of his holiness and six on the other. The Pope bent his head upon the prie-dieu, and seemed to spend three or four minutes in prayer; then rose, and all the purple cardinals and bishops and priests, of whatever degree, rose behind and beside him. Next, he went to kiss St. Peter's toe—at least, I believe he kissed it, but I was not near enough to be certain; and lastly, he knelt down, and directed his devotions towards the high altar. This completed the ceremonies, and his holiness left the church by a side door, making a short passage into the Vatican.

I am very glad I have seen the Pope, because now he may be crossed out of the list of sights to be seen. His proximity impressed me kindly and favourably towards him, and I did not see one face among all his cardinals (in whose number, doubtless, is his successor) which I would so soon trust as that of Pio Nono.

This morning I walked as far as the gate of San Paolo, and, on approaching it, I saw the grey, sharp pyramid of Caius Cestius pointing upward, close to the two dark-brown, battlemented, Gothic towers of the gateway, each of these very different pieces of architecture looking the more picturesque for the contrast of the other. Before approaching the gateway and pyramid, I walked onward, and soon came in sight of Monte Testaccio, the artificial hill made of potsherds. There is a gate admitting into the grounds around the hill, and a road encircling its base. At a distance, the hill looks greener than any other part of the landscape, and has all the curved outlines of a natural hill, resembling in shape a headless sphynx, or Saddleback mountain, as I used to see it from Lenox. It is of very considerable height —two or three hundred feet at least, I should say— and well entitled, both by its elevation and the space it covers, to be reckoned among the hills of Rome. Its base is almost entirely surrounded with small structures, which seem to be used as farm-buildings. On the summit is a large iron cross, the Church having thought it expedient to redeem these shattered pipkins from the power of paganism, as it has so many other Roman ruins. There was a pathway up the hill, but I did not choose to ascend it under the hot sun, so steeply did it clamber up. There appears to be a good depth of soil on most parts of Monte Testaccio, but on some of the sides you observe precipices, bristling with fragments of red or brown earthenware, or pieces of vases of white unglazed clay; and it is evident that this immense pile is entirely composed of broken crockery, which I should hardly have thought would have aggregated to such a heap had it all been thrown here—urns, teacups, porcelain, or earthen—since the beginning of the world.

I walked quite round the hill, and saw, at no great distance from it, the enclosure of the Protestant burial-ground, which lies so close to the pyramid of Caius Cestius that the latter may serve as a general monument to the dead. Deferring, for the present, a visit to the cemetery, or to the interior of the pyramid, I returned to the gateway of San Paolo, and passing through it, took a view of it from the outside of the city wall. It is itself a portion of the wall, having been built into it by the Emperor Aurelian, so that about half of it lies within and half without. The brick or red stone material of the wall being so unlike the marble of the pyramid, the latter is as distinct, and seems as insulated, as if it stood alone in the centre of a plain; and really I do not think there is a more striking architectural object in Rome. It is in perfect condition, just as little ruined or decayed as on the day when the builder put the last peak on the summit; and it ascends steeply from its base, with a point so sharp that it looks as if it would hardly afford foothold to a bird. The marble was once white, but is now covered with a grey coating like that which has gathered upon the statues of Castor and Pollux on Monte Cavallo. Not one of the great blocks is displaced, nor seems likely to be through all time to come. They rest one upon another, in straight and even lines, and present a vast smooth triangle, ascending from a base of a hundred feet, and narrowing to an apex at the height of a hundred and twenty-five, the junctures of the marble slabs being so close that, in all these twenty centuries, only a few little tufts of grass, and a trailing plant or two, have succeeded in rooting themselves into the interstices.

It is good and satisfactory to see anything which, being built for an enduring monument, has endured so faithfully, and has a prospect of such an interminable futurity before it. Once, indeed, it seemed likely to be buried; for three hundred years ago, it had become covered to the depth of sixteen feet, but the soil has since been dug away from its base, which is now lower than that of the road which passes through the neighbouring gate of San Paolo. Midway up the pyramid, cut in the marble, is an inscription in large Roman letters, still almost as legible as when first wrought.

I did not return through the Paolo gateway, but kept onward, round the exterior of the wall, till I came to the gate of San Sebastiano. It was a hot and not a very interesting walk, with only a high bare wall of brick, broken by frequent square towers, on one side of the road, and a bank and hedge or a garden-wall on the other. Roman roads are most inhospitable, offering no shade, and no seat, and no pleasant views of rustic domiciles; nothing but the wheel-track of white dust, without a footpath running by its side, and seldom any grassy margin to refresh the wayfarer's feet.

April 3rd.—A few days ago we visited the studio of Mr. ——, an American, who seems to have a good deal of vogue as a sculptor. We found a figure of Pocohontas, which he has repeated several times; another, which he calls "The Wept of the Wish-ton-Wish," a figure of a smiling girl playing with a cat and dog, and a schoolboy mending a pen. These two last were the only ones that gave me any pleasure, or that really had any merit; for his cleverness and ingenuity appear in homely subjects, but are quite lost in attempts at a higher ideality. Nevertheless, he has a group of the Prodigal Son, possessing more merit than I should have expected from Mr. ——, the son reclining his head on his father's breast, with an expression of utter weariness, at length finding perfect rest, while the father bends his benign countenance over him, and seems to receive him calmly into himself. This group (the plaster-cast standing beside it) is now taking shape out of an immense block of marble, and will be as indestructible as the Laocoon; an idea at once awful and ludicrous, when we consider that it is at best but a respectable production. I have since been told that Mr. —— had stolen—adopted, we will rather say— the attitude and idea of the group from one executed by a student of the French Academy, and to be seen there in plaster.*

Mr. —— has now been ten years in Italy, and, after all this time, he is still entirely American in everything but the most external surface of his manners; scarcely Europeanised, or much modified even in that. He is a native of ——, but had his early breeding in New York, and might, for any polish or refinement that I can discern in him, still be a country shopkeeper in the interior of New York State or New England. How strange! For one expects to find the polish, the close grain and white purity of marble, in the artist who works in that noble material; but, after all, he handles *clay*, and, judging by the specimens I have seen here, is apt to *be* clay—not of the finest—himself. Mr. —— is

* We afterwards saw it in the Medici Casino.

sensible, shrewd, keen, clever; an ingenious workman, no doubt; with tact enough, and not destitute of taste; very agreeable and lively in his conversation, talking as fast and as naturally as a brook runs, without the slightest affectation. His naturalness is, in fact, a rather striking characteristic, in view of his lack of culture, while yet his life has been concerned with idealities and a beautiful art. What degree of taste he pretends to, he seems really to possess, nor did I hear a single idea from him that struck me as otherwise than sensible.

He called to see us last evening, and talked for about two hours in a very amusing and interesting style, his topics being taken from his own personal experience, and shrewdly treated. He spoke much of Greenough, whom he described as an excellent critic of art, but possessed of not the slightest inventive genius. His statue of Washington, at the Capitol, is taken precisely from the Phillian Jupiter; his Chanting Cherubs are copied in marble from two figures in a picture by Raphael. He did nothing that was original with himself. . . . . To-day we took R——, and went to see Miss Hosmer, and as her studio seems to be mixed up with Gibson's, we had an opportunity of glancing at some of his beautiful works. We saw a Venus and a Cupid, both of them tinted; and, side by side with them, other statues identical with these, except that the marble was left in its pure whiteness.

We found Miss —— in a little upper room. She has a small, brisk, wide-awake figure, not ungraceful; frank, simple, straightforward, and downright. She had on a robe, I think, but I did not look so low, my attention being chiefly drawn to a sort of man's sack of purple or plum-coloured broadcloth, into the side pockets of which her hands were thrust as she came forward to greet us. She withdrew one hand, however, and presented it cordially to my wife (whom she already knew) and to myself, without waiting for an introduction. She had on a shirt-front, collar, and cravat like a man's, with a brooch of Etruscan gold, and on her curly head was a picturesque little cap of black velvet, and her face was as bright and merry, and as small of feature as a child's. It looked in one aspect youthful, and yet there was something worn in it too. There never was anything so jaunty as her movement and action; she was very peculiar, but she seemed to be her actual self, and nothing affected or made up; so that, for my part, I gave her full leave to wear what may suit her best, and to behave as her inner woman prompts. I don't quite see, however, what see is to do when she grows older, for the decorum of age will not be consistent with a costume that looks pretty and excusable enough in a young woman.

Miss —— led us into a part of the extensive studio or collection of studios, where some of her own works were to be seen: Beatrice Cenci, which did not very greatly impress me; and a monumental design, a female figure—wholly draped even to the stockings and shoes—in a quiet sleep. I liked this last. There was also a Puck, doubtless full of fun; but I had hardly time to glance at it. Miss —— evidently has good gifts in her profession, and doubtless she derives great advantage from her close association with a consummate artist like Gibson; nor yet does his influence seem to interfere with the originality of her own conceptions. In one way, at least, she can hardly fail to profit—that is by the opportunity of showing her works to the throngs of people who go to see Gibson's own; and these are just such people as an artist would most desire to meet, and might never see in a lifetime, if left to himself. I shook hands with this frank and pleasant little person, and took leave, not without purpose of seeing her again.

Within a few days, there have been many pilgrims in Rome, who come hither to attend the ceremonies of holy week, and to perform their vows, and undergo their penances. I saw two of them near the Forum yesterday, with their pilgrim staves, in the fashion of a thousand years ago. . . . . I sat down on a bench near one of the chapels, and a woman immediately came up to me to beg. I at first refused; but she knelt down by my side, instead of praying to the saint prayed to me; and being thus treated as a canonised personage, I thought it incumbent on me to be gracious to the extent of half a paul. My wife, some time ago, came in contact with a pickpocket at the entrance of a church; and failing in his enterprise upon her purse, he passed in, dipped his thieving fingers in the holy water, and paid his devotions at a shrine. Missing the purse, he said his prayers, in the hope, perhaps, that the saint would send him better luck another time.

April 10*th.*—I have made no entries in my journal recently, being exceedingly lazy, partly from indisposition, as well as from an atmosphere that takes the vivacity out of everybody. Not much has happened or been effected. Last Sunday, which was Easter Sunday, I went with J—— to St. Peter's, where we arrived at about nine o'clock, and found a multitude of people already assembled in the church. The interior was arrayed in festal guise, there being a covering of scarlet damask over the pilasters of the nave, from base to capital, giving an effect of splendour, yet with a loss as to the apparent dimensions of the interior. A guard of soldiers occupied the nave, keeping open a wide space for the passage of a procession that was momently expected, and soon arrived. The crowd was too great to allow of my seeing it in detail; but I could perceive that there were priests, cardinals, Swiss guards—some of them with corslets on—and by-and-by the Pope himself was borne up the nave, high over the heads of all, sitting under a canopy, crowned with his tiara. He floated slowly along, and was set down in the neighbourhood of the high altar; and the procession being broken up, some of its scattered members might be seen here and there about the church: officials in antique Spanish dresses, Swiss guards in polished steel breastplates, serving men in richly embroidered liveries, officers in scarlet coats and military boots, priests, and divers other shapes of men; for the papal ceremonies seem to forego little or nothing that belongs to times past, while it includes everything appertaining to the present. I ought to have waited to witness the papal benediction from the balcony in front of the church, or, at least, to hear the famous silver trumpets sounding from the dome; but J—— grew weary (to say the truth, so did I), and we went on a long walk, out of the nearest city gate, and back through the Janiculum, and, finally, homeward over the Ponto Rotto. Standing on the bridge, I saw the arch of the Cloaca Maxima, close by the Temple of Vesta, with the water rising within two or three feet of its keystone.

The same evening we went to Monte Cavallo, where, from the gateway of the Pontifical Palace, we saw the illumination of St. Peter's. Mr. Akers, the sculptor, had recommended this position to us, and accompanied us thither, as the best point from which the illumination could be witnessed at a distance, without the incommodity of such a crowd as would be assembled at the Pincian. The first illumination — the silver one, as it is called — was very grand and delicate, describing the outline of the great edifice and crowning dome in light, while the day was not yet wholly departed. As —— finely remarked, it seemed like the glorified spirit of the Church made visible; or, as I will add, it looked as this famous and never-to-be-forgotten structure will look to the imaginations of men, through the waste and gloom of future ages, after it shall have gone quite to decay and ruin — the brilliant, though scarcely distinct gleam of a statelier dome than ever was seen, shining on the background of the night of Time. This simile looked prettier in my fancy than I have made it look on paper.

After we had enjoyed the silver illumination a good while, and when all the daylight had given place to the constellated night, the distant outline of St. Peter's burst forth, in the twinkling of an eye, into a starry blaze, being quite the finest effect that I ever witnessed. I stayed to see it, however, only a few minutes; for I was quite ill and feverish with a cold— which, indeed, I have seldom been free from, since my first breathing of the genial atmosphere of Rome. This pestilence kept me within doors all the next day, and prevented me from seeing the beautiful fireworks that were exhibited in the evening from the platform on the Pincian, above the Piazza del Popolo.

On Thursday, I paid another visit to the sculpture gallery of the Capitol, where I was particularly struck with a bust of Cato the Censor, who must have been the most disagreeable, stubborn, ugly-tempered, pig-headed, narrow-minded, strong-willed, old Roman that ever lived. The collection of busts here and at the Vatican are most interesting, many of the individual heads being full of character, and commending themselves by intrinsic evidence as faithful portraits of the originals. These stone people have stood face to face with Cæsar, and all the other emperors, and with statesmen, soldiers, philosophers, and poets of the antique world, and have been to them like their reflections in a mirror. It is the next thing to seeing the men themselves.

We went afterwards into the Palace of the Conservatori, and saw, among various other interesting things, the bronze wolf suckling Romulus and Remus, who sit beneath her dugs, with open mouths, to receive the milk.

On Friday we all went to see the Pope's palace on the Quirinal. There was a vast hall and an interminable suite of rooms, cased with marble, floored with marble or mosaics or inlaid wood, adorned with frescoes on the vaulted ceilings; and many of them lined with Gobelin tapestry — not wofully faded, like almost all that I have hitherto seen, but brilliant as pictures. Indeed, some of them so closely resembled paintings that I could hardly believe they were not so; and the effect was even richer than that of oil paintings. In every room there was a crucifix; but I did not see a single nook or corner where anybody could have dreamed of being comfortable. Nevertheless, as a stately and solemn residence for his Holiness, it is quite a satisfactory affair. Afterwards we went into the pontifical gardens connected with the palace. They are very extensive, and laid out in straight avenues, bordered with walls of box, as impervious as if of stone,—not less than twenty feet high, and pierced with lofty archways, cut in the living wall. Some of the avenues were overshadowed with trees, the tops of which bent over and joined one another from either side, so as to resemble a side aisle of a Gothic cathedral. Marble sculptures, much weather-stained, and generally broken-nosed, stood along these stately walks; there were many fountains gushing up into the sunshine; we likewise found a rich flower-garden, containing rare specimens of exotic flowers, and gigantic cactuses, and also an aviary, with vultures, doves, and singing birds. We did not see half the garden, but, stiff and formal as its general arrangement is, it is a beautiful place,—a delightful, sunny, and serene seclusion. Whatever it may be to the Pope, two young lovers might find the Garden of Eden here, and never desire to stray out of its precincts. They might fancy angels standing in the long, glimmering vistas of the avenues.

It would suit me well enough to have my daily walk along such straight paths; for I think them favourable to thought, which is apt to be disturbed by variety and unexpectedness.

April 12*th.*—We all, except R——, went to-day to the Vatican, where we found our way to the Stawne of Raphael; these being four rooms or halls, painted with frescoes. No doubt they were once very brilliant and beautiful; but they have encountered hard treatment since Raphael's time; especially when the soldiers of the Constable de Bourbon occupied these apartments, and made fires on the mosaic floors. The entire walls and ceilings are covered with pictures; but the handiwork or designs of Raphael consist of paintings on the four sides of each room, and include several works of art. The School of Athens is perhaps the most celebrated; and the longest side of the largest hall is occupied by a battle-piece, of which the Emperor Constantine is the hero, and which covers almost space enough for a real battle-field. There was a wonderful light in one of the pictures—that of St. Peter awakened in his prison by the angel; it really seemed to throw a radiance into the hall below. I shall not pretend, however, to have been sensible of any particular rapture at the sight of these frescoes, so faded as they are, so battered by the mischances of years; insomuch that, through all the power and glory of Raphael's designs, the spectator cannot but be continually sensible that the groundwork of them is an old plaster wall. They have been scrubbed, I suppose—brushed, at least—a thousand times over, till the surface, brilliant or soft, as Raphael left it, must have been quite rubbed off, and with it, all the consummate finish, and everything that made them originally delightful. The sterner features remain, the skeleton of thought, but not the beauty that once clothed it. In truth, the frescoes—excepting a few figures —never had the real touch of Raphael's own hand upon them, having been merely designed by him, and finished by his scholars, or by other artists.

The halls themselves are specimens of antique magnificence, paved with elaborate mosaics; and wherever there is any woodwork, it is richly carved with foliage and figures. In their newness, and probably for a hundred years afterwards, there could not have been so brilliant a suite of rooms in the world.

Connected with them—at any rate, not far distant —is the little Chapel of San Lorenzo, the very site of which, among the thousands of apartments of the Vatican, was long forgotten, and its existence only known by tradition. After it had been walled up, however, beyond the memory of man, there was still a rumour of some beautiful frescoes by Fra Angelico, in an old chapel of Pope Nicholas V., that had strangely disappeared out of the palace; and search at length being made, it was discovered, and entered through a window. It is a small, lofty room, quite covered over with frescoes of sacred subjects, both on the walls and ceiling, a good deal faded, yet pretty distinctly preserved. It would have been no misfortune to me, if the little old chapel had remained still hidden.

We next issued into the Loggie, which consist of a long gallery, or arcade or colonnade, the whole extent of which was once beautifully adorned by Raphael. These pictures are almost worn away, and so defaced as to be untraceable and unintelligible along the side wall of the gallery; although traceries of arabesque, and compartments where there seem to have been rich paintings, but now only an indistinguishable waste of dull colour, are still to be seen. In the coved ceiling, however, there are still some bright frescoes, in better preservation than any others; not particularly beautiful, nevertheless. I remember to have seen (indeed, we ourselves possess them) a series of very spirited and energetic engravings, old and coarse, of these frescoes, the subject being the Creation, and the early Scripture history; and I really think that their translation of the pictures is better than the original. On reference to Murray, I find that little more than the designs is attributed to Raphael, the execution being by Giulio Romano and other artists.

Escaping from these forlorn splendours, we went into the sculpture gallery, where I was able to enjoy, in some small degree, two or three wonderful works of art; and had a perception that there were a thousand other wonders around me. It is as if the statues kept, for the most part, a veil about them, which they sometimes withdraw, and let their beauty gleam upon my sight;—only a glimpse, or two or three glimpses, or a little space of calm enjoyment, and then I see nothing but a discoloured marble image again. The Minerva Medici revealed herself to-day. I wonder whether other people are more fortunate than myself, and can invariably find their way to the inner soul of a work of art. I doubt it; they look at these things for just a minute, and pass on, without any pang of remorse, such as I feel, for quitting them so soon and so willingly. I am partly sensible that some unwritten rules of taste are making their way into my mind; that all this Greek beauty has done something towards refining me, though I am still, however, a very sturdy Goth. . . . .

April 15*th.*—Yesterday I went with J—— to the Forum, and descended into the excavations at the base of the Capitol, and on the site of the basilica of Julia. The essential elements of old Rome are there: columns, single or in groups of two or three, still erect, but battered and bruised at some forgotten time with infinite pains and labour; fragments of other columns lying prostrate, together with rich capitals and friezes; the bust of a colossal female statue, showing the bosom and upper part of the arms, but headless; a long, winding space of pavement, forming part of the ancient ascent to the Capitol, still as firm and solid as ever; the foundation of the Capitol itself, wonderfully massive, built of immense square blocks of stone, doubtless three thousand years old, and durable for whatever may be the lifetime of the world; the arch of Septimius Severus, with bas-reliefs of Eastern wars; the column of Phocas, with the rude series of steps ascending on four sides to its pedestal; the floor of beautiful and precious marbles in the basilica of Julia, the slabs cracked across,—the greater part of them torn up and removed, the grass and weeds growing up through the chinks of what remain; heaps of bricks, shapeless bits of granite, and other ancient rubbish, among which old men are lazily rummaging for specimens that a stranger may be induced to buy, this being an employment that suits the indolence of a modern Roman. The level of these excavations is about fifteen feet, I should judge, below the present street which passes through the Forum, and only a very small part of this alien surface has been removed, though there can be no doubt that it hides numerous treasures of art and monuments of history. Yet these remains do not make that impression of antiquity upon me which Gothic ruins do. Perhaps it is so because they belong to quite another system of society and epoch of time, and in view of them we forgot all that has intervened betwixt them and us, being morally unlike and disconnected with them, and not belonging to the same train of thought; so that we look across a gulf to the Roman ages, and do not realise how wide the gulf is. Yet in that intervening valley lie Christianity, the dark ages, the feudal system, chivalry and romance, and a deeper life of the human race than Rome brought to the verge of the gulf.

To-day we went to the Colonna Palace, where we saw some fine pictures, but, I think, no masterpieces. They did not depress and dishearten me so much as the pictures in Roman palaces usually do; for they were in remarkably good order as regards frames and varnish; indeed, I rather suspect some of them had been injured by the means adopted to preserve their beauty. The palace is now occupied by the French Ambassador, who probably looks upon the pictures as articles of furniture and household adornment, and does not choose to have squares of black and forlorn canvas upon his walls. There were a few noble portraits by Vandyke, a very striking one by Holbein, one or two by Titian, also by Guercino, and some pictures by Rubens, and other *forestieri* painters, which refreshed my weary eyes. But what chiefly interested me was the magnificent and stately hall of the palace, fifty-five of my paces in length, besides a large apartment at either end, opening into it through a pillared space as wide as the gateway of a city. The pillars are of giallo antico, and there are pilasters of the same all the way up and down the walls, forming a perspective of the richest aspect, especially as the broad cornice flames with gilding, and the spaces between the pilasters are emblazoned with heraldic achievements and emblems in gold, and there are Venetian looking-glasses, richly decorated over the surface with beautiful pictures of flowers and Cupids, through which you catch the gleam of the mirror; and two rows of splendid chandeliers extend from end to end of the hall, which, when lighted up, if ever it be lighted up, nowanights, must be the most brilliant interior that ever mortal eye beheld. The ceiling glows with pictures in fresco, representing scenes connected with the history of the Colonna family; and the floor is paved with beautiful marbles, polished and arranged in square and circular compartments; and each of the many windows is set in a great architectural frame of precious marble, as large as the portal of a door. The apartment at the farther end of the hall is elevated above it, and is attained by several marble steps, whence it must have been glorious in former days to have looked down upon a gorgeous throng of princes, cardinals, warriors, and ladies, in such rich attire as might be worn when the palace was built. It is singular how much freshness and brightness it still retains; and the only objects to mar the effect were some ancient statues and busts, not very good in themselves, and now made dreary of aspect by their corroded surfaces,—the result of long burial under ground.

In the room at the entrance of the hall are two cabinets, each a wonder in its way: one being adorned with precious stones; the other with ivory carvings of Michael Angelo's Last Judgment, and of the frescoes of Raphael's Loggie. The world has ceased to be so magnificent as it once was. Men make no such marvels nowadays. The only defect that I remember in this hall, was in the marble steps that ascend to the elevated apartment at the end of it; a large piece had been broken out of one of them, leaving a rough, irregular gap in the polished marble stair. It is not easy to conceive what violence can have done this, without also doing mischief to all the other splendour around it.

April 16*th*.—We went this morning to the Academy of St. Luke (the Fine Arts Academy at Rome), in the Via Bonella, close by the Forum. We rang the bell at the house-door; and after a few moments it was unlocked or unbolted by some unseen agency from above, no one making his appearance to admit us. We ascended two or three flights of stairs, and entered a hall, where was a young man, the custode, and two or three artists engaged in copying some of the pictures. The collection not being vastly large, and the pictures being in more presentable condition than usual, I enjoyed them more than I generally do; particularly a Virgin and Child by Vandyke, where two angels are singing and playing, one on a lute and the other on a violin, to remind the holy infant of the strains he used to hear in heaven. It is one of the few pictures that there is really any pleasure in looking at. There were several paintings by Titian, mostly of a voluptuous character, but not very charming; also two or more by Guido, one of which, representing Fortune, is celebrated. They did not impress me much, nor do I find myself strongly drawn towards Guido, though there is no other painter who seems to achieve things so magically and inscrutably as he sometimes does. Perhaps it requires a finer taste than mine to appreciate him; and yet I do appreciate him so far as to see that his Michael, for instance, is perfectly beautiful. . . . . . In the gallery, there are whole rows of portraits of members of the Academy of St. Luke, most of whom, judging by their physiognomies, were very commonplace people—a fact which makes itself visible in a portrait, however much the painter may try to flatter his sitter. Several of the pictures by Titian, Paul Veronese, and other artists, now exhibited in the gallery, were formerly kept in a secret cabinet in the Capitol, being considered of a too voluptuous character for the public eye. I did not think them noticeably indecorous, as compared with a hundred other pictures that are shown and looked at without scruple,—Calypso and her nymphs, a knot of nude women by Titian, is perhaps as objectionable as any.

But even Titian's flesh tints cannot keep, and have not kept their warmth through all these centuries. The illusion and life-likeness effervesces and exhales out of a picture as it grows old; and we go on talking of a charm that has for ever vanished.

From St. Luke's we went to San Pietro in Vinioli, occupying a fine position on or near the summit of the Esquiline mount. A little abortion of a man (and, by-the-bye, there are more diminutive and ill-shapen men and women in Rome than I ever saw elsewhere—a phenomenon to be accounted for, perhaps, by their custom of wrapping the new-born infant in swaddling clothes)—this two-foot abortion hastened before us, as we drew nigh, to summon the sacristan to open the church door. It was a needless service, for which we rewarded him with two baiocchi. San Pietro is a simple and noble church, consisting of a nave divided from the side aisles by rows of columns, that once adorned some ancient temple; and its wide, unincumbered interior affords better breathing space than most churches in Rome. The statue of Moses occupies a niche in one of the side aisles on the right, not far from the high altar. I found it grand and sublime, with a beard flowing down like a cataract; a truly majestic figure, but not so benign as it were desirable that such strength should be. The horns, about which so much has been said, are not a very prominent feature of the statue, being merely two diminutive tips rising straight up over his forehead, neither adding to the grandeur of the head, nor detracting sensibly from it. The whole force of this statue is not to be felt in one brief visit, but I agree with an English gentleman who, with a large party, entered the church while we were there, in thinking that Moses has "very fine features"—a compliment for which the colossal Hebrew ought to have made the Englishman a bow.

Besides the Moses, the church contains some attractions of a pictorial kind, which are reposited in the sacristy, into which we passed through a side door. The most remarkable of these pictures is a face and bust of Hope, by Guido, with beautiful eyes lifted upwards; it has a grace which artists are continually trying to get into their innumerable copies, but always without success; for, indeed, though nothing is more true than the existence of this charm in the picture, yet if you try to analyse it, or even look too intently at it, it vanishes, till you look again with more trusting simplicity.

Leaving the church, we wandered to the Coliseum, and to the public grounds contiguous to them, where a score and more of French drummers were beating each man his drum, without reference to any rub-a-dub but his own. This seems to be a daily or periodical practice and point of duty with them. After resting ourselves on one of the marble benches, we came slowly home, through the basilica of Constantine, and along the shady sides of the streets and piazzas, sometimes perforce striking boldly through the white sunshine, which, however, was not so hot as to shrivel us up bodily. It has been a most beautiful and perfect day as regards weather—clear and bright, very warm in the sunshine, yet freshened throughout by a quiet stir in the air. Still there is something in this air malevolent, or, at least, not friendly. The Romans lie down and fall asleep in it —in any vacant part of the streets, and wherever they can find any spot sufficiently clean, and among the ruins of temples. I would not sleep in the open air for whatever my life may be worth.

On our way home, sitting in one of the narrow streets, we saw an old woman spinning with a distaff —a far more ancient implement than the spinning-wheel, which the housewives of other nations have long since laid aside.

April 18*th*.—Yesterday, at noon, the whole family of us set out on a visit to the Villa Borghese and its grounds, the entrance to which is just outside of the

Porta del Popolo. After getting within the grounds, however, there is a long walk before reaching the Casino, and we found the sun rather uncomfortably hot, and the road dusty and white in the sunshine; nevertheless, a footpath ran alongside of it most of the way through the grass and among the young trees. It seems to me that the trees do not put forth their leaves with nearly the same magical rapidity in this southern land at the approach of summer as they do in more northerly countries. In these latter, having a much shorter time to develop themselves, they feel the necessity of making the most of it. But the grass, in the lawns and enclosures along which we passed, looked already fit to be mowed, and it was interspersed with many flowers.

Saturday being, I believe, the only day of the week on which visitors are admitted to the Casino, there were many parties in carriages, artists on foot, gentlemen on horseback, and miscellaneous people, to whom the door was opened by a custode on ringing a bell. The whole of the basement-floor of the Casino, comprising a suite of beautiful rooms, is filled with statuary. The entrance-hall is a very splendid apartment, brightly frescoed, and paved with ancient mosaics, representing the combats with beasts and gladiators in the Coliseum,—curious, though very rudely and awkwardly designed, apparently after the arts had begun to decline. Many of the specimens of sculpture displayed in these rooms are fine, but none of them, I think, possess the highest merit. An Apollo is beautiful; a group of a fighting Amazon, and her enemies trampled under her horse's feet, is very impressive; a Faun, copied from that of Praxiteles, and another, who seems to be dancing, were exceedingly pleasant to look at. I like these strange, sweet, playful, rustic creatures, ... linked so prettily, without monstrosity, to the lower tribes. . . . . Their character has never, that I know of, been wrought out in literature; and something quite good, funny, and philosophical, as well as poetic, might very likely be educed from them. . . . . The faun is a natural and delightful link betwixt human and brute life, with something of a divine character intermingled.

The gallery, as it is called, on the basement floor of the Casino, is sixty feet in length, by perhaps a third as much in breadth, and is (after all I have seen at the Colonna Palace and elsewhere) a more magnificent hall than I imagined to be in existence. It is floored with rich marbles, in beautifully-arranged compartments, and the walls are almost entirely cased with marble of various sorts, the prevailing kind being giallo antico, intermixed with verde antique, and I know not what else; but the splendour of the giallo antico gives the character to the room, and the large and deep niches along the walls appear to be lined with the same material. Without coming to Italy, one can have no idea of what beauty and magnificence are produced by these fittings up of polished marble. Marble to an American means nothing but white limestone.

This hall, moreover, is adorned with pillars of oriental alabaster, and wherever is a space vacant of precious and richly-coloured marble it is frescoed with arabesque ornaments; and over the whole is a coved and vaulted ceiling, glowing with picture. There never can be anything richer than the whole effect. As to the sculpture here, it was not very fine, so far as I can remember, consisting chiefly of busts of the emperors in porphyry; but they served a good purpose in the upholstery way. There were also magnificent tables, each composed of one great slab of porphyry; and also vases of nero antico, and other rarest substance. It remains to be mentioned that, on this almost summer-day, I was quite chilled in passing through these glorious halls; no fire-place anywhere; no possibility of comfort; and in the hot season, when their coolness might be agreeable, it would be death to inhabit them.

Ascending a long winding staircase we arrived at another suite of rooms, containing a good many not very remarkable pictures, and a few more pieces of statuary. Among the latter is Canova's statue of Pauline, the sister of Bonaparte, who is represented with but little drapery, and in the character of Venus, holding the apple in her hand. It is admirably done, and, I have no doubt, a perfect likeness; very beautiful too; but it is wonderful to see how the artificial elegance of the woman of this world makes itself perceptible in spite of whatever simplicity she could find in almost utter nakedness. The statue does not afford pleasure in the contemplation.

In one of these upper rooms are some works of Bernini: two of them—Æneas and Anchises, and David on the point of slinging a stone at Goliah—have great merit, and do not tear and rend themselves quite out of the laws and limits of marble, like his later sculpture. Here is also his Apollo overtaking Daphne, whose feet take root, whose fingertips sprout into twigs, and whose tender body roughens round about with bark as he embraces her. It did not seem very wonderful to me; not so good as Hilliard's description of it made me expect; and one does not enjoy these freaks in marble.

We were glad to emerge from the Casino into the warm sunshine; and, for my part, I made the best of my way to a large fountain, surrounded by a circular stone seat, of wide sweep, and sat down in a sunny segment of the circle. Around grew a solemn company of old trees,—ilexes, I believe,—with huge, contorted trunks and evergreen branches, ... deep groves, sunny openings, the airy gush of fountains, marble statues, dimly visible in recesses of foliage, great urns and vases, terminal figures, temples—all these works of art looking as if they had stood there long enough to feel at home, and to be on friendly and familiar terms with the grass and trees. It is a most beautiful place, ... and the Malaria is its true master and inhabitant!

April 22nd.—We have been recently to the studio of Mr. Brown,* the American landscape painter, and were altogether surprised and delighted with his pictures. He is a plain, homely Yankee, quite unpolished by his many years' residence in Italy; he talks ungrammatically, and in Yankee idioms; walks with a strange, awkward gait and stooping shoulders; is altogether unpicturesque; but wins one's confidence by his very lack of grace. It is not often that we see an artist so entirely free from affectation in his

* Now dead.

aspect and deportment. His pictures were views of Swiss and Italian scenery, and were most beautiful and true. One of them, a moonlight picture, was really magical—the moon shining so brightly, that it seemed to throw a light even beyond the limits of the picture; and yet his sunrises and sunsets, and noontides too, were no wise inferior to this, although their excellence required somewhat longer study to be fully appreciated. I seemed to receive more pleasure from Mr. Brown's pictures than from any of the landscapes by the old masters; and the fact serves to strengthen me in the belief that the most delicate, if not the highest, charm of a picture is evanescent; and that we continue to admire pictures prescriptively and by tradition, after the qualities that first won them their fame have vanished. I suppose Claude was a greater landscape painter than Brown, but, for my own pleasure, I would prefer one of the latter artist's pictures; those of the former being quite changed from what he intended them to be, by the effect of time on his pigments. Mr. Brown showed us some drawings from nature, done with incredible care and minuteness of detail, as studies for his paintings. We complimented him on his patience, but he said, "Oh, it's not patience—it's love!" In fact, it was a patient and most successful wooing of a beloved object, which at last rewarded him by yielding itself wholly.

We have likewise been to Mr. B——'s* studio, where we saw several pretty statues and busts, and among them an Eve, with her wreath of fig leaves lying across her poor nudity; comely in some points, but with a frightful volume of thighs and calves. I do not altogether see the necessity of ever sculpturing another nakedness. Man is no longer a naked animal; his clothes are as natural to him as his skin, and sculptors have no more right to undress him than to flay him.

Also, we have seen again William Story's "Cleopatra;" a work of genuine thought and energy, representing a terribly dangerous woman—quiet enough for the moment, but very likely to spring upon you like a tigress. It is delightful to escape to his creations from this universal prettiness, which seems to be the highest conception of the crowd of modern sculptors, and which they almost invariably attain.

Miss Bremer called on us the other day. We find her very little changed from what she was when she came to take tea and spend an evening at our little red cottage among the Berkshire hills, and went away so dissatisfied with my conversational perform-

* Now dead.

ances, and so laudatory of my brow and eyes, while so severely criticising my poor mouth and chin. She is the funniest little old fairy in person whom one can imagine, with a huge nose, to which all the rest of her is but an insufficient appendage; but you feel at once that she is most gentle, kind, womanly, sympathetic, and true. She talks English fluently, in a low quiet voice, but with such an accent that it is impossible to understand her without the closest attention. This was the real cause of the failure of our Berkshire interview; for I could not guess, half the time, what she was saying, and, of course, had to take an uncertain aim with my responses. A more intrepid talker than myself would have shouted his ideas across the gulf; but, for me, there must first be a close and unembarrassed contiguity with my companion, or I cannot say one real word. I doubt whether I have ever really talked with half a dozen persons in my life, either men or women.

To-day my wife and I have been at the picture and sculpture galleries of the Capitol. I rather enjoyed looking at several of the pictures, though at this moment I particularly remember only a very beautiful face of a man, one of two heads on the same canvas, by Vandyke. Yes; I did look with new admiration at Paul Veronese's "Rape of Europa." It must have been, in its day, the most brilliant and rejoicing picture, the most voluptuous, the most exuberant, that ever put the sunshine to shame. The bull has all Jupiter in him, so tender and gentle, yet so passionate, that you feel it indecorous to look at him; and Europa, under her thick, rich stuffs and embroideries, is all a woman. What a pity that such a picture should fade, and perplex the beholder with such splendour, shining through such forlornness.

We afterwards went into the sculpture gallery, where I looked at the Faun of Praxiteles, and was sensible of a peculiar charm in it; a sylvan beauty and homeliness, friendly and wild at once. The lengthened, but not preposterous ears, and the little tail which we infer, have an exquisite effect, and make the spectator smile in his very heart. This race of fauns was the most delightful of all that antiquity imagined. It seems to me that a story, with all sorts of fun and pathos in it, might be contrived on the idea of their species having become intermingled with the human race; a family with the faun blood in them having prolonged itself from the classic era till our own days. The tail might have disappeared by dint of constant intermarriages with ordinary mortals, but the pretty hairy ears should occasionally reappear in members of the family; and the moral instincts and intellectual characteristics of the faun might be most picturesquely brought out, without detriment to the human interest of the story. Fancy this combination in the person of a young lady!

I have spoken of Mr. Gibson's coloured statues. It seems (at least Mr. Nichols tells me) that he stains them with tobacco juice. . . . . Were he to send a Cupid to America, he need not trouble himself to stain it beforehand.

April 25th.—Night before last my wife and I took a moonlight ramble through Rome, it being a very beautiful night, warm enough for comfort, and with no perceptible dew or dampness. We set out at about nine o'clock, and our general direction being towards the Coliseum, we soon came to the Fountain of Trevi, full on the front of which the moonlight fell, making Bernini's sculptures look stately and beautiful; though the semicircular gush and fall of the cascade, and the many jets of the water, pouring and bubbling into the great marble basin, are of far more account than Neptune and his steeds, and the rest of the figures. . . . .

We ascended the Capitoline hill, and I felt a satisfaction in placing my hand on those immense blocks of stone, the remains of the ancient Capitol, which form the foundation of the present edifice, and will make a sure basis for as many edifices as posterity may choose to rear upon it till the end of the world. It is wonderful, the solidity with which those old Romans built; one would suppose they contemplated the whole course of Time as the only limit of their individual life. This is not so strange in the days of the Republic, when, probably, they believed in the permanence of their institutions; but they still seemed to build for eternity in the reigns of the emperors, when neither rulers nor people had any faith or moral substance, or laid any earnest grasp on life.

Reaching the top of the Capitoline hill, we ascended the steps of the portal of the Palace of the Senator, and looked down into the piazza, with the equestrian statue of Marcus Aurelius in the centre of it. The architecture that surrounds the piazza is very ineffective; and so, in my opinion, are all the other architectural works of Michael Angelo, including St. Peter's itself, of which he has made as little as could possibly be made of such a vast pile of material. He balances everything in such a way that it seems but half of itself.

We soon descended into the piazza, and walked round and round the statue of Marcus Aurelius, contemplating it from every point and admiring it in all. .... On these beautiful moonlight nights, Rome appears to keep awake and stirring, though in a quiet and decorous way. It is, in fact, the pleasantest time for promenades, and we both felt less wearied than by any promenade in the day-time, of similar extent, since our residence in Rome. In future, I mean to walk often after nightfall.

Yesterday, we set out betimes, and ascended the dome of St. Peter's. The best view of the interior of the church, I think, is from the first gallery beneath the dome. The whole inside of the dome is set with mosaic-work, the separate pieces being, so far as I could see, about half an inch square. Emerging on the roof, we had a fine view of all the surrounding Rome, including the Mediterranean Sea in the remote distance. Above us still rose the whole mountain of the great dome, and it made an impression on me of greater height and size than I had yet been able to receive. The copper ball at the summit looked hardly bigger than a man could lift; and yet, a little while afterwards, U——, J——, and I stood all together in that ball, which could have contained a dozen more along with us. The esplanade of the roof is, of course, very extensive; and along the front of it are ranged the statues which we see from below, and which, on nearer examination, prove to be roughly-hewn giants. There is a small house on the roof, where, probably, the custodes of this part of the edifice reside; and there is a fountain gushing abundantly into a stone trough, that looked like an old sarcophagus. It is strange where the water comes from at such a height. The children tasted it, and pronounced it very warm and disagreeable. After taking in the prospect on all sides we rang a bell, which summoned a man, who directed us towards a door in the side of the dome, where a custode was waiting to admit us. Hitherto the ascent had been easy, along a slope without stairs, up which, I believe, people sometimes ride on donkeys. The rest of the way we mounted steep and narrow staircases, winding round within the wall, or between the two walls of the dome, and growing narrower and steeper, till, finally, there is but a perpendicular iron ladder, by means of which to climb into the copper ball. Except through small windows and peep-holes, there is no external prospect of a higher point than the roof of the church. Just beneath the ball there is a circular room capable of containing a large company, and a door which ought to give access to a gallery on the outside; but the custode informed us that this door is never opened. As I have said, U——, J——, and I clambered into the copper ball, which we found as hot as an oven; and, after putting our hands on its top, and on the summit of St. Peter's, were glad to clamber down again. I have made some mistake, after all, in my narration. There certainly is a circular balcony at the top of the dome, for I remember walking round it, and looking not only across the country, but downwards along the ribs of the dome; to which are attached the iron contrivances for illuminating it on Easter Sunday. . . . .

Before leaving the church we went to look at the mosaic copy of the Transfiguration, because we were going to see the original in the Vatican, and wished to compare the two. Going round to the entrance of the Vatican, we went first to the manufactory of mosaics, to which we had a ticket of admission. We found it a long series of rooms, in which the mosaic artists were at work, chiefly in making some medallions of the heads of saints for the new church of St. Paul's. It was rather coarse work, and it seemed to me that the mosaic copy was somewhat stiffer and more wooden than the original, the bits of stone not flowing into colour quite so freely as paint from a brush. There was no large picture now in process of being copied; but two or three artists were employed on small and delicate subjects. One had a

Holy Family of Raphael in hand; and the Sibyls of Guercino and Domenichino were hanging on the wall, apparently ready to be put into mosaic. Wherever great skill and delicacy on the artists' part were necessary, they seemed quite adequate to the occasion; but, after all, a mosaic of any celebrated picture is but a copy of a copy. The substance employed is a stone-paste, of innumerable different views, and in bits of various sizes, quantities of which were seen in cases along the whole series of rooms.

We next ascended an amazing height of staircases, and walked along I know not what extent of passages, ... till we reached the picture gallery of the Vatican, into which I had never been before. There are but three rooms, all lined with red velvet, on which hung about fifty pictures, each one of them, no doubt, worthy to be considered a masterpiece. In the first room were three Murillos, all so beautiful that I could have spent the day happily in looking at either of them; for, methinks, of all painters he is the tenderest and truest. I could not enjoy these pictures now, however, because in the next room, and visible through the open door, hung the Transfiguration. Approaching it, I felt that the picture was worthy of its fame, and was far better than I could at once appreciate; admirably preserved, too, though I fully believe it must have possessed a charm when it left Raphael's hand that has now vanished for ever. As church furniture and an external adornment, the mosaic copy is preferable to the original, but no copy could ever reproduce all the life and expression which we see here. Opposite to it hangs the Communion of St. Jerome—the aged, dying saint, half torpid with death already, partaking of the sacrament, and a sunny garland of cherubs in the upper part of the picture, looking down upon him, and quite comforting the spectator with the idea that the old man needs only to be quite dead in order to flit away with them. As for the other pictures, I did but glance at, and have forgotten them.

The Transfiguration is finished with great minuteness and detail, the weeds and blades of grass in the foreground being as distinct as if they were growing in a natural soil. A partly-decayed stick of wood, with the bark, is likewise given in close imitation of nature. The reflection of a foot of one of the Apostles is seen in a pool of water at the verge of the picture. One or two heads and arms seem almost to project from the canvas. There is great lifelikeness and reality, as well as higher qualities. The face of Jesus, being so high aloft and so small in the distance, I could not well see; but I am impressed with the idea that it looks too much like human flesh and blood to be in keeping with the celestial aspect of the figure, or with the probabilities of the scene, when the divinity and immortality of the Saviour beamed from within him through the earthly features that ordinarily shaded him. As regards the composition of the picture, I am not convinced of the propriety of its being in two so distinctly separate parts — the upper portion not thinking of the lower, and the lower portion not being aware of the higher. It symbolises, however, the spiritual shortsightedness of mankind that, amid the trouble and grief of the lower picture, not a single individual, either of those who seek help or those who would willingly afford it, lifts his eyes to that region, one glimpse of which would set everything right. One or two of the disciples point upward, but without really knowing what abundance of help is to be had there.

April 27th.—To-day we have all been with Mr. Akers to some studios of painters; first to that of Mr. Wilde, an artist originally from Boston. His pictures are principally of scenes from Venice, and are miracles of colour, being as bright as if the light were transmitted through rubies and sapphires. And yet, after contemplating them awhile, we became convinced that the painter had not gone in the least beyond nature, but, on the contrary, had fallen short of brilliancies which no palette, or skill, or boldness in using colour, could attain. I do not quite know whether it is best to attempt these things. They may be found in nature, no doubt, but always so tempered by what surrounds them—so put out of sight even while they seem full before our eyes— that we question the accuracy of a faithful reproduction of them on canvas. There was a picture of sunset, the whole sky of which would have outshone any gilded frame that could have been put around it. There was a most gorgeous sketch of a handful of weeds and leaves, such as may be seen strewing acres of forest-ground in an American autumn. I doubt whether any other man has ever ventured to paint a picture like either of these two —the Italian sunset or the American autumnal foliage. Mr. Wilde, who is still young, talked with genuine feeling and enthusiasm of his art, and is certainly a man of genius.

We next went to the studio of an elderly Swiss artist, named Müller, I believe, where we looked at a great many water-colour and crayon drawings of scenes in Italy, Greece, and Switzerland. The artist was a quiet, respectable, somewhat heavy-looking old gentleman, from whose aspect one would expect a plodding pertinacity of character rather than quickness of sensibility. He must have united both these qualities, however, to produce such pictures as these—such faithful transcripts of whatever Nature has most beautiful to show, and which she shows only to those who love her deeply and patiently. They are wonderful pictures—compressing plains, seas, and mountains, with miles and miles of distance, into the space of a foot or two without crowding anything or leaving out a feature, and diffusing the free, blue atmosphere throughout. The works of the English water-colour artists which I saw at the Manchester Exhibition seemed to me nowise equal to these. Now, here are three artists—Mr. Browne, Mr. Wilde, and Mr. Müller—who have smitten me with vast admiration within these few days past, while I am continually turning away disappointed from the landscapes of the most famous among the old masters, unable to find any charm or illusion in them. Yet I suppose Claude, Poussin, and Salvator Rosa must have won their renown by real achievements. But the glory of a picture fades like that of a flower.

Contiguous to Mr. Müller's studio was that of a

young German artist, not long resident in Rome, and Mr. Akers proposed that we should go in there, as a matter of kindness to the young man, who is scarcely known at all, and seldom has a visitor to look at his pictures. His studio comprised his whole establishment; for there was his little bed, with its white drapery, in a corner of the small room, and his dressing-table, with its brushes and combs, while the easel and the few sketches of Italian scenes and figures occupied the foreground. I did not like his pictures very well, but would gladly have bought them all if I could have afforded it—the artist looked so cheerful, patient, and quiet, doubtless amidst huge discouragement. He is probably stubborn of purpose, and is the sort of man who will improve with every year of his life. We could not speak his language, and were therefore spared the difficulty of paying him any compliments; but Miss Shepard said a few kind words to him in German, and seemed quite to win his heart, insomuch that he followed her with bows and smiles a long way down the staircase. It is a terrible business, this looking at pictures, whether good or bad, in the presence of the artists who paint them; it is as great a bore as to hear a poet read his own verses. It takes away all my pleasure in seeing the pictures, and even makes me question the genuineness of the impressions which I receive from them.

After this latter visit Mr. Akers conducted us to the shop of the jeweller Castellani, who is a great reproducer of ornaments in the old Roman and Etruscan fashion. These antique styles are very fashionable just now, and some of the specimens he showed us were certainly very beautiful, though I doubt whether their quaintness and old-time curiousness, as patterns of gewgaws dug out of immemorial tombs, be not their greatest charm. We saw the toilette-case of an Etruscan lady—that is to say, a modern imitation of it—with her rings for summer and winter, and for every day of the week, and for thumb and fingers; her ivory comb; her bracelets; and more knickknacks than I can half remember. Splendid things of our own time were likewise shown us; a necklace of diamonds worth eighteen thousand scudi, together with emeralds and opals and great pearls. Finally we came away, and my wife and Miss Shepard were taken up by the Misses Weston, who drove with them to visit the Villa Albani. During their drive my wife happened to raise her arm, and Miss Shepard espied a little Greek cross of gold which had attached itself to the lace of her sleeve. . . . Pray heaven the jeweller may not discover his loss before we have time to restore the spoil! He is apparently so free and careless in displaying his precious wares—putting inestimable gems and brooches great and small into the hands of strangers like ourselves, and leaving scores of them strewn on the top of his counter—that it would seem easy enough to take a diamond or two; but I suspect there must needs be a sharp eye somewhere. Before we left the shop he requested me to honour him with my autograph in a large book that was full of the names of his visitors. This is probably a measure of precaution.

April 30*th*.—I went yesterday to the sculpture gallery of the Capitol, and looked pretty thoroughly through the busts of the illustrious men, and less particularly at those of the emperors and their relatives. I likewise took particular note of the Faun of Praxiteles, because the idea keeps recurring to me of writing a little romance about it, and for that reason I shall endeavour to set down a somewhat minutely itemized detail of the statue and its surroundings. . . . . .

We have had beautiful weather for two or three days, very warm in the sun, yet always freshened by the gentle life of a breeze, and quite cool enough the moment you pass within the limit of the shade. . .

In the morning, there are few people there (on the Pincian) except the gardeners, lazily trimming the borders, or filling their watering-pots out of the marble-brimmed basin of the fountain; French soldiers, in their long mixed blue surtouts, and wide scarlet pantaloons, chatting with here and there a nursery-maid and playing with the child in her care; and perhaps a few smokers, . . . choosing each a marble seat or wooden bench in sunshine or shade as best suits him. In the afternoon, especially within an hour or two of sunset, the gardens are much more populous, and the seats, except when the sun falls full upon them, are hard to come by. Ladies arrive in carriages, splendidly dressed; children are abundant, much impeded in their frolics, and rendered stiff and stately by the finery which they wear; English gentlemen, and Americans with their wives and families; the flower of the Roman population, too, both male and female, mostly dressed with great nicety; but a large intermixture of artists, shabbily picturesque; and other persons, not of the first stamp. A French band, comprising a great many brass instruments, by-and-by begins to play; and what with music, sunshine, a delightful atmosphere, flowers, grass, well-kept pathways, bordered with box-hedges, pines, cypresses, horse-chestnuts, flowering-shrubs, and all manner of cultivated beauty, the scene is a very lively and agreeable one. The fine equipages that drive round and round through the carriage-paths are another noticeable item. The Roman aristocracy are magnificent in their aspect, driving abroad with beautiful horses, and footmen in rich liveries, sometimes as many as three behind and one sitting by the coachman.

May 1st.—This morning, I wandered for the thousandth time through some of the narrow intricacies of Rome, stepping here and there into a church. I do not know the name of the first one, nor had it anything that in Rome could be called remarkable, though, till I came here, I was not aware that any such churches existed—a marble pavement in variegated compartments, a series of shrines and chapels round the whole floor, each with its own adornment of sculpture and pictures, its own altar with tall wax tapers before it, some of which were burning; a great picture over the high altar, the whole interior of the church ranged round with pillars and pilasters, and lined, every inch of it, with rich yellow marble. Finally, a frescoed ceiling over the nave and transepts, and a dome rising high above the central part, and filled with frescoes brought to such perspective illusion, that the edges seem to project into the air.

Two or three persons are kneeling at separate shrines; there are several wooden confessionals placed against the walls, at one of which kneels a lady, confessing to a priest who sits within; the tapers are lighted at the high altar and at one of the shrines; an attendant is scrubbing the marble pavement with a broom and water—a process, I should think, seldom practised in Roman churches. By-and-by the lady finishes her confession, kisses the priest's hand, and sits down in one of the chairs which are placed about the floor, while the priest, in a black robe, with a short white loose jacket over his shoulders, disappears by a side door out of the church. I, likewise, finding nothing attractive in the pictures, take my departure. Protestantism needs a new apostle to convert it into something positive...

I now found my way to the Piazza Navona. It is to me the most interesting piazza in Rome; a large oblong space, surrounded with tall shabby houses, among which there are none that seem to be palaces. The sun falls broadly over the area of the piazza, and shows the fountains in it;—one, a large basin with great sea-monsters, probably of Bernini's inventions, squirting very small streams of water into it; another of the fountains I do not at all remember; but the central one is an immense basin, over which is reared an old Egyptian obelisk, elevated on a rock, which is cleft into four arches. Monstrous devices in marble, I know not of what purport, are clambering about the cloven rock or burrowing beneath it; one and all of them are superfluous and impertinent, the only essential thing being the abundant supply of water in the fountain. This whole Piazza Navona is usually the scene of more business than seems to be transacted anywhere else in Rome; in some parts of it rusty iron is offered for sale, locks and keys, old tools, and all such rubbish; in other parts vegetables, comprising, at this season, green peas, onions, cauliflowers, radishes, artichokes, and others with which I have never made acquaintance; also, stalls or wheelbarrows containing apples, chestnuts (the meats dried and taken out of the shells), green almonds in their husks, and squash seeds—salted and dried in an oven —apparently a favourite delicacy of the Romans. There are also lemons and oranges; stalls of fish, mostly about the size of smelts, taken from the Tiber; cigars of various qualities, the best at a baioccho and a half a-piece; bread in loaves or in small rings, a great many of which are strung together on a long stick, and thus carried round for sale. Women and men sit with these things for sale, or carry them about in trays or on boards on their heads, crying them with shrill and hard voices. There is a shabby crowd and much babble; very little picturesqueness of costume or figure, however, the chief exceptions being, here and there, an old white-bearded beggar. A few of the men have the peasant costume—a short jacket and breeches of light-blue cloth and white stockings —the ugliest dress I ever saw. The women go bareheaded, and seem fond of scarlet and other bright colours, but are homely and clumsy in form. The piazza is dingy in its general aspect, and very dirty, being strewn with straw, vegetable-tops, and the rubbish of a week's marketing; but there is more life in it than one sees elsewhere in Rome.

On one side of the piazza is the church of St. Agnes, traditionally said to stand on the site of the house where that holy maiden was exposed to infamy by the Roman soldiers, and where her modesty and innocence were saved by miracle. I went into the church, and found it very splendid, with rich marble columns, all as brilliant as if just built; a frescoed dome above; beneath, a range of chapels all round the church, ornamented not with pictures but basreliefs, the figures of which almost step and struggle out of the marble. They did not seem very admirable as works of art, none of them explaining themselves or attracting me long enough to study out their meaning; but, as part of the architecture of the church, they had a good effect. Out of the busy square two or three persons had stepped into this bright and calm seclusion to pray and be devout for a little while; and, between sunrise and sunset of the bustling market day, many doubtless snatch a moment to refresh their souls.

In the Pantheon [to-day] it was pleasant, looking up to the circular opening, to see the clouds flitting across it, sometimes covering it quite over, then permitting a glimpse of sky, then showing all the circle of sunny blue. Then would come the ragged edge of a cloud, brightened throughout with sunshine, passing and changing quickly—not that the divine smile was not always the same, but continually variable through the medium of earthly influences. The great slanting beam of sunshine was visible all the way down to the pavement, falling upon motes of dust, or a thin smoke of incense imperceptible in the shadow. Insects were playing to and fro in the beam, high up toward the opening. There is a wonderful charm in the naturalness of all this, and one might fancy a swarm of cherubs coming down through the opening and sporting in the broad ray, to gladden the faith of worshippers on the pavement beneath; or angels bearing prayers upward, or bringing down responses to them, visible with dim brightness as they pass through the pathway of heaven's radiance, even the many hues of their wings discernible by a trusting eye; though, as they pass into the shadow they vanish like the motes. So the sunbeam would represent those rays of divine intelligence which enable us to see wonders, and to know that they are natural things.

Consider the effect of light and shade in a church when the windows are open and darkened with curtains that are occasionally lifted by a breeze, letting in the sunshine, which whitens a carved tombstone on the pavement of the church, disclosing, perhaps, the letters of the name and inscription, a death's head, a crosier, or other emblem; then the curtain falls and the bright spot vanishes.

May 8th.—This morning my wife and I went to breakfast with Mrs. William Story at the Barberini Palace, expecting to meet Mrs. Jameson, who has been in Rome for a month or two. We had a very pleasant breakfast, but Mrs. Jameson was not present on account of indisposition, and the only other guests were Mrs. A—— and Miss H——, two sensible American ladies. Mrs. Story, however, received a note from Mrs. Jameson, asking her to bring us to see her at her lodgings; so in the course of the afternoon she called for us, and took us thither in her carriage. Mrs. Jameson lives on the first piano of an old Piazzo on the Via di Ripetta, nearly opposite the ferryway across the Tiber, and affording a pleasant view of the yellow river and the green bank and fields on the other side. I had expected to see an elderly lady, but not quite so venerable a one as Mrs. Jameson proved to be; a rather short, round, and massive personage, of benign and agreeable aspect, with a sort of black skull-cap on her head, beneath which appeared her hair, which seemed once to have been fair, and was now almost white. I should take her to be about seventy years old. She began to talk to us with affectionate familiarity, and was particularly kind in her manifestations towards myself, who, on my part, was equally gracious towards her. In truth, I have found great pleasure and profit in her works, and was glad to hear her say that she liked mine. We talked about art, and she showed us a picture leaning up against the wall of the room; a quaint old Byzantine painting, with a gilded background, and two stiff figures (our Saviour and St. Catherine) standing shyly at a sacred distance from one another, and going through the marriage ceremony. There was a great deal of expression in their faces and figures; and the spectator feels, moreover, that the artist must have been a devout man, an impression which we seldom receive from modern pictures, however awfully holy the subject, or however consecrated the place they hang in. Mrs. Jameson seems to be familiar with Italy, its people and life, as well as with its picture galleries. She is said to be rather irascible in her temper; but nothing could be sweeter than her voice, her look, and all her manifestations to-day. When we were coming away she clasped my hand in both of hers, and again expressed the pleasure of having seen me, and her gratitude to me for calling on her; nor did I refrain from responding Amen to these effusions. . . . .

Taking leave of Mrs. Jameson, we drove through the city, and out of the Lateran gate; first, however, waiting a long while at Monaldini's book-store in the Piazza di Spagna for Mr. Story, whom we finally took up in the street after losing nearly an hour.

Just two miles beyond the gate is a space on the green Campagna where, for some time past, excavations have been in progress, which thus far have resulted in the discovery of several tombs, and the old, buried, and almost forgotten church or basilica of San Stefano. It is a beautiful spot—that of the excavations—with the Alban hills in the distance, and some heavy, sun-lighted clouds hanging above, or recumbent at length upon them, and behind the city and its mighty dome. The excavations are an object of great interest both to the Romans and to strangers, and there were many carriages, and a great many visitors viewing the progress of the works, which are carried forward with greater energy than anything else I have seen attempted at Rome. A short time ago the ground in the vicinity was a green surface, level, except here and there a little hillock, or scarcely perceptible swell; the tomb of Cecilia Metella showing itself a mile or two distant, and other rugged ruins of great tombs rising on the plain. Now the whole site of the basilica is uncovered, and they have dug into the depths of several tombs, bringing to light precious marbles, pillars, a statue, and elaborately wrought sarcophagi; and if they were to dig into almost every other inequality that frets the surface of the Campagna, I suppose the result might be the same. You cannot dig six feet downward anywhere into the soil—deep enough to hollow out a grave—without finding some precious relic of the past; only they lose somewhat of their value when you think that you can almost spurn them out of the ground with your foot. It is a very wonderful arrangement of Providence that these things should have been preserved for a long series of coming generations by that accumulation of dust and soil and grass and trees and houses over them, which will keep them safe, and cause their reappearance above ground to be gradual, so that the rest of the world's lifetime may have for one of its enjoyments the uncovering of old Rome.

The tombs were accessible by long flights of steps, going steeply downward, and they were thronged with so many visitors that we had to wait some little time for our own turn. In the first into which we descended we found two tombs side by side, with only a partition wall between; the outer tomb being, as is supposed, a burial-place constructed by the early Christians, while the adjoined and minor one was a work of pagan Rome about the second century after Christ. The former was much less interesting than the latter. It contained some large sarcophagi, with sculpture upon them of rather heathenish aspect; and in the centre of the front of each sarcophagus was a bust in bas-relief, the features of which had never been wrought, but were left almost blank, with only the faintest indications of a nose, for instance. It is supposed that sarcophagi were kept in hand by the sculptors, and were bought ready made, and that it was customary to work out the portrait of the deceased upon the blank face in the centre; but when there was a necessity for sudden burial, as may have been the case in the present instance, this was dispensed with.

The inner tomb was found without any earth in it, just as it had been left when the last old Roman was buried there; and it being only a week or two since it was opened, there was very little intervention of persons—though much of time—between the departure of the friends of the dead and our own visit. It is a square room, with a mosaic pavement, and is six or seven paces in length and breadth, and as much in height to the vaulted roof. The roof and upper walls are beautifully ornamented with frescoes, which were very bright when first discovered, but have rapidly faded since the admission of the air, though the graceful and joyous designs, flowers and fruits and trees, are still perfectly discernible. The room must have been anything but sad and funereal; on the contrary, as cheerful a saloon, and as brilliant, if lighted up, as one could desire to feast in. It contained several marble sarcophagi, covering indeed almost the whole floor, and each of them as much as three or four feet in length, and two much longer. The longer ones I did not particularly examine, and they seemed comparatively plain; but the smaller sarcophagi were covered with the most delicately

wrought and beautiful bas-reliefs that I ever beheld—
a throng of glad and lovely shapes in marble, clustering thickly and chasing one another round the sides of these old stone coffins. The work was as perfect as when the sculptor gave it his last touch; and if he had wrought it to be placed in a frequented hall, to be seen and admired by continual crowds as long as the marble should endure, he could not have chiselled with better skill and care, though his work was to be shut up in the depths of a tomb for ever. This seems to me the strangest thing in the world, the most alien from modern sympathies. If they had built their tombs above-ground, one could understand the arrangement better; but no sooner had they adorned them so richly, and furnished them with such exquisite productions of art, than they annihilated them with darkness. It was an attempt, no doubt, to render the physical aspect of death cheerful, but there was no good sense in it.

We went down also into another tomb close by, the walls of which were ornamented with medallions in stucco. These works presented a numerous series of graceful designs, wrought with the hand in the short space [Mr. Story said it could not have been more than five or ten minutes] while the wet plaster remained capable of being moulded; and it was marvellous to think of the fertility of the artist's fancy, and the rapidity and accuracy with which he must have given substantial existence to his ideas. These too—all of them such adornments as would have suited a festal hall—were made to be buried forthwith in eternal darkness. I saw and handled in this tomb a great thigh-bone, and measured it with my own; it was one of many such relics of the guests who were laid to sleep in these rich chambers. The sarcophagi that served them for coffins could not now be put to a more appropriate use than as wine-coolers in a modern dining-room; and it would heighten the enjoyment of a festival to look at them.

We would gladly have stayed much longer; but it was drawing towards sunset, and the evening, though bright, was unusually cool, so we drove home; and on the way, Mr. Story told us of the horrible practices of the modern Romans with their dead—how they place them in the church, where, at midnight, they are stripped of their last rag of funeral attire, put into the rudest wooden coffins, and thrown into a trench—a half a mile, for instance, of promiscuous corpses. This is the fate of all, except those whose friends choose to pay an exorbitant sum to have them buried under the pavement of a church. The Italians have an excessive dread of corpses, and never meddle with those of their nearest and dearest relatives. They have a horror of death, too, especially of sudden death, and most particularly of apoplexy; and no wonder, as it gives no time for the last rites of the Church, and so exposes them to a fearful risk of perdition for ever. On the whole, the ancient practice was, perhaps, the preferable one; but Nature has made it very difficult for us to do anything pleasant and satisfactory with a dead body. God knows best; but I wish He had so ordered it that our mortal bodies, when we have done with them, might vanish out of sight and sense, like bubbles. A person of delicacy hates to think of leaving such a burthen as his decaying mortality to the disposal of his friends; but, I say again, how delightful it would be, and how helpful towards our faith in a blessed futurity, if the dying could disappear like vanishing bubbles, leaving, perhaps, a sweet fragrance diffused for a minute or two throughout the death-chamber. This would be the odour of sanctity! And if sometimes the evaporation of a sinful soul should leave an odour not so delightful, a breeze through the open windows would soon waft it quite away.

Apropos of the various methods of disposing of dead bodies, William Story recalled a newspaper paragraph respecting a ring, with a stone of a new species in it, which a widower was observed to wear upon his finger. Being questioned as to what the gem was, he answered, "It is my wife." He had procured her body to be chemically resolved into this stone. I think I could make a story on this idea: the ring should be one of the widower's bridal gifts to a second wife; and, of course, it should have wondrous and terrible qualities, symbolising all that disturbs the quiet of a second marriage—on the husband's part, remorse for his inconstancy, and the constant comparison between the dead wife of his youth, now idealised, and the grosser reality which he had now adopted into her place; while on the new wife's finger it should give pressures, shooting pangs into her heart, jealousies of the past, and all such miserable emotions.

By-the-bye, the tombs which we looked at and entered, may have been originally above-ground, like that of Cecilia Metella, and a hundred others along the Appian Way; though, even in this case, the beautiful chambers must have been shut up in darkness. Had there been windows, letting in the light upon the rich frescoes and exquisite sculptures, there would have been a satisfaction in thinking of the existence of so much visual beauty, though no eye had the privilege to see it. But darkness, to objects of sight, is annihilation, as long as the darkness lasts.

May 9th.—Mrs. Jameson called this forenoon to ask us to go and see her this evening ; .... so that I had to receive her alone, devolving part of the burthen on Miss Shepard and the three children, all of whom I introduced to her notice. Finding that I had not been farther beyond the walls of Rome than the tomb of Cecilia Metella, she invited me to take a drive of a few miles with her this afternoon. . . . . . The poor lady seems to be very lame ; and I am sure I was grateful to her for having taken the trouble to climb up the seventy steps of our staircase, and felt pain at seeing her go down them again. It looks fearfully like the gout, the affection being apparently in one foot. Her hands, by the way, are white, and must once have been—perhaps now are—beautiful. She must have been a perfectly pretty woman in her day —a blue or grey-eyed, fair-haired beauty. I think that her hair is not white, but only flaxen in the extreme.

At half-past four, according to appointment, I arrived at her lodgings, and had not long to wait before her little one-horse carriage drove up to the door, and we set out, rumbling along the Via Scrofa, and through the densest part of the city, past the theatre of Marcellus, and thence along beneath the Palatine Hill, and by the Baths of Caracalla, through the gate of San Sebastiano. After emerging from the gate, we soon came to the little church of "Dominè, quo vadis?" Standing on the spot where St. Peter is said to have seen a vision of our Saviour bearing his cross, Mrs. Jameson proposed to alight; and going in, we saw a cast from Michel Angelo's statue of the Saviour; and not far from the threshold of the church, yet perhaps in the centre of the edifice, which is extremely small, a circular stone is placed, a little raised above the pavement, and surrounded by a low wooden railing. Pointing to this stone, Mrs. Jameson showed me the prints of two feet side by side, impressed into its surface, as if a person had stopped short while pursuing his way to Rome. These, she informed me, were supposed to be the miraculous prints of the Saviour's feet; but on looking into Murray, I am mortified to find that they are merely facsimiles of the original impressions, which are treasured up among the relics of the neighbouring basilica of St. Sebastiano. The marks of sculpture seemed to me, indeed, very evident in these prints, nor did they indicate such beautiful feet as should have belonged to the bearer of the best of glad tidings.

Hence we drove on a little way farther, and came to the basilica of San Sebastiano, where also we alighted, and, leaning on my arm, Mrs. Jameson went in. It is a stately and noble interior, with a spacious unincumbered nave, and a flat ceiling frescoed and gilded. In a chapel at the left of the entrance is the tomb of St. Sebastian—a sarcophagus containing his remains, raised on high before the altar, and beneath it a recumbent statue of the saint pierced with gilded arrows. The sculpture is of the school of Bernini— done after the design of Bernini himself, Mrs. Jameson said, and is more agreeable, and in better taste than most of his works. We walked round the basilica, glancing at the pictures in the various chapels, none of which seemed to be of remarkable merit, although Mrs. Jameson pronounced rather a favourable verdict on one of St. Francis. She says that she can read a picture like the page of a book; in fact, without perhaps assuming more taste and judgment than really belong to her, it was impossible not to perceive that she gave her companion no credit for knowing one single simplest thing about art. Nor, on the whole, do I think she underrated me; the only mystery is, how she came to be so well aware of my ignorance on artistical points.

In the basilica the Franciscan monks were arranging benches on the floor of the nave, and some peasant children and grown people besides were assembling, probably to undergo an examination in the catechism, and we hastened to depart, lest our presence should interfere with their arrangements. At the door a monk met us, and asked for a contribution in aid of his church, or some other religious purpose. Boys, as we drove on, ran stoutly along by the side of the chaise, begging as often as they could find breath, but were constrained finally to give up the pursuit. The great ragged bulks of the tombs along the Appian Way now hove in sight, one with a farmhouse on its summit, and all of them preposterously huge and massive. At a distance, across the green Campagna on our left, the Claudian aqueduct strode away over miles of space, and doubtless reached even to that circumference of blue hills which stand afar off, girdling Rome about. The tomb of Cecilia Metella came in sight a long while before we reached it, with the warm buff hue of its travertine, and the grey battlemented wall which the Gaetanis erected on the top of its circular summit six hundred years ago. After passing it, we saw an interminable line of tombs on both sides of the way, each of which might, for aught I know, have been as massive as that of Cecilia Metella, and some perhaps still more monstrously gigantic, though now dilapidated and much reduced in size. Mrs. Jameson had an engagement to dinner at half-past six, so that we could go but a little farther along this most interesting road, the borders of which are strewn with broken marbles, fragments of capitals, and nameless rubbish that once was beautiful. Methinks the Appian Way should be the only entrance to Rome—through an avenue of tombs.

The day had been cloudy, chill, and windy, but was now grown calmer and more genial, and brightened by a very pleasant sunshine, though great dark clouds were still lumbering up the sky. We drove homeward, looking at the distant dome of St. Peter's, and talking of many things—painting, sculpture, America, England, spiritualism, and whatever else came up. She is a very sensible old lady, and sees a great deal of truth; a good woman, too, taking elevated views of matters; but I doubt whether she has the highest and finest perceptions in the world. At any rate, she pronounced a good judgment on the American sculptors now in Rome, condemning them in the mass as men with no high aims, no worthy conception of the purposes of their art, and desecrating marble by the things they wrought in it. William Story, I presume, is not to be included in this censure, as she had spoken highly of his sculpturesque faculty in our previous conversation. On my part, I suggested that the English sculptors were little or nothing better than our own, to which she acceded generally, but said that Gibson had produced works equal to the antique—which I did not dispute, but still questioned whether the world needed Gibson, or was any the better for him. We had a great dispute about the propriety of adopting the costume of the day in modern sculpture, and I contended that either the art ought to be given up (which possibly would be the best course), or else should be used for idealising the man of the day to himself; and that, as Nature makes us sensible of the fact when men and women are graceful, beautiful, and noble, through whatever costume they wear, so it ought to be the test of the sculptor's genius that he should do the same. Mrs. Jameson decidedly objected to buttons, breeches, and all other items of modern costume; and, indeed, they do degrade the marble, and make high sculpture utterly impossible. Then let the art perish as one that the world has done with, as it has done with many other beautiful things that belonged to an earlier time.

It was long past the hour of Mrs. Jameson's dinner engagement when we drove up to her door in the Via

Ripetta. I bade her farewell with much good feeling on my own side, and, I hope, on hers, excusing myself, however, from keeping the previous engagement to spend the evening with her, for, in point of fact, we had mutually had enough of one another for the time being. I am glad to record that she expressed a very favourable opinion of our friend Mr. Thompson's pictures.

May 12th.—To-day we have been to the Villa Albani, to which we had a ticket of admission through the agency of Mr. Cass (the American Minister). We set out between ten and eleven o'clock, and walked through the Via Felice, the Piazza Barberini, and a long, heavy, dusty range of streets beyond, to the Porta Salara, whence the road extends, white and sunny, between two high blank walls to the gate of the villa, which is at no great distance. We were admitted by a girl, and went first to the Casino, along an aisle of overshadowing trees, the branches of which met above our heads. In the portico of the Casino, which extends along its whole front, there are many busts and statues, and, among them, one of Julius Cæsar, representing him at an earlier period of life than others which I have seen. His aspect is not particularly impressive; there is a lack of chin, though not so much as in the older statues and busts. Within the edifice there is a large hall, not so brilliant, perhaps, with frescoes and gilding as those at the Villa Borghese, but lined with the most beautiful variety of marbles. But, in fact, each new splendour of this sort outshines the last, and unless we could pass from one to another all in the same suite, we cannot remember them well enough to compare the Borghese with the Albani, the effect being more on the fancy than on the intellect. I do not recall any of the sculpture, except a colossal bas-relief of Antinous, crowned with flowers, and holding flowers in his hand, which was found in the ruins of Hadrian's Villa. This is said to be the finest relic of antiquity next to the Apollo and the Laocoon; but I could not feel it to be so—partly, I suppose, because the features of Antinous do not seem to me beautiful in themselves; and that heavy downward look is repeated till I am more weary of it than of anything else in sculpture. We went up-stairs and down-stairs, and saw a good many beautiful things, but none, perhaps, of the very best and beautifullest; and second-rate statues, with the corroded surface of old marble that has been dozens of centuries under the ground, depress the spirits of the beholder. The bas-relief of Antinous has at least the merit of being almost as white and fresh, and quite as smooth, as if it had never been buried and dug up again. The real treasures of this villa, to the number of nearly three hundred, were removed to Paris by Napoleon, and, except the Antinous, not one of them ever came back.

There are some pictures in one or two of the rooms, and among them I recollect one by Perugino, in which is a St. Michael, very devout and very beautiful; indeed, the whole picture (which is in compartments, representing the three principal points of the Saviour's history) impresses the beholder as being painted devoutly and earnestly by a religious man. In one of the rooms there is a small bronze Apollo, supposed by Winkelmann to be an original of Praxiteles; but I could not make myself in the least sensible of its merit.

The rest of the things in the Casino I shall pass over, as also those in the coffee-house—an edifice which stands a hundred yards or more from the Casino, with an ornamental garden, laid out in walks and flower-plats between. The coffee-house has a semicircular sweep of porch with a good many statues and busts beneath it, chiefly of distinguished Romans. In this building, as in the Casino, there are curious mosaics, large vases of rare marble, and many other things worth long pauses of admiration; but I think that we were all happier when we had done with the works of art, and were at leisure to ramble about the grounds. The Villa Albani itself is an edifice separate from both the coffee-house and Casino, and is not opened to strangers. It rises, palace-like, in the midst of the garden, and, it is to be hoped, has some possibility of comfort amidst its splendours. Comfort, however, would be thrown away upon it; for besides that the site shares the curse that has fallen upon every pleasant place in the vicinity of Rome, . . . it really has no occupant except the servants who take care of it. The Count of Castelbarco, its present proprietor, resides at Milan. The grounds are laid out in the old fashion of straight paths, with borders of box, which form hedges of great height and density, and as even as a brick-wall at the top and sides. There are also alleys forming long vistas between the trunks and beneath the boughs of oaks, ilexes, and olives; and there are shrubberies and tangled wildernesses of palm, cactus, rhododendron, and I know not what; and a profusion of roses that bloom and wither with nobody to pluck and few to look at them. They climb about the sculpture of fountains, rear themselves against pillars and porticos, run brimming over the walls, and strew the paths with their falling leaves. We stole a few, and feel that we have wronged our consciences in not stealing more. In one part of the grounds we saw a field actually ablaze with scarlet poppies. There are great lagunas; fountains presided over by naiads, who squirt their little jets into basins; sunny lawns; a temple, so artificially ruined that we half believed it a veritable antique; and at its base a reservoir of water, in which stone swans seemed positively to float; groves of cypress; balustrades and broad flights of stone stairs, descending to lower levels of the garden; beauty, peace, sunshine, and antique repose on every side; and far in the distance the blue hills that encircle the Campagna of Rome. The day was very fine for our purpose—cheerful, but not too bright, and tempered by a breeze that seemed even a little too cool when we sat long in the shade. We enjoyed it till three o'clock. . . . .

At the Capitol there is a sarcophagus with a most beautiful bas-relief of the discovery of Achilles by Ulysses, in which there is even an expression of mirth on the faces of many of the spectators. And to-day at the Albani a sarcophagus was ornamented with the nuptials of Peleus and Thetis.

Death strides behind every man, to be sure, at more or less distance, and, sooner or later, enters upon any event of his life; so that, in this point of view, they might each and all serve for bas-reliefs on a sarcophagus; but the Romans seem to have treated Death as lightly and playfully as they could, and tried to cover his dart with flowers, because they hated it so much.

May 15*th.*—My wife and I went yesterday to the Sistine Chapel, it being my first visit. It is a room of noble proportions, lofty and long, though divided in the midst by a screen or partition of white marble, which rises high enough to break the effect of spacious unity. There are six arched windows on each side of the chapel, throwing down their light from the height of the walls, with as much as twenty feet of space (more I should think) between them and the floor. The entire walls and ceiling of this stately chapel are covered with paintings in fresco, except the space about ten feet in height from the floor, and that portion was intended to be adorned by tapestries from pictures by Raphael, but the design being prevented by his immature death, the projected tapestries have no better substitute than paper hangings. The roof, which is flat at top, and coved or vaulted at the sides, is painted in compartments by Michel Angelo, with frescoes representing the whole progress of the world and of mankind from its first formation by the Almighty . . . .

till after the flood. On one of the sides of the chapel are pictures by Perugino, and other old masters, of subsequent events in sacred history; and the entire wall behind the altar, a vast expanse from the ceiling to the floor, is taken up with Michel Angelo's summing up of the world's history and destinies in his "Last Judgment."

There can be no doubt that while these frescoes continued in their perfection, there was nothing else to be compared with the magnificent and solemn beauty of this chapel. Enough of ruined splendour still remains to convince the spectator of all that has departed; but methinks I have seen hardly anything else so forlorn and depressing as it is now, all dusky and dim, even the very lights having passed into shadows, and the shadows into utter blackness; so that it needs a sunshiny day, under the bright Italian heavens, to make the designs perceptible at all. As we sat in the chapel there were clouds flitting across the sky; when the clouds came the pictures vanished; when the sunshine broke forth the figures sadly glimmered into something like visibility—the Almighty moving in chaos—the noble shape of Adam, the beautiful Eve; and, beneath where the roof curves, the mighty figures of sibyls and prophets, looking as if they were necessarily so gigantic because the thought within them was so massive. In the "Last Judgment" the scene of the greater part of the picture lies in the upper sky, the blue of which glows through betwixt the groups of naked figures; and above sits Jesus, not looking in the least like the Saviour of the world, but, with uplifted arm, denouncing eternal misery on those whom he came to save. I fear I am myself among the wicked, for I found myself inevitably taking their part, and asking for at least a little pity, some few regrets, and not such a stern denunciatory spirit on the part of Him who had thought us worth dying for. Around him stand grim saints, and, far beneath, people are getting up sleepily out of their graves, not well knowing what is about to happen; many of them, however, finding themselves clutched by demons before they are half awake. It would be a very terrible picture to one who should really see Jesus, the Saviour, in that inexorable judge; but it seems to me very undesirable that he should ever be represented in that aspect, when it is so essential to our religion to believe him infinitely kinder and better towards us than we deserve. At the last day —I presume, that is, in all future days, when we see ourselves as we are—man's only inexorable judge will be himself, and the punishment of his sins will be the perception of them.

In the lower corner of this great picture, at the right hand of the spectator, is a hideous figure of a damned person, girdled about with a serpent, the folds of which are carefully knotted between his thighs, so as, at all events, to give no offence to decency. This figure represents a man who suggested to Pope Paul III. that the nudities of the "Last Judgment" ought to be draped, for which offence Michel Angelo at once consigned him to hell. It shows what a debtor's prison and dungeon of private torment men would make of hell if they had the control of it. As to the nudities, if they were ever more nude than now, I should suppose, in their fresh brilliancy, they might well have startled a not very squeamish eye. The effect, such as it is, of this picture is much injured by the high altar and its canopy, which stands close against the wall, and intercepts a considerable portion of the sprawl of nakedness with which Michel Angelo has filled his sky. However, I am not unwilling to believe, with faith beyond what I can actually see, that the greatest pictorial miracles ever yet achieved have been wrought upon the walls and ceiling of the Sistine Chapel.

In the afternoon I went with Mr. Thompson to see what bargain could be made with vetturinos for taking myself and family to Florence. We talked with three or four, and found them asking prices of various enormity, from a hundred and fifty scudi down to little more than ninety; but Mr. Thompson says that they always begin in this way, and will probably come down to somewhere about seventy-five. Mr. Thompson took me into the Via Portoghese, and showed me an old palace, above which rose—not a very customary feature of the architecture of Rome—a tall, battlemented tower. At one angle of the tower we saw a shrine of the Virgin, with a lamp, and all the appendages of those numerous shrines which we see at the street corners, and in hundreds of places about the city. Three or four centuries ago this palace was inhabited by a nobleman who had an only son and a large pet monkey, and one day the monkey caught the infant up and clambered to this lofty turret, and sat there with him in his arms, grinning and chattering like the devil himself. The father was in despair, but was afraid to pursue the monkey lest he should fling down the child from the height of the tower and make his escape. At last he vowed that if the boy were safely restored to him he would build a shrine at the summit of the tower, and cause it to be kept as a sacred place for ever. By-and-by the monkey came down and deposited the child on the ground; the father fulfilled his vow, built the shrine, and made it obligatory on all future possessors of the palace to keep the lamp burning before it. Centuries have passed, the property has changed hands; but, still, there is the shrine on the giddy top of the tower, far aloft over the street, on the very spot where the monkey sat, and there burns the lamp, in memory of the father's vow. This being the tenure by which the estate is held, the extinguishment of that flame might yet turn the present owner out of the palace.

May 21st.—Mamma and I went, yesterday forenoon, to the Spada Palace, which we found among the intricacies of central Rome; a dark and massive old edifice, built around a court, the fronts giving on which are adorned with statues in niches and sculptured ornaments. A woman led us up a staircase, and ushered us into a great, gloomy hall, square and lofty, and wearing a very grey and ancient aspect, its walls being painted in chiaroscuro, apparently a great many years ago. The hall was lighted by small windows, high upward from the floors, and admitting only a dusky light. The only furniture or ornament, so far as I recollect, was the colossal statue of Pompey, which stands on its pedestal at one side, certainly the sternest and severest of figures, and producing the most awful impression on the spectator. Much of the effect, no doubt, is due to the sombre obscurity of the hall, and to the loneliness in which the great naked statue stands. It is entirely nude, except for a cloak that hangs down from the left shoulder; in the left hand, it holds a globe; the right arm is extended. The whole expression is such as the statue might have assumed, if, during the tumult of Cæsar's murder, it had stretched forth its marble hand, and motioned the conspirators to give over the attack, or to be quiet, now that their victim had fallen at its feet. On the left leg, about midway above the ankle, there is a dull red stain, said to be Cæsar's blood; but, of course, it is just such a red stain in the marble as may be seen on the statue of Antinous at the Capitol. I could not see any resemblance in the face of the statue to that of the bust of Pompey, shown as such at the Capitol, in which there is not the slightest moral dignity, or sign of intellectual eminence. I am glad to have seen this statue, and glad to remember it in that grey, dim, lofty hall; glad that there were no bright frescoes on the walls, and that the ceiling was wrought with massive beams, and the floor paved with ancient brick.

From this ante-room we passed through several saloons containing pictures, some of which were by eminent artists; the Judith of Guido, a copy of which used to weary me to death, year after year, in the Boston Athenæum; and many portraits of cardinals in the Spada family, and other pictures by Guido. There were some portraits, also of the family, by Titian; some good pictures by Guercino; and many which I should have been glad to examine more at leisure; but, by-and-by, the custode made his appearance, and began to close the shutters, under pretence that the sunshine would injure the paintings—an effect, I presume, not very likely to follow after two or three centuries exposure to light, air, and whatever else might hurt them. However, the pictures seemed to be in much better condition, and more enjoyable, so far as they had merit, than those in most Roman picture galleries; although the Spada Palace itself has a decayed and impoverished aspect, as if the family had dwindled from its former state and grandeur, and now, perhaps, smuggled itself into some out-of-the-way corner of the old edifice. If such be the case, there is something touching in their still keeping possession of Pompey's statue, which makes their house famous, and the sale of which might give them the means of building it up anew; for surely it is worth the whole sculpture gallery of the Vatican.

In the afternoon, Mr. Thompson and I went, for the

third or fourth time, to negotiate with vetturinos.
. . . . So far as I know them, they are a very tricky
set of people, bent on getting as much as they can,
by hook or by crook, out of the unfortunate individual
who falls into their hands. They begin, as I have
said, by asking about twice as much as they ought to
receive : and anything between this exorbitant amount
and the just price is what they thank heaven for, as
so much clear gain. Nevertheless, I am not quite
sure that the Italians are worse than other people
even in this matter. In other countries, it is the
custom of persons in trade to take as much as they
can get from the public, fleecing one man to exactly
the same extent as another; here, they take what
they can obtain from the individual customer. In
fact, Roman tradesmen do not pretend to deny that
they ask and receive different prices from different
people, taxing them according to their supposed
means of payment; the article supplied being the
same in one case as in another. A shopkeeper
looked into his books to see if we were of the class
who paid two pauls, or only a paul and a half for
candles; a charcoal dealer said that seventy baiocchi
was a very reasonable sum for us to pay for charcoal,
and that some persons paid eighty; and Mr. Thompson
recognising the rule, told the vetturino that "a

hundred and fifty scudi was a very proper charge for carrying a prince to Florence, but not for carrying me, who was merely a very good artist." The result is well enough; the rich man lives expensively, and pays a larger share of the profits which people of a different system of trade-morality would take equally from the poor man. The effect on the conscience of the vetturino, however, and of tradesmen of all kinds, cannot be good; their only intent being, not to do justice between man and man, but to go as deep as they can into all pockets, and to the very bottom of some.

We had nearly concluded a bargain, a day or two ago, with a vetturino to take or send us to Florence, *viâ* Perugia, in eight days, for a hundred scudi; but he now drew back, under pretence of having misunderstood the terms, though, in reality, no doubt, he was in hopes of getting a better bargain from somebody else. We made an agreement with another man, whom Mr. Thompson knows and highly recommends, and immediately made it sure and legally binding by exchanging a formal written contract, in which everything is set down, even to milk, butter, bread, eggs, and coffee, which we are to have for breakfast, the vetturino being to pay every expense for himself, his horses, and his passengers, and include it within ninety-five scudi, and five crowns in addition for *buon-mano*. . . . .

May 22nd.—Yesterday, while we were at dinner, Mr. —— called. I never saw him but once before, and that was at the door of our little red cottage in Lenox; he sitting in a waggon with one or two of the Sedgewicks, merely exchanging a greeting with me from under the brim of his straw hat, and driving on. He presented himself now with a long white beard, such as a palmer might have worn as the growth of his long pilgrimages, a brow almost entirely bald, and what hair he has quite hoary; a forehead impending, yet not massive; dark, bushy eyebrows and keen eyes, without much softness in them; a dark and sallow complexion; a slender figure, bent a little with age; but at once alert and infirm. It surprised me to see him so venerable; for, as poets are Apollo's kinsmen, we are inclined to attribute to them his enviable quality of never growing old. There was a weary look in his face, as if he were tired of seeing things and doing things, though with certainly enough still to see and do, if need were. My family gathered about him, and he conversed with great readiness and simplicity about his travels, and whatever other subject came up; telling us that he had been abroad five times, and was now getting a little

home-sick, and had no more eagerness for sights,
though his "gals" (as he called his daughter and
another young lady) dragged him out to see the
wonders of Rome again. His manners and whole
aspect are very particularly plain, though not affect-
edly so; but it seems as if, in the decline of life, and
the security of his position, he had put off whatever
artificial polish he may have heretofore had, and resumed the simpler habits and deportment of his early
New England breeding. Not but what you discover,
nevertheless, that he is a man of refinement, who has
seen the world, and is well aware of his own place in
it. He spoke with great pleasure of his recent visit
to Spain. I introduced the subject of Kansas, and
methought his face forthwith assumed something of the
bitter keenness of the editor of a political newspaper,
while speaking of the triumph of the administration
over the free soil opposition. I inquired whether he
had seen S——, and he gave a very sad account of
him as he appeared at their last meeting, which was
in Paris. S——, he thought, had suffered terribly,
and would never again be the man he was; he was
getting fat; he talked continually of himself, and of
trifles concerning himself, and seemed to have no
interest for other matters; and Mr. —— feared that
the shock upon his nerves had extended to his intel-

lect, and was irremediable. He said that S—— ought to retire from public life, but had no friend true enough to tell him so. This is about as sad as anything can be. I hate to have S—— undergo the fate of a martyr; because he was not naturally of the stuff that martyrs are made of, and it is altogether by mistake that he has thrust himself into the position of one. He was merely, though with excellent abilities, one of the best of fellows, and ought to have lived and died in good fellowship with all the world.

—— was not in the least degree excited about this or any other subject. He uttered neither passion nor poetry; but excellent good sense, and accurate information on whatever subject transpired; a very pleasant man to associate with; but rather cold, I should imagine, if one should seek to touch his heart with one's own. He shook hands kindly all round, but not with any warmth of gripe; although the ease of his deportment had put us all on sociable terms with him.

At seven o'clock, we went by invitation to take tea with Miss Bremer. After much search, and lumbering painfully up two or three staircases in vain, and at last going about in a strange circuity, we found her in a small chamber of a large old building, situated a little way from the brow of the Tarpeian rock.

It was the tiniest and humblest domicile that I have seen in Rome, just large enough to hold her narrow bed, her tea-table, and a table covered with books— photographs of Roman ruins, and some pages written by herself. I wonder whether she be poor. Probably so; for she told us that her expense of living here is only five pauls a day. She welcomed us, however, with the greatest cordiality and ladylike simplicity, making no allusion to the humbleness of her environment (and making us also lose sight of it, by the absence of all apology) any more than if she were receiving us in a palace. There is not a better-bred woman; and yet one does not think whether she has any breeding or no. Her little bit of a round table was already spread for us with her blue earthenware tea-cups; and after she had got through an interview with the Swedish minister, and dismissed him with a hearty pressure of his hand between both her own, she gave us our tea, and some bread, and a mouthful of cake. Meanwhile, as the day declined, there had been the most beautiful view over the Campagna, out of one of her windows; and, from the other, looking towards St. Peter's, the broad gleam of a mildly glorious sunset; not so pompous and magnificent as many that I have seen in America, but softer and sweeter in all its changes. As its lovely hues died slowly away, the half-moon shone out brighter and brighter; for there was not a cloud in the sky, and it seemed like the moonlight of my younger days. In the garden, beneath her window, verging upon the Tarpeian Rock, there was shrubbery and one large tree, softening the brow of the famous precipice, adown which the old Romans used to fling their traitors, or sometimes, indeed, their patriots.

Miss Bremer talked plentifully in her strange manner—good English enough for a foreigner, but so oddly intonated and accented, that it is impossible to be sure of more than one word in ten. Being so little comprehensible, it is very singular how she contrives to make her auditors so perfectly certain, as they are, that she is talking the best sense, and in the kindliest spirit. There is no better heart than hers, and not many sounder heads; and a little touch of sentiment comes delightfully in, mixed up with a quick and delicate humour and the most perfect simplicity. There is also a very pleasant atmosphere of maidenhood about her; we are sensible of a freshness and odour of the morning still in this little withered rose—its recompense for never having been gathered and worn, but only diffusing fragrance on its stem. I forget mainly what we talked about—a good deal about art, of course, although that is a subject of which Miss Bremer evidently knows nothing. Once we spoke of fleas—insects that, in Rome, come home to everybody's business and bosom, and are so common and inevitable, that no delicacy is felt about alluding to the sufferings they inflict. Poor little Miss Bremer was tormented with one while turning out our tea. . . . . She talked, among other things, of the winters in Sweden, and said that she liked them, long and severe as they are; and this made me feel ashamed of dreading the winters of New England, as I did before coming from home, and do now still more, after five or six mild English Decembers.

By-and-by, two young ladies came in — Miss Bremer's neighbours, it seemed—fresh from a long walk on the Campagna, fresh and weary at the same time. One apparently was German, and the other French, and they brought her an offering of flowers, and chattered to her with affectionate vivacity; and, as we were about taking leave, Miss Bremer asked them to accompany her and us on a visit to the edge of the Tarpeian Rock. Before we left the room, she took a bunch of roses that were in a vase, and gave them to Miss Shepard, who told her that she should make her six sisters happy by giving one to each. Then we went down the intricate stairs, and, emerging into the garden, walked round the brow of the hill, which plunges headlong with exceeding abruptness; but, so far as I could see in the moonlight, is no longer quite a precipice. Then we re-entered the house, and went up-stairs and down again, through intricate passages, till we got into the street, which was still peopled with the ragamuffins who infest and burrow in that part of Rome. We returned through an archway, and descended the broad flight of steps into the Piazza of the Capitol; and from the extremity of it, just at the head of the long graded way, where Castor and Pollux and the old milestones stand, we turned to the left, and followed a somewhat winding path, till we came into the court of a palace. This court is bordered by a parapet, leaning over which we saw the sheer precipice of the Tarpeian Rock, about the height of a four-story house. . . . .

On the edge of this, before we left the court, Miss Bremer bade us farewell, kissing my wife most affectionately on each cheek, ... and then turning towards myself, ... she pressed my hand, and we parted, probably never to meet again. God bless her good heart! . . . . She is a most amiable little woman, worthy to be the maiden aunt of the whole human race. I suspect, by-the-bye, that she does not like me half so well as I do her; it is my impression that she thinks me unamiable, or that there is something or other not quite right about me. I am sorry if it be so, because such a good, kindly, clear-sighted, and delicate person is very apt to have reason at the bottom of her harsh thoughts, when, in rare cases, she allows them to harbour with her.

To-day, and for some days past, we have been in quest of lodgings for next winter; a weary search, up interminable staircases, which seduce us upward to no successful result. It is very disheartening not to be able to place the slightest reliance on the integrity of the people we are to deal with; not to believe in any connection between their words and their purposes; to know that they are certainly telling you falsehoods, while you are not in a position to catch hold of the lie, and hold it up in their faces.

This afternoon we called on Mr. and Mrs. —— at the Hôtel de l'Europe, but found only the former at home. We had a pleasant visit, but I made no observations of his character save such as I have already sufficiently recorded; and when we had been with him a little while, Mrs. Chapman, the artist's wife, Mr. Terry, and my friend, Mr. Thompson, came in. —— received them all with the same good degree of cordiality that he did ourselves—not cold, not very warm, not annoyed, not ecstatically delighted; a man, I should suppose, not likely to have ardent individual preferences, though perhaps capable of stern individual dislikes. But I take him, at all events, to be a very upright man, and pursuing a narrow track of integrity; he is a man whom I would never forgive (as I would a thousand other men) for the slightest moral delinquency. I would not be bound to say, however, that he has not the little sin of a fretful and peevish habit; and yet perhaps I am a sinner myself for thinking so.

May 23rd.—This morning I breakfasted at William Story's, and met there Mr. Bryant, Mr. T—— (an English gentleman), Mr. and Mrs. Apthorp, Miss Hosmer, and one or two other ladies. Bryant was very quiet, and made no conversation audible to the general table. Mr. T—— talked of English politics and public men; the *Times*, and other newspapers, English clubs and social habits generally; topics in which I could well enough bear my part of the discussion. After breakfast, and aside from the ladies, he mentioned an illustration of Lord Ellenborough's lack of administrative ability — a proposal seriously made by his lordship in reference to the refractory Sepoys. . . . . .

We had a very pleasant breakfast, and certainly a breakfast is much preferable to a dinner, not merely in the enjoyment while it is passing, but afterwards. I made a good suggestion to Miss Hosmer for the design of a fountain—a lady bursting into tears— water gushing from a thousand pores, in literal translation of the phrase; and to call the statue "Niobe, all tears." I doubt whether she adopts the idea; but Bernini would have been delighted with it. I should think the gush of water might be so arranged as to form a beautiful drapery about the figure, swaying and fluttering with every breath of wind, and re-arranging itself in the calm, in which case the lady might be said to have "a habit of weeping." . . . . Apart, with William Story, he and I talked of the unluckiness of Friday, &c. I like him particularly well. . . . .

We have been plagued to-day with our preparations for leaving Rome to-morrow, and especially with verifying the inventory of furniture, before giving up the house to our landlord. He and his daughter have been examining every separate article, down even to the kitchen skewers, I believe, and charging us to the amount of several scudi for cracks and breakages, which very probably existed when we came into possession. It is very uncomfortable to have dealings with such a mean people (though our landlord is German) — mean in their business transactions; mean even in their beggary; for the beggars seldom ask for more than a mezzo baioccho, though they sometimes grumble when you suit your gratuity exactly to their petition. It is pleasant to record that the Italians have great faith in the honour of the English and Americans, and never hesitate to trust entire strangers, to any reasonable extent, on the strength of their being of the honest Anglo-Saxon race.

This evening, U—— and I took a farewell walk in the Pincian gardens to see the sunset; and found them crowded with people, promenading and listening to the music of the French band. It was the feast of Whitsunday, which probably brought a greater throng than usual abroad.

When the sun went down, we descended into the Piazza del Popolo, and thence into the Via Ripetta, and emerged through a gate to the shore of the Tiber, along which there is a pleasant walk beneath a grove of trees. We traversed it once and back again, looking at the rapid river, which still kept its mud-puddly aspect even in the clear twilight, and beneath the brightening moon. The great bell of St. Peter's tolled with a deep boom,—a grand

and solemn sound; the moon gleamed through the branches of the trees above us; and U—— spoke with somewhat alarming fervour of her love for Rome, and regret at leaving it. We shall have done the child no good office in bringing her here, if the rest of her life is to be a dream of this "city of the soul," and an unsatisfied yearning to come back to it. On the other hand, nothing elevating and refining can be really injurious, and so I hope she will always be the better for Rome, even if her life should be spent where there are no pictures, no statues—nothing but the dryness and meagreness of a New England village.

JOURNEY TO FLORENCE.

CIVITA CASTELLANA, *May* 24*th*.—We left Rome this morning, after troubles of various kinds, and a dispute in the first place with Lalla, our female servant, and her mother. . . . . Mother and daughter exploded into a livid rage, and cursed us plentifully, wishing that we might never come to our journey's end, and that we might all break our necks or die of apoplexy—the most awful curse that an Italian knows how to invoke upon his enemies, because it precludes the possibility of extreme unction. However, as we are heretics, and certain of damnation therefore anyhow, it does not much matter to us; and also the anathemas may have been blown back upon those who invoked them, like the curses that were flung out from the balcony of St. Peter's during Holy Week, and wafted by heaven's breezes right into the faces of some priests who stood near the Pope. Next we had a disagreement with two men who brought down our luggage, and put it on the vetturo; . . . . and, lastly, we were infested with beggars, who hung round the carriages with doleful petitions, till we began to move away; but the previous warfare had put me into too stern a mood for almsgiving, so that they also were doubtless inclined to curse more than to bless, and I am persuaded that we drove off under a perfect shower of anathemas.

We passed through the Porta del Popolo at about eight o'clock; and after a moment's delay, while the passport was examined, began our journey along the Flaminian Way, between two such high and inhospitable walls of brick or stone as seem to shut in all the avenues to Rome. We had not gone far before we heard military music in advance of us, and saw the road blocked up with people, and then the glitter of muskets, and soon appeared the drummers, fifers, and trumpeters, and then the first battalion of a

French regiment, marching into the city, with two mounted officers at their head; then appeared a second and then a third battalion, the whole seeming to make almost an army, though the number on their caps showed them all to belong to one regiment—the 1st; then came a battery of artillery, then a detachment of horse—these last, by the crossed keys on their helmets, being apparently papal troops. All were young, fresh, good-looking men, in excellent trim as to uniform and equipments, and marched rather as if they were setting out on a campaign than returning from it; the fact being, I believe, that they have been encamped or in barracks within a few miles of the city. Nevertheless, it reminded me of the military processions of various kinds which so often, two thousand years ago and more, have entered Rome over the Flaminian Way, and over all the roads that led to the famous city—triumphs oftenest, but sometimes the downcast train of a defeated army, like those who retreated before Hannibal. On the whole, I was not sorry to see the Gauls still pouring into Rome; but yet I begin to find that I have a strange affection for it, and so did we all—the rest of the family in a greater degree than myself even. It is very singular, the sad embrace with which Rome takes possession of the soul. Though we intend to return in a few months, and for a longer residence than this has been, yet we felt the city pulling at our heartstrings far more than London did, where we shall probably never spend much time again. It may be because the intellect finds a home there more than in any other spot in the world, and wins the heart to stay with it, in spite of a good many things strewn all about to disgust us.

The road in the earlier part of the way was not particularly picturesque—the country undulated, but scarcely rose into hills, and was destitute of trees; there were a few shapeless ruins, too indistinct for us to make out whether they were Roman or mediæval. Nothing struck me so much, in the forenoon, as the spectacle of a peasant woman riding on horseback as if she were a man. The houses were few, and those of a dreary aspect, built of grey stone, and looking bare and desolate, with not the slightest promise of comfort within doors. We passed two or three locandas or inns, and finally came to the village (if village it were, for I remember no houses except our osteria) of Castel Nuovo di Porta, where we were to take a *déjeûner à la fourchette*, which was put upon the table between twelve and one. On this journey, according to the custom of travellers in Italy, we pay the vetturino a certain sum, and live at his expense;

and this meal was the first specimen of his catering on our behalf. It consisted of a beefsteak, rather dry and hard, but not unpalatable, and a large omelette; and for beverage, two quart bottles of red wine, which, being tasted, had an agreeable acid flavour.
. . . . The locanda was built of stone, and had what looked like an old Roman altar in 'the basement-hall, and a shrine, with a lamp before it, on the staircase; and the large public saloon in which we ate had a brick floor, a ceiling with cross-beams, meagrely painted in fresco, and a scanty supply of chairs and settees.

After lunch, we wandered out into a valley or ravine near the house, where we gathered some flowers, and J—— found a nest with the young birds in it, which, however, he put back into the bush whence he took it.

Our afternoon drive was more picturesque and noteworthy. Soracte rose before us, bulging up quite abruptly out of the plain, and keeping itself entirely distinct from a whole horizon of hills. Byron well compares it to a wave just on the bend, and about to break over towards the spectator.' As we approached it nearer and nearer, it looked like the barrenest great rock that ever protruded out of the substance of the earth, with scarcely a strip or a

spot of verdure upon its steep and grey declivities.
The road kept trending towards the mountain, following the line of the old Flaminian Way, which
we could see, at frequent intervals, close beside the
modern track. It is paved with large flag-stones,
laid so accurately together that it is still, in some
places, as smooth and even as the floor of a church;
and everywhere the tufts of grass find it difficult
to root themselves into the interstices. Its course
is straighter than that of the road of to-day, which
often turns aside to avoid obstacles which the ancient
one surmounted. Much of it, probably, is covered
with the soil and overgrowth, deposited in later
years; and, now and then, we could see its flag-
stones partly protruding from the bank, through
which our road has been cut, and thus showing that
the thickness of this massive pavement was more
than a foot of solid stone. We lost it over and over
again; but still it reappeared, now on one side of
us, now on the other; perhaps from beneath the
roots of old trees, or the pasture land of a thousand
years old, and leading on towards the base of
Soracte. I forget where we finally lost it. Passing
through a town called Rignano, we found it dressed
out in festivity, with festoons of foliage along both
sides of the street, which ran beneath a triumphal

arch, bearing an inscription in honour of a ducal personage of the Massinii family. I know no occasion for the feast, except that it is Whitsuntide. The town was thronged with peasants, in their best attire, and we met others on their way thither, particularly women and girls, with heads bare in the sunshine; but there was no tiptoe jollity, nor, indeed, any more show of festivity than I have seen in my own country at a cattle show or muster,— really, I think, not half so much.

The road still grew more and more picturesque, and now lay along ridges, at the bases of which were deep ravines and hollow valleys. Woods were not wanting—wilder forest than I have seen since leaving America, of oak trees chiefly; and among the green foliage grew golden tufts of broom, making a gay and lovely combination of hues. I must not forget to mention the poppies, which burned like live coals along the wayside, and lit up the landscape, even a single one of them, with wonderful effect. At other points we saw olive trees, hiding their eccentricity of boughs under thick masses of foliage of a livid tint, which is caused, I believe, by their turning their reverse sides to the light and to the spectator. Vines were abundant; but were of little account in the scene. By-and-by, we came in sight of the high, flat table-land on which stands Città Castellana, and beheld, straight downward, between us and the town, a deep level valley, with a river winding through it. It was the valley of the Treja. A precipice, hundreds of feet in height, falls perpendicularly upon the valley, from the site of Città Castellana; there is an equally abrupt one, probably, on the side from which we saw it; and a modern road, skilfully constructed, goes winding down to the stream, crosses it by a narrow stone bridge, and winds upward into the town. After passing over the bridge, I alighted, with J—— and R——, . . . and made the ascent on foot, along walls of natural rock, in which old Etruscan tombs were hollowed out. There are likewise antique remains of masonry, whether Roman or of what earlier period I cannot tell. At the summit of the acclivity, which brought us close to the town, our vetturino took us into the carriage again, and quickly brought us to what appears to be really a good hotel, where all of us are accommodated with sleeping chambers in a range, beneath an arcade, entirely secluded from the rest of the population of the hotel. After a splendid dinner, (that is, splendid, considering that it was ordered by our hospitable vetturino), Una, Miss Shepard,

J—— and I, walked out of the little town, in the opposite direction from our entrance, and crossed a bridge at the height of the table-land, instead of at its base. On either side, we had a view down into a profound gulf, with sides of precipitous rock, and heaps of foliage in its lap, through which ran the snowy track of a stream; here snowy, there dark; here hidden among the foliage, there quite revealed in the broad depths of the gulf. This was wonderfully fine. Walking on a little farther, Soracte came fully into view, starting with bold abruptness out of the middle of the country; and before we got back, the bright Italian moon was throwing a shower of silver over the scene, and making it so beautiful that it seemed miserable not to know how to put it into words; a foolish thought, however, for such scenes are an expression in themselves, and need not be translated into any feebler language. On our walk, we met parties of labourers, both men and women, returning from the fields, with rakes and wooden forks over their shoulders, singing in chorus. It is very customary for women to be labouring in the fields.

TO TERNI.—BORGHETTO.

May 25th.—We were aroused at four o'clock this morning; had some eggs and coffee, and were ready to start between five and six; being thus matutinary, in order to get to Terni in time to see the falls. The road was very striking and picturesque; but I remember nothing particularly, till we came to Borghetto, which stands on a bluff, with a broad valley sweeping round it, through the midst of which flows the Tiber. There is an old castle on a projecting point; and we saw other battlemented fortresses, of mediæval date, along our way, forming more beautiful ruins than any of the Roman remains to which we have become accustomed. This is partly, I suppose, owing to the fact that they have been neglected, and allowed to mantle their decay with ivy, instead of being cleaned, propped up, and restored. The antiquarian is apt to spoil the objects that interest him.

Sometimes we passed through wildernesses of various trees, each contributing a different hue of verdure to the scene; the vine, also, marrying itself to the fig tree, so that a man might sit in the shadow of both at once, and temper the luscious sweetness of the one fruit with the fresh flavour of the other. The wayside incidents were such as meeting a man and woman borne along as prisoners, handcuffed, and in a cart; two men reclining across one another, asleep, and lazily lifting their heads to gaze at us as we passed by; a woman spinning with a distaff as she walked along the road. An old tomb or tower stood in a lonely field, and several caves were hollowed in the rocks, which might have been either sepulchres or habitations. Soracte kept us company, sometimes a little on one side, sometimes behind, looming up again and again, when we thought that we had done with it, and so becoming rather tedious at last, like a person who presents himself for another and another leave-taking, after the one which ought to have been final. Honeysuckles sweetened the hedges along the road.

After leaving Borghetto, we crossed the broad valley of the Tiber, and skirted along one of the ridges that border it, looking back upon the road that we had passed, lying white behind us. We saw a field covered with buttercups, or some other yellow flower, and poppies burned along the road-side, as they did yesterday, and there were flowers of a delicious blue, as if the blue Italian sky had been broken into little bits, and scattered down upon the green earth. Otricoli by-and-by appeared, situated on a bold promontory above the valley, a village of a few grey houses and huts, with one edifice gaudily painted in white and pink. It looked more important at a distance than we found it on our nearer approach. As the road kept ascending, and as the hills grew to be mountains, we had taken two additional horses, making six in all, with a man and boy running beside them, to keep them in motion. The boy had two club feet, so inconveniently disposed that it seemed almost inevitable for him to stumble over them at every step; besides which, he seemed to tread upon his ankles, and moved with a disjointed gait, as if each of his legs and thighs had been twisted round together with his feet. Nevertheless, he had a bright, cheerful, intelligent face, and was exceedingly active, keeping up with the horses at their trot, and inciting them to better speed when they lagged. I conceived a great respect for this poor boy, who had what most Italian peasants would consider an enviable birthright in those two club feet, as giving him a sufficient excuse to live on charity, but yet took no advantage of them; on the contrary, putting his poor misshapen hoofs to such good use, as might have shamed many a better provided biped. When he quitted us, he asked no alms of the travellers; but merely applied to Gaetano for some slight recompense for his well-performed service. This behaviour contrasted most favourably with that of some other boys and girls, who ran begging beside the carriage-door, keeping up a low, miserable murmur, like that of a kennel-stream, for a long, long way. Beggars, indeed, started up at every point when we stopped for a moment, and whenever a hill imposed a slower pace upon us; each village had its deformity or its infirmity, offering his wretched petition at the step of the carriage; and even a venerable, white-headed patriarch—the grandfather of all the beggars—seemed to grow up by the roadside; but was left behind from inability to join in the race with his light-footed juniors. No shame is attached to begging in Italy. In fact, I rather imagine it to be held an honourable profession, inheriting some of the odour of sanctity that used to be attached to a mendicant and idle life in the days of early Christianity, when every saint lived upon Providence, and deemed it meritorious to do nothing for his support.

Murray's guide-book is exceedingly vague and unsatisfactory along this route; and whenever we asked Gaetano the name of a village or a castle, he gave some one which we had never heard before, and could find nothing of in the book. We made out the river Nar, however, or what I supposed to be such, though he called it Nera. It flows through a most stupendous mountain gorge; winding its narrow passage between high hills, the broad sides of which descend steeply upon it, covered with trees and shrubbery, that mantle a host of rocky roughnesses, and make all look smooth. Here and there a precipice juts sternly forth. We saw an old castle on a hill-side, frowning down into the gorge; and farther on, the grey tower of Narni stands upon a height, imminent over the depths below, and with its battlemented castle above, now converted into a prison, and therefore kept in excellent repair. A long, winding street passes through Narni, broadening at one point into a market-place, where an old cathedral showed its venerable front, and the great dial of its clock, the figures on which were numbered in two semicircles of twelve points each; one, I suppose, for noon, and the other for midnight. The town has, so far as its principal street is concerned, a city-like aspect, with large, fair edifices, and shops as good as most of those at Rome, the smartness of which contrasts strikingly with the rude and lonely scenery of mountain and stream, through which we had come to reach it. We drove through Narni without stopping, and came out from it on the other side, where a broad, level valley opened before us, most unlike the wild, precipitous gorge which had brought us to the town. The road went winding down into the peaceful vale, through the midst of which flowed the same stream that cuts its way between the impending hills, as already described. We passed a monk and a soldier—the two curses of Italy, each in his way—walking sociably side by side; and from Narni to Terni I remember nothing that need be recorded.

Terni, like so many other towns in the neighbourhood, stands in a high and commanding position, chosen doubtless for its facilities of defence, in days long before the mediæval warfares of Italy made such sites desirable. I suppose that, like Narni and Otricoli, it was a city of the Umbrians. We reached it between eleven and twelve o'clock, intending to employ the afternoon on a visit to the famous falls of Terni; but, after lowering all day, it has begun to rain, and we shall probably have to give them up.

Half-past Eight o'clock.—It has rained in torrents during the afternoon, and we have not seen the Cascade of Terni; considerably to my regret, for I think I felt the more interest in seeing it, on account of its being artificial. Methinks nothing was more characteristic of the energy and determination of the old Romans, than thus to take a river, which they wished to get rid of, and fling it over a giddy precipice, breaking it into ten million pieces by the fall. . . . . We are in the Hôtel delle tre Colonne, and find it reasonably good, though not, so far as we are concerned, justifying the rapturous commendations of previous tourists, who probably travelled at their own charges. However, there is nothing really to be complained of, either in our accommodations or table, and the only wonder is how Gaetano contrives to get any profit out of our contract, since the hotel-bills would alone cost us more than we pay him for the journey and all. It is worth while to record as history of vetturino commissary customs, that for breakfast this morning we had coffee, eggs, and bread and butter; for lunch an omelette, some stewed veal, and a dessert of figs and grapes, besides two decanters of a light-coloured, acid wine, tasting very like indifferent cider; for dinner, an excellent vermicelli soup, two young fowls, fricasseed, and a hind quarter of roast lamb, with fritters, oranges and figs, and two more decanters of the wine aforesaid.

This hotel is an edifice with a gloomy front upon a narrow street, and enterable though an arch, which admits you into an enclosed court; around the court, on each story, run the galleries, with which the parlours and sleeping apartments communicate. The whole house is dingy—probably old, and seems not very clean; but yet bears traces of former magnificence; for instance, in our bedroom, the door of which is ornamented with gilding, and the cornices with frescoes, some of which appear to represent the cascade of Terni; the roof is crossed with carved beams, and is painted in the interstices; the floor has a carpet, but rough tiles underneath it, which show themselves at the margin. The windows admit the wind; the door shuts so loosely as to leave great cracks; and, during the rain to-day, there was a heavy shower through our ceiling, which made a flood upon the carpet. We see no chamber-maids; nothing of the comfort and neatness of an English hotel, nor of the smart splendours of an American one; but still, this dilapidated palace affords us a better shelter than I expected to find in the decayed country towns of Italy. In the album of the hotel, I find the names of more English travellers than of any other nation except the Americans, who, I think, even exceed the former; and the route being the favourite one for tourists between Rome and Florence, whatever merit the inns have is probably owing to the demands of the Anglo-Saxons. I doubt not, if we chose to pay for it, this hotel would supply us with any luxury we might ask for; and perhaps even a gorgeous saloon and state bed-chamber.

After dinner, J—— and I walked out in the dusk to see what we could of Terni. We found it compact and gloomy (but the latter characteristic might well enough be attributed to the dismal sky), with narrow streets, paved from wall to wall of the houses, like those of all the towns in Italy; the blocks of paving-stone larger than the little square torments of Rome. The houses are covered with dingy stucco, and mostly low, compared with those of Rome, and inhospitable as regards their dismal aspects and uninviting doorways. The streets are intricate as well as narrow, insomuch that we quickly lost our way, and could not find it again, though the town is of so small dimensions that we passed through it in two directions in the course of our brief wanderings. There are no lampposts in Terni; and as it was growing dark, and beginning to rain again, we at last inquired of a person in the principal piazza, and found our hotel, as I expected, within two minutes' walk of where we stood.

FOLIGNO.

May 26th.—At six o'clock this morning we packed ourselves into our vetturo, my wife and I occupying the coupé, and drove out of the city-gate of Terni. There are some old towers near it, ruins of I know not what, and care as little, in the plethora of antiquities and other interesting objects. Through the arched gateway, as we approached, we had a view of one of the great hills that surround the town, looking partly bright in the early sunshine, and partly catching the shadows of the clouds that floated about the sky. Our way was now through the vale of Terni, as I believe it is called, where we saw somewhat of the fertility of Italy: vines trained on poles, or twining round mulberry and other trees, ranged regularly like orchards; groves of olives and fields of grain. There are interminable shrines in all sorts of situations; some under arched niches, or little penthouses, with a brick-tiled roof, just large enough to cover them; or perhaps in some bit of old Roman masonry, on the wall of a wayside inn, or in a shallow cavity of the natural rock; or high upward in the deep cuts of the road; everywhere, in short, so that nobody need be at a loss when he feels the religious sentiment stir within him. Our way soon began to wind among the hills, which rose steep and lofty from the scanty, level space that lay between; they continually thrust themselves across the passage, and appeared as if determined to shut us completely in. A great hill would put its foot right before us; but, at the last moment, would grudgingly withdraw it, and allow us just room enough to creep by. Adown their sides we discerned the dry beds of mountain torrents, which had lived too fierce a life to let it be a long one. On here and there a hill-side or promontory we saw a ruined castle or a convent, looking from its commanding height upon the road, which very likely some robber-knight had formerly infested with his banditti, retreating with his booty to the security of such strongholds. We came, once in a while, to wretched villages, where there was no token of prosperity or comfort, but perhaps there may have been more than we could appreciate; for the Italians do not seem to have any of that sort of pride which we find in New England villages, where every man, according to his taste and means, endeavours to make his homestead an ornament to the place. We miss nothing in Italy more than the neat door-steps and pleasant porches and thresholds and delightful lawns or grass-plots, which hospitably invite the imagination into a sweet domestic interior. Everything, however sunny and luxuriant may be the scene around, is especially dreary and disheartening in the immediate vicinity of an Italian home.

At Strettura (which, as the name indicates, is a very narrow part of the valley) we added two oxen to our horses, and began to ascend the Monte Somma, which, according to Murray, is nearly four thousand feet high where we crossed it. When we came to the steepest part of the ascent, Gaetano, who exercises a pretty decided control over his passengers, allowed us to walk; and we all, with one exception, alighted, and began to climb the mountain on foot. I walked on briskly, and soon left the rest of the party behind, reaching the top of the pass in such a short time that I could not believe it, and kept onward, expecting still another height to climb. But the road began to descend, winding among the depths of the hills as heretofore; now beside the dry, gravelly bed of a departed stream, now crossing it by a bridge, and perhaps passing through some other gorge, that yet gave no decided promise of an outlet into the world beyond. A glimpse might occasionally be caught, through a gap between the hill-tops, of a company of distant mountain peaks, pyramidal, as these hills are apt to be, and resembling the camp of an army of giants. The landscape was not altogether savage: sometimes a hill-side was covered with a rich field of grain, or an orchard of olive trees, looking not unlike puffs of smoke, from the peculiar hue of their foliage; but oftener there was a vast mantle of trees and shrubbery from top to bottom, the golden tufts of the broom shining out amid the verdure, and gladdening the whole. Nothing was dismal except the houses; those were always so, whether the compact, grey lines of village hovels, with a narrow street between, or the lonely farm-house, standing far apart from the road, built of stone, with window-gaps high in the wall, empty of glass; or the half-castle, half-dwelling, of which I saw a specimen or two, with what looked like a defensive rampart drawn around its court. I saw no look of comfort anywhere; and continually, in this wild and solitary region, I met beggars, just as if I were still in the streets of Rome. Boys and girls kept beside me, till they delivered me into the hands of others like themselves; hoary grandsires and grandmothers caught a glimpse of my approach, and tottered as fast as they could to intercept me; women came out of the cottages, with rotten cherries on a plate, entreating me to buy them for a mezzo baiocco; a man, at work on the road, left his toil to beg, and was grateful for the value of a cent; in short, I was never safe from importunity as long as there was a house or a human being in sight.

We arrived at Spoleto before noon, and while our *déjeûner* was being prepared, looked down from the window of the inn into the narrow street beneath, which, from the throng of people in it, I judged to be the principal one; priests, papal soldiers, women with no bonnets on their heads; peasants in breeches and mushroom hats; maids and matrons drawing water at a fountain; idlers smoking on a bench under the window; a talk, a bustle, but no genuine activity. After lunch we walked out to see the lions of Spoleto, and found our way up a steep and narrow street that led us to the city gate, at which, it is traditionally said, Hannibal sought to force an entrance after the battle of Thrasymene, and was repulsed. The gateway has a double arch, on the inner one of which is a tablet recording the above tradition as an unquestioned historical fact. From the gateway we went in search of the Duomo or Cathedral, and were kindly directed thither by an officer, who was descending into the town from the citadel, which is an old castle, now converted into a prison. The Cathedral seemed small, and did not much interest us, either by the Gothic front or its modernised interior. We saw nothing else in Spoleto, but went back to the inn and resumed our journey, emerging from the city into the classic valley of the Clitumnus, which we did not view under the best of auspices, because it was overcast, and the wind as chill as if it had the east in it. The valley, though fertile, and smilingly picturesque, perhaps, is not such as I should wish to celebrate, either in prose or poetry. It is of such breadth and extent that its frame of mountains and ridgy hills hardly serve to shut it in sufficiently, and the spectator thinks of a boundless plain rather than of a secluded vale. After passing Le Vene, we came to the little temple which Byron describes, and which has been supposed to be the one immortalised by Pliny. It is very small, and stands on a declivity that falls immediately from the road, right upon which rises the pediment of the temple, while the columns of the other front find sufficient height to develop themselves in the lower ground. A little farther down than the base of the edifice we saw the Clitumnus, so recently from its source in the marble rock that it was still as pure as a child's heart, and as transparent as truth itself. It looked airier than nothing, because it had not substance enough to brighten, and it was clearer than the atmosphere. I remember nothing else of the valley of Clitumnus, except that the beggars in this region of proverbial fertility are well-nigh profane in the urgency of their petitions; they absolutely fall down on their knees as you approach, in the same attitude as if they were praying to their Maker, and beseech you for alms with a fervency which I am afraid they seldom use before an altar or shrine. Being denied, they ran hastily beside the carriage, but got nothing, and finally gave over.

I am so very tired and sleepy that I mean to mention nothing else to-night, except the city of Trevi, which, on the approach from Spoleto, seems completely to cover a high, peaked hill, from its pyramidal tip to its base. It was the strangest situation in which to build a town, where, I should suppose, no horse can climb, and whence no inhabitant would think of descending into the world, after the approach of age should begin to stiffen his joints. On looking back on this most picturesque of towns (which the road, of course, did not enter, as evidently no road could), I saw that the highest part of the hill was quite covered with a crown of edifices, terminating in a church tower; while a part of the northern side was apparently too steep for building; and a cataract of houses flowed down the western and southern slopes. There seemed to be palaces, churches, everything that a city should have; but my eyes are heavy, and I can write no more about them; only that I suppose the summit of the hill was artificially tenured, so as to prevent its crumbling down, and enable it to support the platform of edifices which crowns it.

May 27th.—We reached Foligno in good season yesterday afternoon. Our inn seemed ancient; and, under the same roof, on one side of the entrance, was the stable, and on the other the coach-house. The house is built round a narrow court, with a well of water at bottom, and an opening in the roof at top, whence the staircases are lighted that wind round the sides of the court, up to the highest story. Our dining-room and bed-rooms were in the latter region, and were all paved with brick, and without carpets; and the characteristic of the whole was an exceeding plainness and antique clumsiness of fitting-up. We found ourselves sufficiently comfortable, however; and, as has been the case throughout our journey, had a very fair and well-cooked dinner. It shows, as perhaps I have already remarked, that it is still possible to live well in Italy, at no great expense, and that the high prices charged to the *forestieri* at Rome and elsewhere are artificial, and ought to be abated. . . . .

The day had darkened since morning, and was now ominous of rain; but as soon as we were established, we sallied out to see whatever was worth looking at. A beggar boy, with one leg, followed us, without asking for anything, apparently only for the pleasure of our company, though he kept at too great a distance for conversation, and indeed did not attempt to speak.

We went first to the cathedral, which has a Gothic front and a modernised interior, stuccoed and whitewashed, looking as neat as a New England meeting-house, and very mean, after our familiarity with the gorgeous churches in other cities. There were some pictures in the chapels, but, I believe, all modern, and I do not remember a single one of them. Next we went, without any guide, to a church attached to a convent of Dominican monks, with a Gothic exterior, and two hideous pictures of Death, the skeleton, leaning on his scythe, one on each side of the door. This church, likewise, was whitewashed, but we understood that it had been originally frescoed all over, and by famous hands; but these pictures, having become much injured, they were all obliterated, as we saw—all, that is to say, except a few specimens of the best preserved, which were spared to show the world what the whole had been. I thanked my stars that the obliteration of the rest had taken place before our visit; for if anything is dreary, and calculated to make the beholder utterly miserable, it is a faded fresco, with spots of the white plaster dotted over it.

Our one-legged boy had followed us into the church, and stood near the door till he saw us ready to come out, when he hurried on before us, and waited a little way off to see whither we should go. We still went on at random, taking the first turn that offered itself, and soon came to another old church—that of St. Mary Within the Walls—into which we entered, and found it whitewashed, like the other two. This was especially fortunate, for the doorkeeper informed us that, two years ago, the whole church (except, I suppose, the roof, which is of timber) had been covered with frescoes by Pinturicchio, all of which had been ruthlessly obliterated, except a very few fragments. These he proceeded to show us; poor, dim ghosts of what may once have been beautiful—now so far gone towards nothingness that I was hardly sure whether I saw a glimmering of the design or not. By-the-bye, it was not Pinturicchio, as I have written above, but Giotto, assisted, I believe, by Cimabue, who painted these frescoes. Our one-legged attendant had followed us also into this church, and again hastened out of it before us; and still we heard the dot ot his crutch upon the pavement, as we passed from street to street. By-and-by a sickly-looking man met us, and begged for "qualehe cosa;" but the boy shouted to him "Niente!" whether intimating that we would give him nothing, or that he himself had a prior claim to all our charity, I cannot tell. However, the beggar-man turned round, and likewise followed our devious course. Once or twice we missed him; but it was only because he could not walk so fast as we; for he appeared again as we emerged from the door of another church. Our one-legged friend we never missed for a moment; he kept pretty near us—near enough to be amused by our indecision whither to go; and he seemed much delighted when it began to rain, and he saw us at a loss how to find our way back to the hotel. Nevertheless, he did not offer to guide us; but stumped on behind with a faster or slower dot of his crutch, according to our pace. I began to think that he must have been engaged as a spy upon our movements by the police, who had taken away my passport at the city gate. In this way he attended us to the door of the hotel, where the beggar had already arrived. The latter again put in his doleful petition ; the one-legged boy said not a word, nor seemed to expect anything, and both had to go away without so much as a mezzo baioccho out of our pockets. The multitude of beggars in Italy makes the heart as obdurate as a paving-stone.

We left Foligno this morning, and, all ready for us at the door of the hotel, as we got into the carriage, were our friends, the beggar-man and the one-legged boy; the latter holding out his ragged hat, and smiling with as confident an air as if he had done us some very particular service, and were certain of being paid for it, as from contract. It was so very funny, so impudent, so utterly absurd, that I could not help giving him a trifle; but the man got nothing,—a fact that gives me a twinge. or. two, for he looked sickly and miserable. But where everybody begs, everybody, as a general rule, must be denied; and, besides, they act misery so well, that you are never sure of the genuine article.

PERUGIA.

May 28th.—As I said last night, we left Foligno betimes in the morning, which was bleak, chill, and very threatening; there being very little blue sky anywhere, and the clouds lying heavily on some of the mountain ridges. The wind blew sharply right in U——'s face and mine, as we occupied the coupé, so that there must have been a great deal of the north in it. We drove through a wide plain—the Umbrian valley, I suppose—and soon passed the old town of Spello, just touching its skirts, and wondering how people who had this rich and convenient plain from which to choose a site, could think of covering a huge island of rock with their dwellings—for Spello tumbled its crooked and narrow streets down a steep descent, and cannot well have a yard of even space within its walls. It is said to contain some rare treasures of ancient pictorial art.

I do not remember much that we saw on our route. The plains and the lower hill-sides seemed fruitful of everything that belongs to Italy, especially the olive and the vine. As usual, there were a great many shrines, and frequently a cross by the wayside. Hitherto it had been merely a plain wooden cross; but now almost every cross was hung with various instruments, represented in wood, apparently symbols of the crucifixion of our Saviour—the spear, the sponge, the crown of thorns, the hammer, a pair of pincers, and always St. Peter's cock made a prominent figure, generally perched on the summit of the cross.

From our first start this morning we had seen mists in various quarters, betokening that there was rain in those spots, and now it began to spatter in our own faces, although within the wide extent of our prospect we could see the sunshine falling on portions of the valley. A rainbow, too, shone out, and remained so long visible that it appeared to have made a permanent stain in the sky.

By-and-by we reached Assissi, which is magnificently situated for pictorial purposes, with a grey castle above it, and a grey wall around it, itself on a mountain, and looking over the great plain which we had been traversing, and through which lay our onward way. We drove through the Piazza Grande to an ancient house a little beyond, where a hospitable old lady receives travellers for a consideration, without exactly keeping an inn.

In the piazza we saw the beautiful front of a temple of Minerva, consisting of several marble pillars, fluted, and with rich capitals supporting a pediment. It was as fine as anything I had seen at Rome, and is now, of course, converted into a Catholic church.

I ought to have said that, instead of driving straight to the old lady's, we alighted at the door of a church near the city gate, and went in to inspect some melancholy frescoes, and thence clambered up a narrow street to the cathedral, which has a Gothic front, old enough, but not very impressive. I really remember not a single object that we saw within, but am pretty certain that the interior had been stuccoed and whitewashed. The ecclesiastics of old time did an excellent thing in covering the interiors of their churches with brilliant frescoes, thus filling the holy places with saints and angels, and almost with the presence of the divinity. The modern ecclesiastics do the next best thing in obliterating the wretched remnants of what has had its day and done its office. These frescoes might be looked upon as the symbol of the living spirit that made Catholicism a true religion, and glorified it so long as it did live; now the glory and beauty have departed from one and the other.

My wife, U——, and Miss Shepard now set out with a cicerone to visit the great Franciscan convent, in the church of which are preserved some miraculous specimens, in fresco and in oils, of early Italian art; but as I had no mind to suffer any further in this way, I stayed behind with J—— and R——, who were equally weary of these things.

After they were gone we took a ramble through the city, but were almost swept away by the violence of the wind, which struggled with me for my hat, and whirled R—— before it like a feather. The people in the public square seemed much diverted at our predicament, being, I suppose, accustomed to these rude blasts in their mountain home. However, the wind blew in momentary gusts, and then became more placable till another fit of fury came, and passed as suddenly as before. We walked out of the same gate through which we had entered—an ancient gate, but recently stuccoed and whitewashed, in wretched contrast to the grey, venerable wall through which it affords ingress—and I stood gazing at the magnificent prospect of the wide valley beneath. It was so vast that there appeared to be all varieties of weather in it at the same instant; fields of sunshine, tracts of storm—here the coming tempest, there the departing one. It was a picture of the world on a vast canvas, for there was rural life and city life within the great expanse, and the whole set in a frame of mountains—the nearest bold and distinct, with the rocky ledges showing through their sides; the distant ones blue and dim—so far stretched this broad valley.

When I had looked long enough—no, not long enough, for it would take a great while to read that page—we returned within the gates, and we clambered up, past the cathedral and into the narrow streets above it. The aspect of everything was immeasurably old; a thousand years would be but a middle age for one of those houses, built so massively with huge stones and solid arches, that I do not see how they are ever to tumble down, or to be less fit for human habitation than they are now. The streets crept between them, and beneath arched passages, and up and down steps of stone or ancient brick, for it would be altogether impossible for a carriage to ascend above the Grand Piazza, though possibly a donkey or a chairman's mule might find foothold. The city seems like a stony growth out of the hill-side, or a fossilised city—so old and singular it is, without enough life and juiciness in it to be susceptible of decay. An earthquake is the only chance of its ever being ruined, beyond its present ruin. Nothing is more strange than to think that this now dead city—dead, as regards the purposes for which men live nowadays—was, centuries ago, the seat and birth-place almost of art, the only art in which the beautiful part of the human mind then developed itself. How came that flower to grow among these wild mountains? I do not conceive, however, that the people of Assissi were ever much more enlightened or cultivated on the side of art than they are at present. The ecclesiastics were then the only patrons; and the flower grew here because there was a great ecclesiastical garden in which it was sheltered and fostered. But it is very curious to think of Assissi, a school of art within, and mountain and wilderness without.

My wife and the rest of the party returned from the convent before noon, delighted with what they had seen, as I was delighted not to have seen it. We ate our *déjeûner*, and resumed our journey, passing beneath the great convent, after emerging from the gate opposite to that of our entrance. The edifice made a very good spectacle, being of great extent, and standing on a double row of high and narrow arches, on which it is built up from the declivity of the hill.

We soon reached the church of St. Mary of the Angels, which is a modern structure, and very spacious, built in place of one destroyed by an earthquake. It is a fine church, opening out a magnificent space in its nave and aisles; and beneath the great dome stands the small old chapel, with its rude stone walls, in which St. Francis founded his order. This chapel and the dome appear to have been the only portions of the ancient church that were not destroyed by the earthquake. The dwelling of St. Francis is said to be also preserved within the church; but we did not see it, unless it were a little dark closet into which we squeezed to see some frescoes by La Spagna. It had an old wooden door, of which U—— picked off a little bit of a chip, to serve as a relic. There is a fresco in the church, on the pediment of the chapel, by Overbeck, representing the Assumption of the Virgin. It did not strike me as wonderfully fine. The other pictures, of which there were many, were modern, and of no great merit.

We pursued our way, and came, by-and-by, to the foot of the high hill on which stands Perugia, and which is so long and steep, that Gaetano took a yoke of oxen to aid his horses in the ascent. We all, except my wife, walked a part of the way up, and I myself, with J—— for my companion, kept on even to the city-gate, a distance, I should think, of two or three miles, at least. The lower part of the road was on the edge of the hill, with a narrow valley on our left; and as the sun had now broken out, its verdure and fertility, its foliage and cultivation shone forth in miraculous beauty, as green as England, as bright as only Italy. Perugia appeared above us, crowning a mighty hill, the most picturesque of cities; and the higher we ascended, the more the view opened before us, as we looked back on the course that we had traversed, and saw the wide valley, sweeping down and spreading out, bounded afar by mountains, and sleeping in sun and shadow. No language, nor any art of the pencil, can give an idea of the scene. When God expressed Himself in the landscape to mankind, He did not intend that it should be translated into any tongue save his own immediate one. J—— meanwhile, whose heart is now wholly in snail-shells, was rummaging for them among the stones and hedges by the roadside; yet, doubtless, enjoyed the prospect more than he knew. The coach lagged far behind us, and when it came up, we entered the gate, where a soldier appeared, and demanded my passport. We drove to the Grand Hôtel de France, which is near the gate, and two fine little boys ran beside the carriage, well dressed and well looking enough to have been a gentleman's sons, but claiming Gaetano for their father. He is an inhabitant of Perugia, and has therefore reached his own home, though we are still little more than midway to our journey's end.

Our hotel proves, thus far, to be the best that we have yet met with. We are only in the outskirts of Perugia, the bulk of the city, where the most interesting churches, and the public edifices are situated, being far above us on the hill. My wife, U——, Miss

Shepard, and R—— streamed forth immediately, and saw a church; but J——, who hates them, and I remained behind; and, for my part, I added several pages to this volume of scribble.

This morning was as bright as morning could be, even in Italy, and in this transparent mountain atmosphere. We at first declined the services of a cicerone, and went out in the hopes of finding our way to whatever we wished to see, by our own instincts. This proved to be a mistaken hope, however; and we wandered about the upper city, much persecuted by a shabby old man who wished to guide us; so, at last, Miss Shepard went back in quest of the cicerone at the hotel, and, meanwhile, we climbed to the summit of the hill of Perugia, and leaning over a wall, looked forth upon a most magnificent view of mountain and valley, terminating in some peaks, lofty and dim, which surely must be the Apennines. There again a young man accosted us, offering to guide us to the Cambio or Exchange; and as this was one of the places which we especially wished to see, we accepted his services. By-the-bye, I ought to have mentioned that we had already entered a church (San Luigi, I believe), the interior of which we found very impressive, dim with the light of stained and painted windows, insomuch that it at first seemed almost dark, and we could only see the bright twinkling of the tapers at the shrines; but, after a few minutes, we discerned the tall octagonal pillars of the nave, marble, and supporting a beautiful roof of crossed arches. The church was neither gothic nor classic, but a mixture of both, and most likely barbarous; yet it had a grand effect in its tinted twilight, and convinced me more than ever how desirable it is that religious edifices should have painted windows.

The door of the Cambio proved to be one that we had passed several times, while seeking for it, and was very near the church just mentioned, which fronts on one side of the same piazza. We were received by an old gentleman, who appeared to be a public officer; and found ourselves in a small room, wainscoted with beautifully carved oak, roofed with a coved ceiling, painted with symbols of the planets, and arabesqued in rich designs by Raphael, and lined with splendid frescoes of subjects, scriptural and historical, by Perugino. When the room was in its first glory, I can conceive that the world had not elsewhere to show, within so small a space, such magnificence and beauty as were then displayed here. Even now, I enjoyed (to the best of my belief, for we can never feel sure that we are not bamboozling ourselves in such matters) some real pleasure in what I saw; and especially seemed to feel, after all these ages, the old painter's devout sentiment still breathing forth from the religious pictures, the work of a hand that had so long been dust.

When we had looked long at these, the old gentleman led us into a chapel, of the same size as the former room, and built in the same fashion, wainscoted likewise with old oak. The walls were also frescoed,—entirely frescoed,—and retained more of their original brightness than those we had already seen, although the pictures were the production of a somewhat inferior hand, a pupil of Perugino. They seemed to be very striking, however, not the less so that one of them provoked an unseasonable smile. It was the decapitation of John the Baptist; and this holy personage was represented as still on his knees, with his hands clasped in prayer, although the executioner was already depositing the head in a charger, and the blood was spouting from the headless trunk, directly, as it were, into the face of the spectator.

While we were in the outer room the cicerone who first offered his services at the hotel had come in, so we paid our chance guide, and expected him to take his leave. It is characteristic of this idle country, however, that if you once speak to a person, or connect yourself with him by the slightest possible tie, you will hardly get rid of him by anything short of main force. He still lingered in the room, and was still there when I came away; for having had as many pictures as I could digest, I left my wife and U—— with the cicerone, and set out on a ramble with J——. We plunged from the upper city down through some of the strangest passages that ever were called streets; some of them, indeed, being arched all over; and going down into the unknown darkness, looked like caverns; and we followed one of them doubtfully, till it opened out upon the light. The houses on each side were divided only by a pace or two, and communicated with one another, here and there, by arched passages. They looked very ancient, and may have been inhabited by Etruscan princes, judging from the massiveness of some of the foundation stones. The present inhabitants, nevertheless, are by no means princely,—shabby men, and the care-worn wives and mothers of the people, one of whom was guiding a child in leading strings through those antique alleys, where hundreds of generations have trod before those little feet. Finally we came out through a gateway, the same gateway at which we entered last night.

I ought to have mentioned, in the narrative of

yesterday, that we crossed the Tiber shortly before reaching Perugia, already a broad and rapid stream, and already distinguished by the same turbid and mud-puddly quality of water that we see in it at Rome. I think it will never be so disagreeable to me hereafter, now that I find this turbidness to be its native colour, and not (like that of the Thames) accruing from city sewers or any impurities of the lowlands.

As I now remember, the small chapel in Santa Maria degli Angeli seems to have been originally the house of St. Francis.

May 29th.—This morning we visited the church of the Dominicans, where we saw some quaint pictures by Fra Angelico, with a good deal of religious sincerity in them; also a picture of St. Columbo by Perugino, which unquestionably is very good. To confess the truth, I took more interest in a fair Gothic monument, in white marble, of Pope Benedict XII., representing him reclining under a canopy, while two angels draw aside the curtain, the canopy being supported by twisted columns, richly ornamented. I like this overflow and gratuity of device with which Gothic sculpture works out its designs, after seeing so much of the simplicity of classic art in marble.

We then tried to find the church of San Pietro in Martire, but without success, although every person of whom we inquired immediately attached himself or herself to us, and could hardly be got rid of by any efforts on our part. Nobody seemed to know the church we wished for, but all directed us to another church of San Pietro, which contains nothing of interest; whereas the right church is supposed to contain a celebrated picture by Perugino.

Finally, we ascended the hill and the city proper of Perugia (for our hotel is in one of the suburbs), and J—— and I set out on a ramble about the city. It was market day, and the principal piazza, with the neighbouring streets, was crowded with people . . . .

The best part of Perugia—that in which the grand piazzas and the principal public edifices stand—seems to be a nearly level plateau on the summit of the hill; but it is of no very great extent, and the streets rapidly run downward on either side. J—— and I followed one of these descending streets, and were led a long way by it, till we at last emerged from one of the gates of the city, and had another view of the mountains and valleys, the fertile and sunny wilderness in which this ancient civilisation stands.

On the right of the gate there was a rude country-path, partly overgrown with grass, bordered by a hedge on one side, and on the other by the grey city wall, at the base of which the tract crept onward. We followed it, hoping that it would lead us to some other gate by which we might re-enter the city; but it soon grew so indistinct and broken, that it was evidently on the point of melting into somebody's olive orchard or wheat-fields or vineyards, all of which lay on the other side of the hedge; and a kindly old woman of whom I inquired told me (if I rightly understood her Italian) that I should find no further passage in that direction. So we turned back, much broiled in the hot sun, and only now and then relieved by the shadow of an angle or a tower.

A lame beggar-man sat by the gate, and as we passed him J—— gave him two baiocchi (which he himself had begged of me to buy an orange with), and was loaded with the pauper's prayers and benedictions as we entered the city. A great many blessings can be bought for very little money anywhere in Italy, and whether they avail anything or no, it is pleasant to see that the beggars have gratitude enough to bestow them in such abundance.

Of all beggars I think a little fellow who rode beside our carriage on a stick—his bare feet scampering merrily, while he managed his steed with one hand, and held out the other for charity, howling piteously the while—amused me most.

PASSIGNANO.

May 29th—We left Perugia at about three o'clock to-day, and went down a pretty steep descent; but I have no particular recollection of the road till it again began to descend, before reaching the village of Mugione. We all, except my wife, walked up the long hill, while the vetturo was dragged after us with the aid of a yoke of oxen. Arriving first at the village, I leaned over the wall to admire the beautiful *pacse* (" le bel piano," as a peasant called it who made acquaintance with me) that lay at the foot of the hill—so level, so bounded within moderate limits by a frame of hills and ridges that it looked like a green lake. In fact, I think it was once a real lake, which made its escape from its bed, as I have known some lakes to have done in America.

Passing through and beyond the village, I saw, on a height above the road, a half ruinous tower, with great cracks running down its walls, half way from top to bottom. Some little children had mounted the hill with us, begging all the way; they were recruited with additional members in the village;

and here, beneath the ruinous tower, a madman, as it seemed, assaulted us, and ran almost under the carriage-wheels in his earnestness to get a baioccho. Ridding ourselves of these annoyances we drove on, and, between five and six o'clock, came in sight of the lake of Thrasymene, obtaining our first view of it, I think, in its longest extent. There were high hills, and one mountain with its head in the clouds, visible on the farther shore, and on the horizon beyond it; but the nearer banks were long ridges, and hills of only moderate height. The declining sun threw a broad sheen of brightness over the surface of the lake, so that we could not well see it for excess of light; but had a vision of headlands and islands floating about in a flood of gold, and blue, airy heights bounding it afar. When we first drew near the lake there was but a narrow tract, covered with vines and olives, between it and the hill that rose on the other side; as we advanced the tract grew wider, and was very fertile, as was the hill-side, with wheat-fields and vines and olives, especially the latter, which, symbol of peace as it is, seemed to find something congenial to it in the soil, stained long ago with blood. Farther onward, the space between the lake and hill grew still narrower, the road skirting along almost close to the water-side; and when we reached the town of Passignano there was but room enough for its dirty and ugly street to stretch along the shore. I have seldom beheld a lovelier scene than that of the lake and the landscape around it; never an uglier one than that of this idle and decaying village, where we were immediately surrounded by beggars of all ages, and by men vociferously proposing to row us out upon the lake. We declined their offers of a boat, for the evening was very fresh and cool, insomuch that I should have liked an outside garment— a temperature that I had not anticipated, so near the beginning of June, in sunny Italy. Instead of a row, we took a walk through the village, hoping to come upon the shore of the lake, in some secluded spot; but an incredible number of beggar children, both boys and girls, but more of the latter, rushed out of every door, and went along with us, all howling their miserable petitions at the same moment. The village street is long, and our escort waxed more numerous at every step, till Miss Shepard actually counted forty of these little reprobates, and more were doubtless added afterwards. At first, no doubt, they begged in earnest hope of getting some baiocchi; but, by-and-by, perceiving that we had determined not to give them anything, they made a joke of the matter, and began to laugh and to babble, and turn heels over head, still keeping about us, like a swarm of flies, and now and then begging again with all their might. There were as few pretty faces as I ever saw among the same number of children; and they were as ragged and dirty little imps as any in the world, and, moreover, tainted the air with a very disagreeable odour from their rags and dirt; rugged and healthy enough, nevertheless, and sufficiently intelligent; certainly bold and persevering too; so that it is hard to say what they needed to fit them for success in life. Yet they begin as beggars, and no doubt will end so, as all their parents and grandparents do; for in our walk through the village, every old woman, and many younger ones, held out their hands for alms, as if they had all been famished. Yet these people kept their houses over their heads; had firesides in winter, I suppose, and food out of their little gardens every day; pigs to kill, chickens, olives, wine, and a great many things to make life comfortable. The children, desperately as they begged, looked in good bodily case, and happy enough; but, certainly, there was a look of earnest misery in the faces of some of the old women, either genuine or exceedingly well acted.

I could not bear the persecution, and went into our

hotel, determining not to venture out again till our departure, at least not in the daylight. My wife, and the rest of the family, however, continued their walk, and at length were relieved from their little pests by three policemen (the very images of those in Rome, in their blue, long-skirted coats, cocked chapeaux bras, white shoulder-belts, and swords), who boxed their ears, and dispersed them. Meanwhile, they had quite driven away all sentimental effusion (of which I felt more, really, than I expected) about the lake of Thrasymene.

The inn of Passignano promised little from its outward appearance; a tall, dark old house, with a stone staircase leading us up from one sombre story to another, into a brick-paved dining-room, with our sleeping chambers on each side. There was a fireplace of tremendous depth and height, fit to receive big forest-logs, and with a queer, double pair of ancient andirons, capable of sustaining them; and, in a handful of ashes lay a small stick of olive-wood; a specimen, I suppose, of the sort of fuel which had made the chimney black, in the course of a good many years. There must have been much shivering and misery of cold around this fire-place. However, we needed no fire now, and there was promise of good cheer in the spectacle of a man cleaning some lake-fish for our dinner, while the poor things flounced and wriggled under the knife.

The dinner made its appearance, after á long while, and was most plentiful, ... so that, having measured our appetite in anticipation of a paucity of food, we had to make more room for such overflowing abundance.

When dinner was over, it was already dusk, and before retiring I opened the window, and looked out on Lake Thrasymene, the margin of which lies just on the other side of the narrow village street. The moon was a day or two past the full, just a little clipt on the edge, but gave light enough to show the lake and its nearer shores, almost as distinctly as by day; and there being a ripple on the surface of the water, it made a sheen of silver over a wide space.

AREZZO.

May 30th.—We started at six o'clock, and left the one ugly street of Passignano, before many of the beggars were awake. Immediately in the vicinity of the village there is very little space between the lake in front and the ridge of hills in the rear, but the plain widened as we drove onward, so that the lake was scarcely to be seen, or often quite hidden among the intervening trees, although we could still discern the summits of the mountains that rise far beyond its shores. The country was fertile, presenting on each side of the road vines trained on fig-trees, wheat-fields and olives, in greater abundance than any other product. On our right, with a considerable width of plain between, was the bending ridge of hills that shut in the Roman army, by its close approach to the lake at Passignano. In perhaps half an hour's drive we reached the little bridge that throws its arch over the Sanguinetto, and alighted there. The stream has but about a yard's width of water, and its whole course, between the hills and the lake, might well have been reddened and swollen with the blood of the multitude of slain Romans. Its name put me in mind of the Bloody Brook at Deerfield, where a company of Massachusetts' men were massacred by the Indians.

The Sanguinetto flows over a bed of pebbles, and J—— crept under the bridge, and got one of them for a memorial, while U——, Miss Shepard, and R—— plucked some olive twigs and oak leaves, and made them into wreaths together—symbols of victory and peace. The tower, which is traditionally named after Hannibal, is seen on a height that makes part of the line of enclosing hills. It is a large, old castle, apparently of the middle ages, with a square front, and a battlemented sweep of wall. The town of Torres (its name, I think), where Hannibal's main army is supposed to have lain, while the Romans came through the pass, was in full view; and I could understand the plan of the battle better than any system of military operations which I have hitherto tried to fathom. Both last night and to-day I found myself stirred more sensibly than I expected by the influences of this scene. The old battle-field is still fertile in thoughts and emotions, though it is so many ages since the blood spilt there has ceased to make the grass and flowers grow more luxuriantly. I doubt whether I should feel so much on the field of Saratoga or Monmouth; but these old classic battle-fields belong to the whole world, and each man feels as if his own forefathers fought them. Mine, by-the-bye, if they fought them at all, must have been on the side of Hannibal; for, certainly, I sympathised with him, and exulted in the defeat of the Romans on their own soil. They excite much the same emotion of general hostility that the English do. Byron has written some very fine stanzas on this battle-field—not so good as others that he has written on classical scenes and subjects, yet wonderfully impressing his own perception of the subject on the reader. Whenever he has to deal with a statue, a ruin, a battle-field, he pounces upon the topic like a vulture, and tears out its heart in a twinkling, so that there is nothing more to be said.

If I mistake not, our passport was examined by the papal officers at the last custom-house in the Pontifical territory, before we traversed the path through which the Roman army marched to its destruction. Lake Thrasymene, of which we took our last view, is not deep set among the hills, but is bordered by long ridges, with loftier mountains receding into the distance. It is not to be compared to Windermere or Loch Lomond for beauty, nor with Lake Champlain and many a smaller lake in my own country, none of which, I hope, will ever become so historically interesting as this famous spot. A few miles onward our passport was countersigned at the Tuscan custom-house, and our luggage permitted to pass without examination on payment of a fee of nine or ten pauls, besides two pauls to the porters. There appears to be no concealment on the part of the officials in thus waiving the exercise of their duty, and I rather imagine that the thing is recognised and permitted by their superiors. At all events, it is very convenient for the traveller.

We saw Cortona, sitting, like so many other cities in this region, on its hill, and arrived about noon at

Arezzo, which also stretches up a high hill-side, and is surrounded, as they all are, by its wall, or the remains of one, with a fortified gate across every entrance.

I remember one little village, somewhere in the neighbourhood of the Clitumnus, which we entered by one gateway, and, in the course of two minutes at the utmost, left by the opposite one, so diminutive was this walled town. Everything hereabouts bears traces of times when war was the prevalent condition, and peace only a rare gleam of sunshine.

At Arezzo we have put up at the Hôtel Royal, which has the appearance of a grand old house, and proves to be a tolerable inn enough. After lunch we wandered forth to see the town, which did not greatly interest me after Perugia, being much more modern and less picturesque in its aspect. We went to the cathedral, a Gothic edifice, but not of striking exterior. As the doors were closed, and not to be opened till three o'clock, we seated ourselves under the trees, on a high grassy space surrounded and intersected with gravel-walks—a public promenade, in short, near the cathedral; and after resting ourselves here we went in search of Petrarch's house, which Murray mentions as being in this neighbourhood. We inquired of several people, who knew nothing about the matter; one woman misdirected us, out of mere fun, I believe, for she afterwards met us and asked how we had succeeded. But finally, through ——'s enterprise and perseverance, we found the spot, not a stone's throw from where we had been sitting.

Petrarch's house stands below the promenade which I have just mentioned, and within hearing of the reverberations between the strokes of the cathedral bell. It is two stories high, covered with a light-coloured stucco, and has not the slightest appearance of antiquity, no more than many a modern and modest dwelling-house in an American city. Its only remarkable feature is a pointed arch of stone, let into the plastered wall, and forming a framework for the doorway. I set my foot on the doorsteps, ascended them, and Miss Shepard and J—— gathered some weeds or blades of grass that grew in the chinks between the steps. There is a long inscription on a slab of marble set in the front of the house, as is the fashion in Arezzo when a house has been the birthplace or residence of a distinguished man.

Right opposite Petrarch's birth-house—and it must have been the well whence the water was drawn that first bathed him—is a well which Boccaccio has introduced into one of his stories. It is surrounded with a stone curb, octagonal in shape, and evidently as ancient as Boccaccio's time. It has a wooden cover, through which is a square opening, and looking down I saw my own face in the water far beneath.

There is no familiar object connected with daily life so interesting as a well; and this well of old Arezzo, whence Petrarch had drank, around which he had played in his boyhood, and which Boccaccio has made famous, really interested me more than the cathedral. It lies right under the pavement of the street, under the sunshine, without any shade of trees about it, or any grass, except a little that grows in the crevices of its stones; but the shape of its stonework would make it a pretty object in an engraving. As I lingered round it I thought of my own townpump in old Salem, and wondered whether my townspeople would ever point it out to strangers, and whether the stranger would gaze at it with any degree of such interest as I felt in Boccaccio's well. Oh, certainly not; but yet I made that humble townpump the most celebrated structure in the good town. A thousand and a thousand people had pumped there, merely to water oxen or fill their tea-kettles; but when once I grasped the handle, a rill gushed forth that meandered as far as England—as far as India—

besides tasting pleasantly in every town and village of our own country. I like to think of this, so long after I did it, and so far from home, and am not without hopes of some kindly local remembrance on this score.

Petrarch's house is not a separate and insulated building, but stands in contiguity and connection with other houses on each side; and all, when I saw them, as well as the whole street, extending down the slope of the hill, had the bright and sunny aspect of a modern town.

As the cathedral was not yet open, and as J—— and I had not so much patience as my wife, we left her and Miss Shepard, and set out to return to the hotel. We lost our way, however, and finally had to return to the cathedral, to take a fresh start; and as the door was now open, we went in. We found the cathedral very stately, with its great arches, and darkly magnificent with the dim rich light coming through its painted windows, some of which are reckoned the most beautiful that the whole world has to show. The hues are far more brilliant than those of any painted glass I saw in England, and a great wheel window looks like a constellation of many coloured gems. The old English glass gets so smoky and dull with dust, that its pristine beauty cannot any longer be even imagined; nor did I imagine it till I saw these Italian windows. We saw nothing of my wife and Miss Shepard; but found afterwards that they had been much annoyed by the attentions of a priest, who wished to show them the cathedral till they finally told him that they had no money with them, when he left them, without another word. The attendants in churches seem to be quite as venal as most other Italians, and, for the sake of their little profit, they do not hesitate to interfere with the great purposes for which their churches were built and decorated; hanging curtains, for instance, before all the celebrated pictures, or hiding them away in the sacristy, so that they cannot be seen without a fee.

Returning to the hotel we looked out of the window, and in the street beneath there was a very busy scene, it being Sunday, and the whole population apparently being astir, promenading up and down the smooth flagstones, which made the breadth of the street one side walk; or at their windows, or sitting before their doors.

The vivacity of the population in these parts is very striking, after the gravity and lassitude of Rome; and the air was made cheerful with the talk and laughter of hundreds of voices. I think the women are prettier than the Roman maids and matrons, who, as I think I have said before, have chosen to be very uncomely since the rape of their ancestresses, by way of wreaking a terrible spite and revenge.

I have nothing more to say of Arezzo, except that, finding the ordinary wine very bad, as black as ink, and tasting as if it had tar and vinegar in it, we called for a bottle of Monte Pulciano, and were exceedingly gladdened and mollified thereby.

INCISA.

We left Arezzo early on Monday morning, the sun throwing the long shadows of the trees across the road, which at first, after we had descended the hill, lay over a plain. As the morning advanced—or as we advanced—the country grew more hilly. We saw many bits of rustic life—such as old women tending pigs or sheep by the roadside, and spinning with a distaff; women sewing under trees, or at their own doors; children leading goats, tied by the horns, while they browse; sturdy, sunburnt creatures, in petticoats, but otherwise manlike, at work side by side with male labourers in the fields. The broad-brimmed, high-crowned hat of Tuscan straw is the customary female head-dress, and is as unbecoming as can possibly be imagined, and of little use, one would suppose, as a shelter from the sun, the brim continually blowing upward from the face. Some of the elder women wore black felt hats, likewise broad-brimmed; and the men wore felt hats also, shaped a good deal like a mushroom, with hardly any brim at all. The scenes in the villages through which we passed were very lively and characteristic, all the population seeming to be out of doors;—some at the butcher's shop, others at the well; a tailor sewing in the open air, with a young priest sitting sociably beside him; children at play; women mending clothes, embroidering, spinning with the distaff at their own doorsteps; many idlers, letting the pleasant morning pass in the sweet-do-nothing; all assembling in the street, as in the common room of one large household, and thus brought close together, and made familiar with one another, as they can never be in a different system of society. As usual, along the road we passed multitudes of shrines, where the Virgin was painted in fresco, or sometimes represented in bas-reliefs, within niches, or under more spacious arches. It would be a good idea to place a comfortable and shady seat beneath all these wayside shrines, where the wayfarer might rest himself, and thank the Virgin for her hospitality; nor can I believe that it would offend her, any more than other incense, if he were to regale himself, even in such consecrated spots, with the fragrance of a pipe or cigar.

In the wire-work screen, before many of the shrines, hung offerings of roses and other flowers, some wilted and withered, some fresh with that morning's dew, some that never bloomed and never faded, being artificial. I wonder that they do not plant rose trees and all kinds of fragrant and flowering shrubs under the shrines, and twine and wreathe them all around, so that the Virgin may dwell within a bower of perpetual freshness; at least put flower-pots, with living plants, into the niche. There are many things in the customs of these people that might be made very beautiful, if the sense of beauty were as much alive now as it must have been when these customs were first imagined and adopted.

I must not forget, among these little descriptive items, the spectacle of women and girls bearing huge bundles of twigs and shrubs, or grass, with scarlet poppies and blue flowers intermixed; the bundles sometimes so huge as almost to hide the woman's figure from head to heel, so that she looked like a locomotive mass of verdure and flowers; sometimes reaching only half way down her back, so as to show the crooked knife slung behind, with which she had been reaping this strange harvest-sheaf. A Pre-Raphaelite painter—the one, for instance, who painted the heap of autumnal leaves, which we saw at the Manchester Exhibition—would find an admirable subject in one of these girls, stepping with a free, erect, and graceful carriage, her burthen on her head; and the miscellaneous herbage and flowers would give him all the scope he could desire for minute and various delineation of nature.

The country houses which we passed had sometimes open galleries or arcades on the second story and above, where the inhabitants might perform their domestic labour in the shade and in the air. The houses were often ancient, and most picturesquely time-stained, the plaster dropping in spots from the old brickwork; others were tinted of pleasant and cheerful hues; some were frescoed with designs in arabesques, or with imaginary windows; some had escutcheons of arms painted on the front. Wherever there was a pigeon-house, a flight of doves were represented as flying into the holes, doubtless for the invitation and encouragement of the real birds.

Once or twice I saw a bush stuck up before the door of what seemed to be a wine shop. If so, it is the ancient custom, so long disused in England, and alluded to in the proverb, "Good wine needs no bush." Several times we saw grass spread to dry on the road, covering half the track, and concluded it to have been cut by the roadside for the winter forage of his ass by some poor peasant, or peasant's wife, who had no grass land, except the margin of the public way.

A beautiful feature of the scene to-day, as the preceding day, were the vines growing on fig trees (?),* and often wreathed in rich festoons from one tree to another, by-and-by to be hung with clusters of purple grapes. I suspect the vine is a pleasanter object of sight under this mode of culture than it can be in countries where it produces a more precious wine, and therefore is trained more artificially. Nothing can be more picturesque than the spectacle of an old grape-vine, with almost a trunk of its own, clinging round its tree, imprisoning within its strong embrace the friend that supported its tender infancy, converting the tree wholly to its own selfish ends, as seemingly flexible natures are apt to do, stretching out its innumerable arms on every bough, and allowing hardly a leaf to sprout except its own. I must not yet quit this hasty sketch, without throwing in, both

* This interrogation mark must mean that Mr. Hawthorne was not sure they were fig trees.—ED.

in the early morning, and later in the forenoon, the mist that dreamed among the hills, and which—now that I have called it mist—I feel almost more inclined to call light, being so quietly cheerful with the sunshine through it. Put in, now and then, a castle on a hill-top; a rough ravine, a smiling valley; a mountain stream, with a far wider bed than it at present needs, and a stone bridge across it, with ancient and massive arches;—and I shall say no more, except that all these particulars, and many better ones which escape me, made up a very pleasant whole.

At about noon we drove into the village of Incisa, and alighted at the albergo where we were to lunch. It was a gloomy old house, as much like my idea of an Etruscan tomb as anything else that I can compare it to. We passed into a wide and lofty entrance-hall, paved with stone, and vaulted with a roof of intersecting arches, supported by heavy columns of stuccoed-brick, the whole as sombre and dingy as can well be. This entrance-hall is not merely the passage-way into the inn, but is likewise the carriage-house, into which our vetturo is wheeled; and it has, on one side, the stable, odorous with the litter of horses and cattle; and on the other the kitchen, and a common sitting-room. A narrow stone staircase leads from it to the dining-room, and chambers above, which are paved with brick, and adorned with rude frescoes instead of paper-hangings. We look out of the windows, and step into a little iron-railed balcony before the principal window, and observe the scene in the village street. The street is narrow, and nothing can exceed the tall, grim ugliness of the village houses, many of them four stories high, contiguous all along, and paved quite across; so that nature is as completely shut out from the precincts of this little town as from the heart of the widest city. The walls of the houses are plastered, grey, dilapidated; the windows small, some of them drearily closed with wooden shutters, others flung wide open, and with women's heads protruding; others merely frescoed, for a show of light and air. It would be a hideous street to look at in a rainy day, or when no human life pervaded it. Now it has vivacity enough to keep it cheerful. People lounge round the door of the albergo, and watch the horses as they drink from a stone trough, which is built against the wall of the house, and filled with the unseen gush of a spring.

At first there is a shade entirely across the street, and all the within-doors of the village empties itself there, and keeps up a babblement that seems quite disproportioned even to the multitude of tongues that make it. So many words are not spoken in a New England village in a whole year as here in this single day. People talk about nothing as if they were terribly in earnest, and laugh at nothing as if it were an excellent joke.

As the hot noon sunshine encroaches on our side of the street, it grows a little more quiet. The loungers now confine themselves to the shady margin (growing narrower and narrower) of the other side, where, directly opposite the albergo, there are two cafés and a wine shop, " vendeta di pane, vino, ed altri generi," all in a row with benches before them. The benchers joke with the women passing by, and are joked with back again. The sun still eats away the shadow inch by inch, beating down with such intensity that finally everybody disappears except a few passers by.

Doubtless the village snatches this half-hour for its siesta. There is a song, however, inside one of the cafés, with a burden in which several voices join. A girl goes through the street, sheltered under her great bundle of freshly-cut grass. By-and-by the song ceases, and two young peasants come out of the café, a little affected by liquor, in their shirt-sleeves and bare feet, with their trousers tucked up. They resume their song in the street, and dance along, one's arm around his fellow's neck, his own waist grasped by the other's arm. They whirl one another quite round about, and come down upon their feet. Meeting a village maid coming quietly along, they dance up and intercept her for a moment, but give way to her sobriety of aspect. They pass on, and the shadow soon begins to spread from one side of the street, which presently fills again, and becomes once more, for its size, the noisiest place I ever knew.

We had quite a tolerable dinner at this ugly inn, where many preceding travellers had written their condemnatory judgments, as well as a few their favourable ones, in pencil on the walls of the diningroom.

TO FLORENCE.

At setting off [from Incisa] we were surrounded by beggars as usual, the most interesting of whom were a little blind boy and his mother, who had besieged us with gentle pertinacity during our whole stay there. There was likewise a man with a maimed hand, and other hurts or deformities; also an old woman who, I suspect, only pretended to be blind, keeping her eyes tightly squeezed together, but directing her hand very accurately where the copper shower was expected to fall. Besides these, there were a good many sturdy little rascals, vociferating in proportion as they needed nothing. It was touching, however, to see several persons — themselves beggars for aught I know—assisting to hold up the little blind boy's tremulous hand, so that he, at all events, might not lack the pittance which we had to give. Our dole was but a poor one after all, consisting of what Roman coppers we had brought into Tuscany with us; and as we drove off, some of the boys ran shouting and whining after us in the hot sunshine, nor stopped till we reached the summit of the hill, which rises immediately from the village-street. We heard Gaetano once say a good thing to a swarm of beggar children who were infesting us, "Are your fathers all dead?" a proverbial expression, I suppose. The pertinacity of beggars does not, I think, excite the indignation of an Italian, as it is apt to do that of Englishmen or Americans. The Italians probably sympathise more, though they give less. Gaetano is very gentle in his modes of repelling them, and, indeed, never interferes at all, as long as there is a prospect of their getting anything.

Immediately after leaving Incisa we saw the Arno, already a considerable river, rushing between deep banks, with the greenish hue of a duck-pond diffused through its water. Nevertheless, though the first impression was not altogether agreeable, we soon became reconciled to this hue, and ceased to think it an indication of impurity; for, in spite of it, the river is still to a certain degree transparent, and is, at any rate, a mountain-stream, and comes uncontaminated from its source. The pure, transparent brown of the New England rivers is the most beautiful colour; but I am content that it should be peculiar to them.

Our afternoon's drive was through scenery less striking than some which we had traversed, but still picturesque and beautiful. We saw deep valleys and ravines, with streams at the bottom; long, wooded hill-sides, rising far and high, and dotted with white dwellings, well towards the summits. By-and-by, we had a distant glimpse of Florence, showing its great dome and some of its towers out of a side-long valley, as if we were between two great waves of the tumultuous sea of hills; while, far beyond, rose in the distance the blue peaks of three or four of the Apennines, just on the remote horizon. There being a haziness in the atmosphere, however, Florence was little more distinct to us than the Celestial City was to Christian and Hopeful, when they spied at it from the Delectable Mountains.

Keeping steadfastly onward, we ascended a winding road, and passed a grand villa, standing very high, and surrounded with extensive grounds. It must be the residence of some great noble; and it has an avenue of poplars or aspens, very light and gay, and fit for the passage of the bridal procession, when the proprietor or his heir brings home his bride; while, in another direction, from the same front of the palace stretches an avenue or grove of cypresses, very long, and exceedingly black and dismal, like a train of gigantic mourners. I have seen few things more striking, in the way of trees, than this grove of cypresses.

From this point we descended, and drove along an ugly, dusty avenue, with a high brick wall on one side or both, till we reached the gate of Florence, into which we were admitted with as little trouble as custom-house officers, soldiers, and policemen can possibly give. They did not examine our luggage, and even declined a fee, as we had already paid one at the frontier custom-house. Thank heaven, and the Grand Duke!

As we hoped that the Casa del Bello had been taken for us, we drove thither in the first place, but found that the bargain had not been concluded. As the house and studio of Mr. Powers were just on the opposite side of the street, I went to it, but found him too much engrossed to see me at the moment; so I returned to the vettura, and we told Gaetano to carry us to a hotel. He established us at the Albergo della Fontana, a good and comfortable house. . . . . Mr. Powers called in the evening—a plain personage, characterised by strong simplicity and warm kindliness, with an impending brow, and large eyes, which kindle as he speaks. He is grey, and slightly bald, but does not seem elderly, nor past his prime. I accept him at once as an honest and trustworthy man, and shall not vary from this judgment. Through his good offices, the next day, we engaged the Casa del Bello, at a rent of fifty dollars a month, and I shall take another opportunity (my fingers and head being tired now) to write about the house, and Mr. Powers, and what appertains to him, and about the beautiful city of Florence. At present, I shall only say further, that this journey from Rome has been one of the brightest and most uncareful interludes of my life; we have all enjoyed it exceedingly, and I am happy that our children have it to look back upon.

June 4*th*.—At our visit to Powers' studio on Tuesday, we saw a marble copy of the Fisher-boy holding a shell to his ear, and the bust of Proserpine, and two or three other ideal busts; various casts of most of the ideal statues and portrait busts which he has executed. He talks very freely about his works, and is no exception to the rule that an artist is not apt to speak in a very laudatory style of a brother artist. He showed us a bust of Mr. Sparks by Persico,—a lifeless and thoughtless thing enough, to be sure,— and compared it with a very good one of the same gentleman by himself; but his chiefest scorn was bestowed on a wretched and ridiculous image of Mr. King, of Alabama, by Clarke Mills, of which he said he had been employed to make several copies for Southern gentlemen. The consciousness of power is plainly to be seen, and the assertion of it by no means withheld, in his simple and natural character; nor does it give me an idea of vanity on his part to see and hear it. He appears to consider himself neglected by his country—by the government of it, at least—and talks with indignation of the by-ways and political intrigue which, he thinks, win the rewards that ought to be bestowed exclusively on merit. An appropriation of twenty-five thousand dollars was made, some years ago, for a work of sculpture by him, to be placed in the Capitol; but the intermediate measures necessary to render it effective have been delayed; while the above-mentioned Clarke Mill—certainly the greatest bungler that ever botched a block of marble—has received an order for an equestrian statue of Washington. Not that Mr. Powers is made bitter or sour by these wrongs, as he considers them: he talks of them with the frankness of his disposition when the topic comes in his way, and is pleasant, kindly, and sunny when he has done with it.

His long absence from our country has made him think worse of us than we deserve; and it is an effect of what I myself am sensible, in my shorter exile: the most piercing shriek, the wildest yell, and all the ugly sounds of popular turmoil, inseparable from the life of a republic, being a million times more audible than the peaceful hum of prosperity and content which is going on all the while.

He talks of going home, but says that he has been talking of it every year since he first came to Italy; and between his pleasant life of congenial labour, and his idea of moral deterioration in America, I think it doubtful whether he ever crosses the sea again. Like most exiles of twenty years, he has lost his native country without finding another; but then it is as well to recognise the truth,—that an individual country is by no means essential to one's comfort.

Powers took us into the farthest room, I believe, of his very extensive studio, and showed us a statue of

Washington that has much dignity and stateliness. He expressed, however, great contempt for the coat and breeches, and masonic emblems, in which he had been required to drape the figure. What would he do with Washington, the most decorous and respectable personage that ever went ceremoniously through the realities of life? Did anybody ever see Washington nude? It is inconceivable. He had no nakedness, but I imagine he was born with his clothes on, and his hair powdered, and made a stately bow on his first appearance in the world. His costume, at all events, was a part of his character, and must be dealt with by whatever sculptor undertakes to represent him. I wonder that so very sensible a man as Powers should not see the necessity of accepting drapery, and the very drapery of the day, if he will keep his art alive. It is his business to idealise the tailor's actual work. But he seems to be especially fond of nudity, none of his ideal statues, so far as I know them, having so much as a rag of clothes. His statue of "California," lately finished, and as naked as Venus, seemed to me a very good work; not an actual woman, capable of exciting passion, but evidently a little out of the category of human nature. In one hand she holds a divining rod. "She says to the emigrants," observed Powers, "'Here is the gold, if you choose to take it.'" But in her face, and in her eyes, very finely expressed, there is a look of latent mischief, rather grave than playful, yet somewhat impish or sprite-like; and, in the other hand, behind her back, she holds a bunch of thorns. Powers calls her eyes Indian. The statue is true to the present fact and history of California, and includes the age-long truth as respects the "auri sacra fames." . . . .

When we had looked sufficiently at the sculpture, Powers proposed that we should now go across the street and see the Casa del Bello. We did so in a body, Powers in his dressing-gown and slippers, and his wife and daughters without assuming any street costume.

The Casa del Bello is a palace of three pianos, the topmost of which is occupied by the Countess of St. George, an English lady, and two lower pianos are to be let, and we looked at both. The upper one would have suited me well enough; but the lower has a terrace, with a rustic summer-house over it, and is connected with a garden, where there are arbours and a willow tree, and a little wilderness of shrubbery and roses, with a fountain in the midst. It has likewise an immense suite of rooms, round the four sides of a small court—spacious, lofty, with frescoed ceilings and rich hangings, and abundantly furnished with arm-chairs, sofas, marble tables, and great looking-glasses. Not that these last are a great temptation, but in our wandering life I wished to be perfectly comfortable myself, and to make my family so, for just this summer, and so I have taken the lower piano, the price being only fifty dollars per month (entirely furnished, even to silver and linen). Certainly this is something like the paradise of cheapness we were told of, and which we vainly sought in Rome. . . . . . .

To me has been assigned the pleasantest room for my study; and when I like I can overflow into the summer-house or an arbour, and sit there dreaming of a story. The weather is delightful—too warm to walk, but perfectly fit to do nothing in, in the coolness of these great rooms. Every day I shall write a little, perhaps—and probably take a brief nap somewhere between breakfast and tea— but go to see pictures and statues occasionally, and so assuage and mollify myself a little after that uncongenial life of the consulate, and before going back to my own hard and dusty New England.

After concluding the arrangement for the Casa del Bello, we stood talking a little while with Powers and his wife and daughter before the door of the house, for they seem so far to have adopted the habits of the Florentines as to feel themselves at home on the shady side of the street. The out-of-door life and free communication with the pavement, habitual apparently among the middle classes, reminds one of the plays of Molière and other old dramatists, in which the street or the square becomes a sort of common parlour, where most of the talk and scenic business of the people is carried on.

June 5th.—For two or three mornings after breakfast I have rambled a little about the city till the shade grew narrow beneath the walls of the houses, and the heat made it uncomfortable to be in motion. To-day I went over the Ponte Carraja, and thence into and through the heart of the city, looking into several churches, in all of which I found people taking advantage of the cool breadth of these sacred interiors to refresh themselves and say their prayers. Florence at first struck me as having the aspect of a very new city in comparison with Rome; but, on closer acquaintance, I find that many of the buildings are antique and massive, though still the clear atmosphere, the bright sunshine, the light, cheerful hues of the stucco, and—as much as anything else, perhaps—the vivacious character of the human life in the streets, take away the sense of its being an ancient city. The streets are delightful to walk in after so many penitential pilgrimages as I have made over those little square, uneven blocks of the Roman pavement, which wear out the boots and torment the soul. I absolutely walk on the smooth flags of Florence for the mere pleasure of walking, and live in its atmosphere for the mere pleasure of living; and, warm as the weather is getting to be, I never feel that inclination to sink down in a heap and never stir again, which was my dull torment and misery as long as I stayed in Rome. I hardly think there can be a place in the world where life is more delicious for its own simple sake than here.

I went to-day into the Baptistery which stands near the Duomo, and, like that, is covered externally with slabs of black and white marble, now grown brown and yellow with age. The edifice is octagonal, and on entering one immediately thinks of the Pantheon—the whole space within being free from side to side, with a dome above; but it differs from the severe simplicity of the former edifice, being elaborately ornamented with marble and frescoes, and lacking that great eye in the roof that looks so nobly and reverently heavenward from the Pantheon. I did little more than pass through the Baptistery, glancing at the famous bronze doors, some perfect and admirable casts of which I had already seen at the Crystal Palace.

The entrance of the Duomo being just across the piazza, I went in there after leaving the Baptistery, and was struck anew—for this is the third or fourth visit—with the dim grandeur of the interior, lighted as it is almost exclusively by painted windows, which seem to me worth all the variegated marbles and rich cabinet-work of St. Peter's. The Florentine cathedral has a spacious and lofty nave, and side aisles divided from it by pillars; but there are no chapels along the aisles, so that there is far more breadth and freedom of interior in proportion to the actual space than is usual in churches. It is woeful to think how the vast capaciousness within St. Peter's is thrown away, and made to seem smaller than it is by every possible device, as if on purpose. The pillars and walls of this Duomo are of a uniform brownish, neutral tint; the pavement, a mosaic work of marble; the ceiling of the dome itself is covered with frescoes, which, being very imperfectly lighted, it is impossible to trace out. Indeed, it is but a twilight region that is enclosed within the firmament of this great dome, which is actually larger than that of St. Peter's, though not lifted so high from the pavement. But looking at the painted windows, I little cared what dimness there might be elsewhere; for certainly the art of man has never contrived any other beauty and glory at all to be compared to this.

The dome sits, as it were, upon three smaller domes—smaller, but still great—beneath which are three vast niches, forming the transepts of the cathedral and the tribune behind the high altar. All round these hollow, dome-covered arches or niches are high and narrow windows crowded with saints, angels, and all manner of blessed shapes, that turn the common daylight into a miracle of richness and splendour as it passes through their heavenly substance. And just beneath the swell of the great central dome is a wreath of circular windows quite round it, as brilliant as the tall and narrow ones below. It is a pity anybody should die without seeing an antique painted window, with the bright Italian sunshine glowing through it. This is "the dim, religious light" that Milton speaks of; but I doubt whether he saw these windows when he was in Italy, or any but those faded or dusty and dingy ones of the English cathedrals, else he would have illuminated that word "dim" with some epithet that should not chase away the dimness, yet should make it shine like a million of rubies, sapphires, emeralds, and topazes—bright in themselves, but dim with tenderness and reverence because God

Himself was shining through them. I hate what I have said.

All the time that I was in the cathedral the space around the high altar, which stands exactly under the dome, was occupied by priests or acolytes in white garments, chanting a religious service.

After coming out, I took a view of the edifice from a corner of the street nearest to the dome, where it and the smaller domes can be seen at once. It is greatly more satisfactory than St. Peter's in any view I ever had of it — striking in its outline, with a mystery, yet not a bewilderment, in its masses and curves and angles, and wrought out with a richness of detail that gives the eyes new arches, new galleries, new niches, new pinnacles, new beauties, great and small, to play with when wearied with the vast whole. The hue, black and white marbles, like the Baptistery, turned also yellow and brown, is greatly preferable to the buff travertine of St. Peter's.

From the Duomo it is but a moderate street's length to the Piazza del Gran Duca, the principal square of Florence. It is a very interesting place, and has on one side the old governmental palace — the Palazzo Vecchio — where many scenes of historic interest have been enacted; for example, conspirators have been hanged from its windows, or precipitated from them upon the pavement of the square below.

It is a pity that we cannot take as much interest in the history of these Italian Republics as in that of England, for the former is much the more picturesque and fuller of curious incident. The sobriety of the Anglo-Saxon race — in connection, too, with their moral sense—keeps them from doing a great many things that would enliven the page of history; and their events seem to come in great masses, shoved along by the agency of many persons rather than to result from individual will and character. A hundred plots for a tragedy might be found in Florentine history for one in English.

At one corner of the Palazzo Vecchio is a bronze equestrian statue of Cosmo di Medici, the first Grand Duke, very stately and majestic; there are other marble statues—one of David, by Michel Angelo— at each side of the palace door; and entering the court I found a rich antique arcade within, surrounded by marble pillars, most elaborately carved, supporting arches that were covered with faded frescoes. I went no farther, but stepped across a little space of the square to the Loggia di Lanzi, which is broad and noble, of three vast arches, at the end of which, I take it, is a part of the Palazzo Uffizi fronting on the piazza. I should call it a portico if it stood before the palace door; but it seems to have been constructed merely for itself, and as a shelter for the people from sun and rain, and to contain some fine specimens of sculpture, as well antique as of more modern times. Benvenuto Cellini's Perseus stands here; but it did not strike me so much as the cast of it in the Crystal Palace.

A good many people were under these great arches; some of whom were reclining, half or quite asleep, on the marble seats that are built against the back of the loggia. A group was reading an edict of the Grand Duke, which appeared to have been just posted on a board at the farther end of it; and I was surprised at the interest which they ventured to manifest, and the freedom with which they seemed to discuss it. A soldier was on guard, and doubtless there were spies enough to carry every word that was said to the ear of absolute authority. Glancing myself at the edict, however, I found it referred only to the furtherance of a project, got up among the citizens themselves, for bringing water into the city; and on such topics, I suppose there is freedom of discussion.

June 7th.—Saturday evening we walked with U—— and J—— into the city, and looked at the exterior of the Duomo with new admiration. Since my former view of it, I have noticed—which, strangely enough, did not strike me before—that the façade is but a great, bare, ugly space, roughly plastered over, with the brickwork peeping through it in spots, and a faint, almost invisible, fresco of colours upon it. This front was once nearly finished with an incrustation of black and white marble, like the rest of the edifice, but one of the city magistrates, Benedetto Uguacione, demolished it three hundred years ago, with the idea of building it again in better style. He failed to do so, and ever since the magnificence of the great church has been marred by this unsightly roughness of what should have been its richest part; nor is there, I suppose, any hope that it will ever be finished now.

The Campanile, or bell-tower, stands within a few paces of the cathedral, but entirely disconnected from it, rising to a height of nearly three hundred feet, a square tower of light marbles, now discoloured by time. It is impossible to give an idea of the richness of effect produced by its elaborate finish; the whole surface of the four sides, from top to bottom, being decorated with all manner of statuesque and architectural sculpture. It is like a toy of ivory, which some ingenious and pious monk might have spent his lifetime in adorning with scriptural designs and figures of saints; and when it was finished, seeing it so beautiful, he prayed that it might be miraculously magnified from the size of one foot to that of three hundred. This idea somewhat satisfies me, as conveying an impression how gigantesque the Campanile is in its mass and height, and how minute and varied in its detail. Surely these mediæval works have an advantage over the classic. They combine the telescope and the microscope.

The city was all alive in the summer evening, and the streets humming with voices. Before the doors of the cafés were tables, at which people were taking refreshment, and it went to my heart to see a bottle of English ale, some of which was poured foaming into a glass: at least, it had exactly the amber hue and the foam of English bitter ale; but perhaps it may have been merely a Florentine imitation.

As we returned home over the Arno, crossing the Ponte di Santa Trinità, we were struck by the beautiful scene of the broad, calm river, with the palaces along its shores repeated in it on either side, and the neighbouring bridges, too, just as perfect in the tide beneath as in the air above—a city of dream and shadow so close to the actual one. God has a meaning, no doubt, in putting this spiritual symbol continually beside us.

Along the river, on both sides, as far as we could see, there was a row of brilliant lamps, which, in the far distance, looked like a cornice of golden light; and this also shone as brightly in the river's depths. The hues of the evening, in the quarter where the sun had gone down, were very soft and beautiful, though not so gorgeous as thousands that I have seen in America. But I believe I must fairly confess that the Italian sky, in the daytime, is bluer and brighter than our own, and that the atmosphere has a quality of showing objects to better advantage. It is more than mere daylight; the magic of moonlight is somehow mixed up with it, although it is so transparent a medium of light.

Last evening, Mr. Powers called to see us, and sat down to talk in a friendly and familiar way. I do not know a man of more facile intercourse, nor with whom one so easily gets rid of ceremony. His conversation, too, is interesting. He talked, to begin with, about Italian food, as poultry, mutton, beef, and their lack of savouriness, as compared with our own; and mentioned an exquisite dish of vegetables, which they prepare from squash or pumpkin blossoms; likewise another dish, which it will be well for us to remember when we get back to the Wayside, where we are overrun with acacias. It consists of the acacia blossoms in a certain stage of its development fried in olive oil. I shall get the receipt from Mrs. Powers, and mean to deserve well of my country by first trying it, and then making it known; only I doubt whether American lard, or even butter, will produce the dish quite so delicately as fresh Florence oil.

Meanwhile, I like Powers all the better, because he does not put his life wholly into marble. We had much talk, nevertheless, on matters of sculpture, for he drank a cup of tea with us, and stayed a good while.

He passed a condemnatory sentence on classic busts in general, saying that they were conventional, and not to be depended upon as true representations of the persons. He particularly excepted none but the bust of Caracalla; and, indeed, everybody that has seen this bust must feel the justice of the exception, and so be the more inclined to accept his opinion about the rest. There are not more than half a dozen — that of Cato the Censor among the others — in regard to which I should like to ask his judgment individually. He seems to think the faculty of making a bust an extremely rare one. Canova put his own likeness into all the busts he made. Greenough could not make a good one; nor Crawford, nor Gibson. Mr. Harte, he observed—an American sculptor, now resident in Florence—is the best man of the day for making busts. Of course, it is to be presumed that he excepts himself; but I would not do Powers the great injustice to imply that there is the slightest professional jealousy in his estimate of what others have done, or are now doing, in his own art. If he saw a better man than himself, he would recognise him at once, and tell the world of him; but he knows well enough that, in this line, there is no better, and probably none so good. It would not accord with the simplicity of his character to blink a fact that stands so broadly before him.

We asked him what he thought of Mr. Gibson's practice of colouring his statues, and he quietly and slyly said that he himself had made wax figures in his earlier days, but had left off making them now. In short, he objected to the practice wholly, and said that a letter of his on the subject had been published in the London *Athenæum*, and had given great offence to some of Mr. Gibson's friends. It appeared to me, however, that his arguments did not apply quite fairly to the case, for he seems to think Gibson aims at producing an illusion of life in the statue, whereas, I think his object is merely to give warmth and softness to the snowy marble, and so bring it a little nearer to our hearts and sympathies. Even so far, nevertheless, I doubt whether the practice is defensible, and I was glad to see that Powers scorned, at all events, the argument drawn from the use of colour by the antique sculptors, on which Gibson relies so much. It might almost be implied, from the contemptuous way in which Powers spoke of colour, that he considers it an impertinence on the face of visible nature, and would rather the world had been made without it; for he said that everything in intellect or feeling can be expressed as perfectly—or more so—by the sculptor in colourless marble, as by the painter with all the resources of his palette. I asked him whether he could model the face of Beatrice Cenci from Guido's picture so as to retain the subtle expression, and he said he could, for that the expression depended entirely on the drawing, "the picture being a badly coloured thing." I inquired whether he could model a blush, and he said "Yes;" and that he had once proposed to an artist to express a blush in marble if he would express it in picture. On consideration, I believe one to be as impossible as the other; the life and reality of the blush being in its tremulousness, coming and going. It is lost in a settled red just as much as in a settled paleness, and neither the sculptor nor painter can do more than represent the circumstances of attitude and expression that accompany the blush. There was a great deal of truth in what Powers said about this matter of colour, and in one of our interminable New England winters it ought to comfort us to think how little necessity there is for any hue but that of the snow.

Mr. Powers, nevertheless, had brought us a bunch of beautiful roses, and seemed as capable of appreciating their delicate blush as we were. The best thing he said against the use of colour in marble was to the effect that the whiteness removed the object represented into a sort of spiritual region, and so gave chaste permission to those nudities which would otherwise suggest immodesty. I have myself felt the truth of this in a certain sense of shame as I looked at Gibson's tinted Venus.

He took his leave at about eight o'clock, being to make a call on the Bryants, who are at the Hôtel de New York, and also on Mrs. Browning, at Casa Guidi.

END OF VOL. I.